The Book of Ruth

by

Samuel Cox and Thomas Fuller

Foreword by
Dr. Cyril J. Barber

Klock & Klock Christian Publishers, Inc.
2527 Girard Avenue North
Minneapolis, Minnesota 55411

Limited Classical Reprint Library

The Book of Ruth

by

Samuel Cox

Klock & Klock Christian Publishers, Inc.
2527 Girard Avenue North
Minneapolis, Minnesota 55411

Originally published by
Religious Tract Society
London, n.d.

ISBN: 0-86524-140-6

Printed by Klock & Klock in the U.S.A.
1982 Reprint

FOREWORD

John Ruskin, the British essayist, art critic and social reformer of the last century, once said, *"All books are divisible into two classes: the books of the hour, and the books of all time."*

In all of literature, the Book of Ruth occupies a prominent place. Its eloquence and symmetry, language and style, commands our attention. It stands with those masterpieces of verbal expression which transcend time and culture, and yet it never loses its relevance or appeal. Anyone attempting to write an exposition of this beautiful pastoral idyll, however, should himself possess gifts of description and an understanding of human nature similar to those exhibited by the original author.

Samuel Cox (1826-1893) and Thomas Fuller (1608-1661) both wrote commentaries on this portion of God's Word. Dr. Cox's work has been one of the chief sources consulted by preachers whenever they have spoken on the Book of Ruth. Dr. Fuller's treatment is very rare. It comprises addresses he gave at St. Benet's Church, Cambridge (1630-1631), during the few months he pastored that church. These studies were not published, however, until 1654, and when they appeared the title page read: *"A Comment on Ruth* by T.F." They are complete only to the end of chapter 2.

Samuel Cox graduated from the University of London and received his doctorate from the University of St. Andrews. He served Baptist and Congregational churches in England where he ministered with great acceptance in a variety of capacities and to an ever-widening group of people.

Dr. Cox married Eliza Tebbutt in 1873, and from this time until his death his wife played an important role in his ministry. She was his most valued critic, his chief counselor, and one who so understood him and the work he was doing that she never failed to stand by him and encourage him. And when her husband was compelled to resign his pastorate because his voice failed and he could no longer speak, she supported him as he sought first one avenue of service and then another.

During these years of enforced absence from the pulpit, Dr. Cox began to minister through *The Expositor*, a journal which he had founded to promote high standards of Bible exposition. Some issues were entirely made up of his material; and others included expository studies by the greatest biblicists of the British Isles.

As a speaker, Dr. Cox's voice has long since been stilled, but as a writer his works live on and are of benefit to succeeding generations. It is with particular pleasure that we welcome the reappearance of his most famous work, *The Book of Ruth: A Popular Exposition*, which is here reissued with Thomas Fuller's *A Comment on Ruth*.

Thomas Fuller was born in Northamptonshire, England, where his father was a minister of the Church of England. He studied at Queens' College, Cambridge, from which he received his Bachelor of Divinity degree. His first pastoral charge was to St. Benet's, Cambridge, and it was here that his lectures on Ruth were first given.

Thomas Fuller's "promotions" within the framework of the Angli-can Communion came so rapidly that, in less than a year, he found him-self prebendary of Salisbury Cathedral, and three years later rector of Broad-Winsor, Dorsetshire. Within eight years he was transferred to London where he became one of the most popular evangelical preachers of his day. In due course his *alma mater* conferred upon him the degree of Doctor of Divinity, and from this time onwards he was known as "Good Dr. Tom Fuller"--a unique title considering the characteristic reserve of the British people.

Dr. Fuller's *Notes Upon Jonah* were added to his study of the Book of Ruth. They are here reproduced exactly as published so many years ago.

Of Dr. Fuller's works, Charles Haddon Spurgeon had this to say:

Weighty, judicious, and full of Gospel truth. . . Quaint, pithy, and lit up with flashes of his irrepressible wit. . . .

We concur and hope that these works on the Book of Ruth will rekin-dle interest in this priceless portion of God's Word.

Cyril J. Barber
Author, *The Minister's Library*

CONTENTS.

PAGE

INTRODUCTION ... ...

TRANSLATION 25

EXPOSITION:

   I. THE SOJOURN IN MOAB 41

   II. THE RETURN TO BETHLEHEM 61

   III. IN THE HARVEST FIELD 81

   IV. IN THE THRESHING-FLOOR 101

   V. IN THE GATE 121

APPENDICES:

   A.—ON CHRIST AS THE MENUCHAH OF THE
      WORLD 149

   B.—ON CHRIST AS THE TRUE GOEL OF MEN... 164

INTRODUCTION.

INTRODUCTION.

IN the whole gallery of Scripture portraits there are few which are more familiar to us, or more attractive, than the sweet figure of "Ruth standing amid the alien corn." Nor is it the least of her attractions to the Christian heart that the blood of Ruth ran in the veins of Jesus of Nazareth. In his genealogy of our Lord, St. Matthew inscribes the names of only four women,—Thamar, Rahab, Ruth, and Bathsheba; and among these four, Ruth easily holds the pre-eminence. Thamar, Rahab, and Bathsheba were all women of dubious virtue, even when judged by the standards of antiquity; but, judged by the moral standard of any age, Ruth is not only pure and sweet as the fields in which she gleaned, she rises to an heroic pitch of unselfish devotion and love. Strength veiled in gentleness, heroism enhanced yet also concealed by humility, is as truly the characteristic of Ruth as it is of the

Son of Man. We may find her aptest emblem in those exquisite wild flowers which hide their perfect blooms under their broad green leaves, and only reveal their presence by the subtile fragrance they shed upon the air. Ruth is a true lily of the valley. It is not improbable, indeed, that her very name may be that of a flower, though not of the flower just mentioned. The common and accepted derivation of the Hebrew word *ruth* is "a friend;" and truly Ruth's face is as the face of a friend to us : but a learned and ingenious scholar has conjectured, with much probability, that *ruth* is an ancient Hebrew form of the Greek ῥόδον, the Latin *rosa*, the English *rose*, a word which denotes the *redness* of the flower; and, to say the least of it, it is very pleasant to think of Ruth as "*the Rose* of Moab."

At what period the events narrated in this Book occurred we are not expressly told. All we are told is that it was " in the days when the Judges judged " (Chap. i. 1). But as Israel was under the Judges for nearly five centuries—as long, let us say, as from the accession of the Plantagenet Henry v. to the present day — the phrase does not go far toward dating the Book. But another phrase in it (Chap. iv. 21, 22), from which we learn that Boaz was the great-grandfather of David, makes it pretty certain that the Judge, in whose days Ruth the alien was admitted to the Commonwealth of Israel, was the venerable but most unhappy Eli. Ruth's son was Jesse's father; Jesse was the father of David. It is very probable, therefore, that, when he was a child, Ruth may have fondled Jesse in her arms. "The Rose of Moab" is closely con- nected with "the Darling of Israel."

We may be reasonably sure that the story of this Book was enacted while Eli was Judge in Israel; but when was it *written?* The question is not in itself of grave importance, perhaps; but to find the answer to it is a good and wholesome exercise for younger students of Scripture. For all the materials of the answer are contained in the Book itself; they need no scholarship to discover them; they are accessible to all. If, then, we read the Book of Ruth carefully, and with the purpose of fixing its date in our minds, surely the very opening words of the Story must arrest our attention: "Now it came to pass, *in the days when the Judges judged,* that there was a famine in the land." Is that the

tone of a man who is writing of the present or of a
past age? Obviously it is the tone of one who
speaks of the past. The Judges are no longer
judging; the whole form of civil government has
changed in the interval between the events narrated
and the time at which the narrator writes. He is
as evidently looking back as we should be were we
to commence a story with the words, " Now it
came to pass in the days when the Lord Protector
sat on the throne of England."

This is our first "note of time," the first hint
we get that a considerable interval must have
elapsed between the time in which Ruth lived and
the time in which the story of her life was told. As
we read on we come on two other hints which confirm our conclusion. In Chap. iv. 6–8 we are told
of a curious legal custom. The next of kin to
Naomi, when he refused to redeem her inheritance,
and to take Ruth to wife, drew off his shoe and
gave it to Boaz, so transferring the right of redemption to him. And the historian pauses to explain
that this was "*formerly*" the legal mode in Israel
" concerning redeeming, and concerning exchanging." But why should he stay to explain the

custom if it had not fallen into disuse,—if it had not been so long disused that his readers had clean forgotten it? Yet old legal customs are very tenacious. They do not soon, or suddenly, become obsolete even with us, and much less in the un-changing East. And, therefore, we may infer that the story of Ruth was written, not only after her death, but long after it.

Verses 17, 21, and 22 of the same Chapter point to the same conclusion. For here we are told that Ruth had a son named Obed, Obed a son named Jesse, and Jesse a son named David. But how should David's name have been written before he was born? The Story—unless at least we have recourse to the clumsy expedient of supposing additions made to the original Scripture by a later hand—must have been composed, at the very earliest, after that great Prince was born : *i.e.* it must have been written at least four generations— say from a hundred and twenty to a hundred and fifty years—after the events it records.

To this extent, then, the Book dates itself. That it could not have been written *before* the time of David may be inferred from the fact that David's name is twice mentioned in it. That it was written *in* his time will become evident, I think, when we have caught the tone and purport of the Story.

Briefly told, that Story runs thus :—Under the pressure of a great famine, an ancient and honourable Hebrew family were threatened with want and misery. All that we are told of them indicates that they were Israelites indeed, devoutly attached to the land and worship of their fathers. We may be sure, therefore, that it cost them many a pang to resolve to abandon their inheritance in the promised land and to seek bread among the idolaters of Moab. They went farther than their neighbours, who were exposed to the same pressure, only to fare worse. In seeking a livelihood they lost life. Three out of the four, Elimelech and his two sons, found a grave in the land in which they sought bread. Naomi is left alone, a childless widow. To all human appearance the family is blotted out from among the tribes of Israel. True, Naomi has her two daughters-in-law left ; but these also are childless : and, moreover, they are strangers and aliens from the Hebrew Commonwealth, and of a race which had long been reckoned among the foes of the elect people. Naomi cannot endure to remain in the land which has proved so fatal to her affections and hopes. She returns to Bethlehem, but she returns "empty and afflicted," in great bitterness of soul, because the Lord has dealt very bitterly with her. Destitute and hopeless, she has but one comfort. Ruth remains with her, and will not be persuaded to leave her. She forsakes all— her country, her friends, her gods—that she may be true to her love for Naomi. But, like Naomi, she too comes to Bethlehem in poverty and sadness of heart.

When they arrive, although "the whole city is moved about them," no one offers them either succour or sympathy. Even the wealthy kinsmen of Elimelech,—one of whom, as we happen to know, was of a very noble and generous temper,—either because they are unaware of the calamities that had overtaken Naomi, or because they had disapproved of Elimelech's sojourn among the Heathen, stand aloof from her. Ruth is her sole stay. But Ruth is willing to work, and even to beg, for her. At the time of harvest she goes into the fields to glean after the reapers. A kindly Providence leads her

to the fields of Boaz, the wealthiest, though not the
nearest, kinsman of Elimelech. Here her virtue
and piety became known. Boaz honours her both
for her unselfish devotion to Naomi, and because
she, a heathen, has come "to trust herself under
the wings of the God of Israel." For Ruth's sake,
Naomi is restored to the goodwill of her kinsmen.
By her modesty, her unselfishness, her pious
reverence for Jehovah, the Moabitish woman
conquers the Hebrew prejudice against the alien
and the stranger. By these same virtues she wins
the heart of Boaz and the rights of a wife and a
mother in Israel. At every turn of the Story we
are made to feel that the Gentile Ruth is its
heroine, and that she is its heroine simply because,
in virtue and in piety, she excels even the Hebrew
women. Yet she is no "saint," no devotee, no
prophetess, but a very woman, and a woman

> "Not too bright and good
> For human nature's daily food."

Wide as is the gulf of time and social habit by
which we are separated from her, nevertheless we
feel that she is such a woman as would even now
be the crown and charm of any household.

And it surely speaks well for those ancient Jews, of whom we are apt to think, not altogether without reason, as the most jealous and exclusive of men, that they should have so frankly recognized the worth and charm of a daughter of Moab ; that they should have preserved the tradition of her extraordinary sweetness and nobility till some holy man of God, moved by the Holy Ghost, raised the tradition into a Scripture.

The Story, moreover, is written in no hostile or grudging spirit. The figure of the Gentile is not placed in the shade of the background, but in the centre and full light of the narrative. The Book is not called, as with some show of reason it might have been called when gathered into the Hebrew annals, the " Book of Naomi," or the " Book of Boaz," or the " Descent of David," but the " Book of Ruth." *She* is placed in the foreground, and kept in it throughout.

No doubt the Story is a love story, and is designed to set forth the power of love to overcome all the alienations, hostilities, and prejudices of nature and of that second nature which we call "habit." But it is not a story of romantic love

between a young man and a young woman. It is
the story of a woman's love for a woman; and,
strangely as it would sound in the ears of our
modern wits, it is the story of a young wife's
passionate and devoted love for her mother-in-law !
Ruth's tender self-sacrificing affection for Naomi is
the very charm of the Story.   It is in the strength
of love that she abandons Moab and her father's
house ; it is in the strength of love that she also
conquers the prejudices and jealousies of Bethlehem, and compels even Hebrews to admire her
virtue and record her fame.   And in that it was by
her love for Naomi that Ruth was brought to know
and serve the only wise and true God, we may see
an illustration of the fact that men and women are
often led to religion by natural affection, and rise
to the love of God through their love for one
another.   The Story, then, is a story in praise of
charity ; and it *shews* the charity it praises.   We
have no reason to doubt that it was written by a
Hebrew ; obviously it is one of the Hebrew Scriptures ; and yet it contains no touch of the common
Hebrew enmity against the Gentile.   It is fair, and
even generous, in the tone it takes toward those

who were outside the Hebrew pale. It has no word of blame for Elimelech, although he left the land of his fathers to sojourn among the Heathen; nor for Orpah, although she turned back from Naomi : on the contrary, it records her kindness and self-devotion in at least intending to remain with her "mother" till Naomi herself dissuaded her; while for Ruth it has no praise too high. It bases itself on the truth, which Christ has made the common property of the race, that in every nation a pure and unselfish love is acceptable to God. So far from asserting the exclusive privilege of the chosen people, it rather invites other races to come and put their trust under the wings of Jehovah, by shewing that, as soon as they trust in Him, the privilege and blessing of Israel become theirs.

Now it is this singular charity for the outside world, this disposition to do justice and to shew kindness to the Gentiles, which most of all renders it probable that the Story of Ruth was rescued from the stammering and uncertain lips of Tradition and fairly written out in the reign of David. For nothing is more characteristic of David and his time, though it is a characteristic too com-

monly overlooked, than the fair and easy terms on
which he met all foreigners, all men of alien races,
and the rare fidelity with which these aliens clave
to his cause, even when it was a losing cause.   It
is very strange, and very instructive when we
think of it, that David, a Hebrew of the Hebrews,
the flower and darling of his race, should have
been wholly free from the Hebrew prejudice
against men of Heathen races,—that he should
have called so many of them to his service,
placed them close to his person, had them constantly about him, and have inspired them with
so profound an attachment that they willingly laid
down their lives for him.   For, from the very first,
from his encounter with the Giant of Gath on-
ward, he displayed a faith in the religious convictions peculiar to Israel which never wavered, which,
if equalled, was never surpassed.   And yet no
prince of Israel was ever on such friendly intimate
terms with the Heathen about him.   He fearlessly
commits his father and mother to the care of the
King of Moab.[1]   He gratefully records the kindness shewn him by the King of Ammon.[2]   When

[1] 1 Samuel xxii. 3   [2] 2 Samuel x. 2.

he took refuge in the cave, or hold, of Adullam
from the vindictive hatred of Saul, his body-guard
was formed of brave men of foreign origin, who
afterward became the captains of his army.[1] He
tarried long in the city of Gath, and gained the goodwill of the king, although he had slain its gigantic
champion; indeed, he so won the hearts of many
of the Gittites that six hundred of them followed
him throughout his chequered career, and were
faithful to him even when Hebrew statesmen and
soldiers deserted him.[2] He had no more loyal
soldier in his host than Uriah *the Hittite.* When
his son Absalom revolted from him, almost the
only men who remained true to him were his
foreign servants and captains. It was *an Am-
monite* who supplied him with provisions for his
hasty flight.[3] It was *a Phœnician* who went back
to the camp of Absalom that he might serve
David by thwarting the intrigues of Ahithophel.[4]
The spirit of utter loyalty and devotion by which
these gallant men were animated received, perhaps,
its finest illustration in the interview of David with

---

[1] The *Cherethites* and the *Pelethites* of 2 Samuel viii. 18.
[2] 1 Samuel xxvii. xxviii. 1, 2 ; xxix. ; and 2 Samuel xv. 18.
[3] 2 Samuel xvii. 27–29.   [4] Ibid. xv. 32–37.

Ittai, *a man of Gath.*[1] When the treasonable designs of Absalom broke out, Ittai had but recently taken service with David. And therefore the king, generous and considerate even in his darkest hour of distress, says to him : "Wherefore goest *thou* with us? Return to thy place, and abide with the king, for thou art a stranger. If thou art banished, go to thy native land. Whereas thou camest but yesterday, should I to-day make thee go up and down with us, seeing I go whither I may? Return thou, and take back thy brethren. Mercy and truth be with thee." "Nay," replied the brave loyal stranger, "as Jehovah liveth, and as my lord the king liveth, in what place the lord my king shall be, whether in death or in life, even there will thy servant be also."

One hardly knows which the more to admire, the man who could inspire a loyalty so pure and devoted, or the men who were capable of feeling it. But one thing is quite certain, viz., that in no other period of Jewish history do such friendly and cordial relations between Jew and Gentile come to view. And, therefore, we may well believe—what

[1] 2 Samuel xv. 19–22.

all the other indications of time in this Scripture suggest—that it was at this period that the Book of Ruth, which commemorates the fidelity and love of a Gentile, and that Gentile an ancestress of David, was written. It breathes the tone of David's life and time—the tone of a time in which all who feared God and wrought righteousness were held in honour, whether they were of Hebrew or of Heathen blood.

Some wonder has been expressed by commentators and divines that the Book of Ruth should have been included in the Sacred Canon ; that a love story, charming and idyllic as it is, should have found a place among the Scriptures of the Prophets. But, though we have a strange and irrational trick of smiling a little contemptuously, or a little ironically, when so much as the name of "love" is mentioned, yet no man who reflects on how great a part love plays in human life, and how much the sweetness and dignity of human life depend upon it, and how closely the love of our neighbour is connected with the love of God, will much marvel that God should have moved a holy man to record the love of Ruth for Naomi, or even

the love of Boaz for Ruth, and so to set us "a
pattern how we ought to live." The place of
Ruth in Holy Writ needs no other vindication
than this,—that, in her, love grew to heroism.
But if it did, an ample vindication might be found
in the facts that this Book shews us that every
pure and unselfish affection leads to God, and is
acceptable to Him; that it reveals Him to us as no
less pleased by the goodness of a Heathen than by
that of a Hebrew: and that it also shews us that,
in their better moods, the very Jews knew that
there was no respect of persons with Him. Nor,
in vindicating the honour conferred on this "love
story," should we omit to note a fact in entire and
happy accord with the catholic spirit of the Book,
that the name of Ruth the Moabitess stands in
the genealogy of that mighty Redeemer and Lord
who broke down the wall of partition which long
divided the "circumcision" from the "uncircum-
cision;" and "in whom there is neither Greek nor
Jew, Barbarian, Scythian, bond nor free," since
men of every race and of every condition become
"one new man" in Him.

TRANSLATION.

TRANSLATION.

CHAPTER I.

NOW it came to pass, in the days when the Judges judged, that there was a famine in the land. And a man of Bethlehem-judah went to sojourn in the Field of Moab, he, and his wife, and his sons. 2. And the name of the man was Elimelech, and the name of his wife Naomi, and the names of his two sons Mahlon and Chilion—Ephrathites of Bethlehem-judah. And they came into the Field of Moab and abode there.

3. And Elimelech, Naomi's husband, died; and she was left, and her two sons. 4. And they took them wives of the women of Moab; the name of the one was Orpah, and the name of the other Ruth : and they dwelt there about ten years. 5. Then, died these two also, Mahlon and Chilion; and

the woman was left of her two sons and her husband.

6. Then she arose with her daughters-in-law, and returned from the Field of Moab; for she had heard in the Field of Moab that the Lord had re-membered his people to give them bread.   7. And she went forth out of the place where she was, and her two daughters-in-law with her; and they went on the way to return to the land of Judah.   8. Then said Naomi to her two daughters-in-law, Go, return each to her mother's house. The Lord deal kindly with you, as ye have dealt with the dead, and with me.   9. The Lord grant you that ye may find an asylum, each in the house of her husband. Then she kissed them; and they lifted up their voice, and wept.   10. And they said unto her, Nay, but we will return with thee unto thy people.   11. And Naomi said, Return, my daughters : why will ye go with me?   Are there yet any more sons in my womb, that they may be your husbands?   12. Return, my daughters, go ; for I am too old to have a husband.   Even if I should say, I have hope; if even to-night I should have a husband, and should also bear sons ; (13) would ye tarry till they were grown? would ye, for them, shut yourselves up from having husbands? Nay, my daughters.

Yet is it much more bitter for me than for you, since the hand of the Lord is gone out against me. 14. And they lifted up their voice and wept again. And Orpah kissed her mother-in-law ; but Ruth clave unto her. 15. And she (*Naomi*) said, Behold, thy sister-in-law has gone back unto her people, and unto her gods ; return thou also after thy sister-in-law. 16. And Ruth said, Intreat me not to leave thee, nor to return from following after thee ; for whither thou goest, I will go ; and where thou lodgest, I will lodge : thy people is my people, and thy God my God : (17) where thou diest I will die, and there will I be buried. The Lord do so to me, and more also, if aught but death part thee and me. 18. So when she saw that she was stedfastly minded to go with her, then she ceased to dissuade her.

19. So they two went on till they came to Bethlehem. And it came to pass, when they were come to Bethlehem, that all the city was moved about them, and they said, This Naomi![1] 20. And she said unto them, Call me not Naomi, call me Mara, for the Lord hath dealt very bitterly with me.

[1] Verse 19.—The last " *they* " is feminine in the Hebrew. It was *the women* of Bethlehem, therefore, who cried, " *This* Naomi !"

21. I went out full, and the Lord hath brought me home again empty. Why, then, call ye me Naomi, seeing the Lord hath testified against me, and the Almighty hath afflicted me? 22. So Naomi returned, and Ruth the Moabitess,[1] her daughter-in-law, with her, who came back out of the Field of Moab. And they came to Bethlehem in the beginning of barley-harvest.

CHAPTER II.

And Naomi had a kinsman of her husband's, a valiant hero, of the family of Elimelech; and his name was Boaz. 2. And Ruth the Moabitess said unto Naomi, Let me now go into the fields, and glean among the ears after him in whose sight I shall find grace. And she said unto her, Go, my daughter. 3. And she went, and came and gleaned in a field after the reapers. And her lot met her in the field of Boaz, who was of the kindred of Elimelech. 4. And, behold, Boaz came from Bethlehem, and said unto the reapers, The

---

[1] Verse 22.—"The Moabitess who came back with Naomi out of the Field of Moab," seems to have been the common designation, or description, of Ruth among the villagers of Bethlehem. Compare Chap. ii. 6.

Lord be with you.   And they answered him, The
Lord bless thee.   5. Then said Boaz unto his servant that was set over the reapers, Whose damsel
is this?   6. And the servant that was set over the
reapers answered and said, She is a Moabitish
damsel who came back with Naomi out of the
Field of Moab; (7) and she said, I pray thee let
me glean, and I will gather after the reapers among
the sheaves : so she came and hath continued (*at
work*) even from the morning until now, save that
she rested a little in the house.   8. Then said
Boaz unto Ruth, Hearest thou not,[1] my daughter?
Go not to glean in another field, neither go from
hence, but abide here fast by my maidens : (9) let
thy eyes be on the field that they do reap, and go
thou (*fearlessly*) after them :[2] have I not charged
the young men that they shall not molest thee?
and when thou art athirst, go unto the vessels and

---

[1] Verse 8.—"*Hearest thou not?*" literally, "*Hast thou not
heard,* my daughter?" the force of the perfect tense being "to
mark the permission to glean as a thing irrevocably fixed, not
subject to uncertainty or change." (*Speaker's Commentary in
loco.*)

[2] Verse 9.—"Let thine eyes be on the field that *they* do reap,
and go thou after *them.*" "They" is masculine in the Hebrew,
and "them" feminine. Ruth, therefore, was to follow the
reapers, but to keep with the gleaners, since thus she was the
more likely to escape molestation.

drink of that which the young men have drawn.
10. Then she bent her face, and bowed herself to
the ground, and said unto him, Why have I found
grace in thine eyes that thou shouldst take note
of me, seeing I am a stranger? 11. And Boaz
answered and said unto her, It hath been fully
shewn me all that thou hast done unto thy mother-
in-law since the death of thine husband, and that
thou hast left thy father and thy mother and the
land of thy nativity, and art come among a people
whom thou knewest not heretofore.¹ 12. The Lord
recompense thy work, and a full reward be given
thee of the Lord God of Israel, under whose wings
thou art come to take refuge.² 13. Then she said,
Let me find favour in thy sight, my lord, for thou
hast comforted me, and hast spoken to the heart
of thine handmaid, though I be not like unto one
of thy handmaidens. 14. And Boaz said unto her
at meal-time, Come thou hither, and eat of the
bread, and dip thy morsel in the vinegar. And
she sat beside the reapers; and he reached her
parched corn,³ and she did eat and was satisfied,

---

¹ Verse 11.—" *Heretofore ;*" literally, " *yesterday, and the third
day,*" *i.e.* " yesterday, and the day before yesterday,"—a common Hebraism for " heretofore."

² Verse 12.—Compare Psalm xci. 4.

³ Verse 14.—The parched corn which Boaz handed to Ruth is

and left (*of that she ate*).   15. And when she was risen up to glean, Boaz commanded the young men, saying, Let her glean even between the sheaves, and shame her not ; (16) and pull out some (*ears*) from the armfuls on purpose for her, and leave them, that she may glean them, and rebuke her not. 17. So she gleaned in the fields until evening, and beat out that she had gleaned ; and it was about an ephah of barley.

18. And she took it up, and came into the city; and her mother-in-law saw what she had gleaned.   And she brought out and gave to her that which she had left (*at meal-time*) after she was satisfied.   19. And her mother-in-law said unto her, Where hast thou gleaned to-day? and where hast thou worked?   Blessed be he that did

prepared thus: a few handfuls of the best ears are plucked and tied into small bundles.   Then a quick fire of dried grass and thorn bushes is kindled, and the corn is held in the blaze till the chaff is mostly burned off.   The grain is then sufficiently roasted to be rubbed out and eaten, and is a well-liked food throughout the East.   The servants of a traveller do not scruple to help themselves and him to sufficient corn from any field they pass ; nor is it thought wrong for them to help themselves to as much as they require.

"The morsel" which Ruth dipped in "vinegar," *i.e.* a mixture of vinegar and oil and water, was, no doubt, a piece of biscuit bread.   And travellers in the East report that it is quite incredible how the biscuit, eaten with vinegar and oil, recruits the weary and exhausted frame.

take note of thee. And she shewed her mother-in-law with whom she had worked, and said, The man's name with whom I worked to-day is Boaz. 20. And Naomi said unto her daughter-in-law, Blessed be he of the Lord, who hath not left off his kindness to the living and to the dead. And Naomi said unto her, The man is akin to us, one of our *goelim.* 21. And Ruth the Moabitess said, Moreover he said unto me, Thou shalt keep fast by my young men until they have ended all my harvest. 22. And Naomi said unto Ruth her daughter-in-law, Good, my daughter; go out only with his maidens, lest in any other field thou be molested. 23. So she kept fast by the maidens of Boaz, gleaning to the end of the barley-harvest and of the wheat-harvest; and then she abode with her mother-in-law.

CHAPTER III.

Then Naomi, her mother-in-law, said unto her, My daughter, shall I not seek an asylum for thee, that it may be well with thee? 2. And, now, is not Boaz of our kindred, with whose maidens thou wast? Behold he winnoweth barley to-night in the threshing - floor.[1]　3. Wash thyself, therefore, and anoint thee, and put thy (*best*) apparel upon thee, and get thee down to the floor, but let not thyself be seen until the man have done eating and drinking.　4. And it shall be that when he lieth down, thou shalt mark the place where he shall lie, and thou shalt go in and uncover (*the place at*) his feet, and lay thee down : and he will tell thee what thou shalt do.　5. And she said unto her, All that thou sayest I will do.　6. And she went down unto the floor, and did according to all that her mother-in-law bade her.

7. And when Boaz had eaten and drunk, and his heart was cheerful, he went to lie down at the end of the heap of corn; and she came softly, and uncovered (*the place at*) his feet, and laid her down.　8. And it came to pass, at midnight, that the man was startled, and bent himself forward ; [2] and, behold, a woman lay at his feet.　9. And he said, Who art thou ?　And she answered, I am Ruth, thine handmaid : spread therefore thy wings

---

[1] Verse 2.—" He winnoweth barley *to-night :*" for the sake of the breeze which springs up at sunset, and greatly facilitates the cleansing of the corn tossed up against the wind.

[2] Verse 8.—"And bent himself *forward*," *i.e.* so as to discover what or who it was at his feet.

over thine handmaid : for thou art a *goel.* 10.
And he said, Blessed be thou of the Lord, my
daughter : for thy latter kindness is better than thy
former, inasmuch as thou didst not go after young
men, whether poor or rich. 11. And, now, my
daughter, fear not ; I will do for thee all that thou
askest : for all the gate of my people doth know
that thou art a brave woman.[1] 12. And, now,
truly indeed I am a *goel ;* howbeit there is a *goel*
nearer than I. 13. Tarry here to-night, and it
shall be, in the morning, that if he will redeem
thee, well ; let him redeem : but if he will not
redeem thee, then, as the Lord liveth, I will redeem thee. Lie down until the morning. 14.
And she lay at his feet till the morning : and she
rose up before a man could recognize his friend.
For he said, Let it not be known that the woman
came into the floor. 15. Also he said, Bring
hither thy shawl that thou hast upon thee, and
hold it out. And when she held it out, he measured six measures of barley,[2] and laid it on her.
And he went into the city.

---

[1] Literally, "*a woman of strength,*" *i.e.* a woman both brave
and good.

[2] Verse 15.—"Six *measures* of barley :" *i.e.* six seahs = two
ephahs, or twice as much as Ruth had been able to glean in a
most fortunate day.　See Chap. ii. 17.

16. And when she came to her mother-in-law, she (*Naomi*) said, How comest thou, my daughter? And she told her all that the man had done unto her. 17. And she said, These six measures of barley gave he me; for he said to me, Go not empty to thy mother-in-law. 18. And she (*Naomi*) said, Stay at home, my daughter, until thou knowest how the matter will go ; for the man will not rest until he have finished it this day.

CHAPTER IV.

And Boaz went up to the gate, and sat him down there : and, behold, the *goel* of whom Boaz spake passed by ; unto whom he said, Ho, So-and-So, turn aside, sit down here. And he turned aside, and sat down. 2. And he (*Boaz*) took ten men of the elders of the city, and said, Sit ye down here. And they sat down. 3. And he said unto the *goel*, Naomi, who is come again out of the Field of Moab, hath put up for sale the parcel of land which was our brother Elimelech's ; (4) and I determined to advertize thee of it,[1] and say,

---

[1] Verse 4.—"And I determined *to advertize* thee :" literally, "And I have said, I will *uncover thine ear ;*" *i.e.* I resolved to tell thee. The metaphor is taken from the Oriental custom of removing the end of the turban in order to whisper into the ear.

Acquire it before those who sit (*in the gate*) and before the elders of my people.   If thou wilt redeem it, redeem it; but if thou wilt not redeem it, tell me, that I may know : for there is none to redeem it but thou, and I, who am next to thee. And he said, I will redeem it.   5. Then said Boaz, What day thou acquirest the field of the hand of Naomi, thou acquirest it also of Ruth the Moabitess, the wife of the dead, to raise up the name of the dead upon his inheritance.   6. And the *goel* said, I cannot redeem it for myself, lest I mar mine own inheritance; redeem thou for thyself that which it is mine to redeem, for I cannot redeem it.   7. Now this was the custom formerly in Israel in cases of redeeming and in cases of exchanging, in order that at all points they might be confirmed : A man plucked off his shoe and gave it to his neighbour : and this was attestation[1] in Israel.   8. When, then, the *goel* said unto Boaz, Do thou acquire it, he drew off his shoe.   9. And Boaz said unto the elders and all the people, Ye are witnesses this day that I have acquired all that was Elimelech's, and all that was Chilion's and Mahlon's, of the hand of Naomi.   10. Moreover, Ruth the Moabitess, the wife of Mahlon, have I acquired to be

---

[1] *Attestation*, *i.e.* the legal form of attestation.

my wife, to raise up the name of the dead upon
his inheritance, that the name of the dead be not
cut off from among his brethren and from the gate
of his place.   Ye are witnesses this day.   11. And
all the people that were in the gate, and the elders,
said, We are witnesses.   The Lord make the woman
that cometh into thy house like Rachel and like
Leah, which two did build the house of Israel;
and mayest thou grow strong in Ephrathah and
win a name in Bethlehem: (12) and may thy
house be like the house of Pharez, whom Tamar
bore unto Judah, of the seed which the Lord shall
give thee of this young woman.

13. So Boaz took Ruth, and she became his
wife; and he went in unto her, and the Lord gave
her conception, and she bare a son.   14. And the
women said unto Naomi, Blessed be the Lord, who
hath not left thee this day without a *goel*, and may
his name be famous in Israel: (15) and may he
be a restorer of thy soul, and the stay of thine old
age; for thy daughter-in-law, who loveth thee, who
is better to thee than seven sons, hath borne him.
16. And Naomi took the child, and laid it in her
bosom, and became nurse unto it.   17. And the
women her neighbours gave it a name, saying,
There is a son born to Naomi; and they called

his name Obed : he is the father of Jesse, the father of David.

18. Now these are the generations of Pharez: Pharez begat Hezron, (19) and Hezron begat Ram, and Ram begat Amminadab, (20) and Amminadab begat Nahshon, and Nahshon begat Salmon, (21) and Salmon begat Boaz, and Boaz begat Obed, (22) and Obed begat Jesse, and Jesse begat David.

I.

THE SOJOURN IN MOAB.

Chapter i. verses 1-5

I.

THE SOJOURN IN MOAB.

Chapter i. verses 1–5.

THE Book of Ruth was, as we have seen, probably written in the time of David, that is, some century and a half after the events narrated in the Book occurred. The opening sentence of the Book shews that the Author was going back for his story to a past age. He speaks of "the days when the Judges judged" as over and gone. He is as obviously telling the story of a bygone time as an author of the present day would be were he to open with the sentence, " Now it came to pass in the days when the Prelates of England were its Statesmen."   And, probably, he indicates the days of the Judges as the date of his Story in order to remind us that in those days, as there was no settled order of government, "every man did tha⁺

which was right in his own eyes." Elimelech might go and come as he pleased, there
being no authority to restrain him.

The home of Elimelech was in Bethlehem
—"*Bethlehem-judah*," as the historian is careful to remark, in order to distinguish it from
another Bethlehem in the territory of the
tribe of Zebulun. Now Bethlehem-in-Judah
was "remarkably well watered in comparison
with other parts of Palestine."[1] The pastures of its limestone downs were famous for
their fine rich grass. and its valleys were
covered over with corn. Its very name—
Bethlehem, *i.e. House of Bread*—indicates its
fertility. And, therefore, the famine which
drove Elimelech from Bethlehem must have
been extraordinarily protracted and severe;
even the most wealthy and fertile parts of the
land must have been consumed by drought :
there was no bread even in the very " House
of Bread."

Elimelech and his household were by no
means likely to be the first to feel the pinch
of want, or to feel it most keenly ; for he

[1] Ritter's "Comparative Geography of Palestine."

came of a good stock, of a family that stood high in the tribe of Judah, and was a man of consideration and wealth. When his sorely-bereaved widow returned to her native place, "*all the city* were moved about her," as about some well-known person once held in general repute, and cried, "*This* Naomi!" She herself confesses, "I went out *full*, and the Lord hath brought me home again empty," evidently contrasting her present penury with her former opulence. The kinsmen of Elimelech, Boaz and that unnamed kinsman who declined to redeem his inheritance, were men conspicuous for high character and large possessions. So that we have every reason to believe that Elimelech was a man well endowed and in good esteem. The probability is that he was rich in flocks and herds, a sheep-master such as Bethlehem has constantly produced; and that it was to find pastures for his famishing flocks that he went to sojourn in Moab.

His own name, and the names of his wife and children, confirm this conclusion. For *Elimelech* is compounded of *El* = God, and

melech = king, and means " My God is my
King;" and Hebrew scholars have noted
that all names compounded with *melech* are
borne by distinguished persons. *Naomi,* or
Noomi, means "the lovely, or gracious,
one." *Mahlon* and *Chilion* probably mean
"joy" and "ornament." And as we know
that the Hebrew names were commonly
expressive of character, and in the earlier
ages even prophetic of character, we may
perhaps infer from these names that the
father was a kingly kind of man, the mother
a lovely and gracious woman, and the two
boys the very pride and joy of their parents'
hearts.

They are all expressly called "*Ephrathites*
of Bethlehem-judah." *Ephrathah* was the
ancient name of the district in which Bethlehem stood; and probably the word denotes
the fruitfulness of this district as insured by
its abundance of water,—*Euphrates* and *Ephrathah* seem to be kindred words. *Ephrathites*, then, are *natives* of the city or district
as distinguished from mere sojourners or
residents; *born* Bethlehemites, and not men

of other districts who had come to settle in it; and possibly the antique word may also here convey an intimation that Elimelech belonged to one of the *ancient* and well-born families of the district.

So that, on the whole, we may conceive of Elimelech as a native of the fertile district of Bethlehem, a member of an ancient, noble, and distinguished family a man of substance and mark, with a lovely wife and two bright promising sons fast rising into manhood.

This man, pinched by famine and fearing to lose his wealth, resolved to emigrate to the Field of Moab, which, untouched by drought, was green with grass and wealthy with corn. But why did he select *Moab*? The usual resort of the clans of Canaan and its vicinity in time of famine was Egypt. Why, then, did not Elimelech, like his great forefathers, either go or send down into Egypt for corn?

The probability is that he would have sent or gone if the road to Egypt had not been closed. All the notes of time in the Book imply that it was while the venerable but miserable Eli was Judge that Elimelech resolved to leave his ancestral fields : and while Eli was Judge there was perpetual war with Philistia. When the Philistines heard that the tribes of Israel were oppressed by famine, they would be sure to guard the high road to Egypt, in order to prevent their famishing foes from procuring supplies from the vast public granaries of that opulent and powerful empire.

With the way to Egypt stopped, Elimelech would naturally turn to the Field of Moab; for Moab had much to attract both the farmer and the shepherd. The name "Moab" stands in the Bible for three districts on the east of the Dead Sea; but we can tell in which of these it was that Elimelech found a home and a grave, for one of these districts is expressly called "The *Field* of Moab,"— which is the technical phrase used throughout this Book; while another was called "The *Land* of Moab," and a third "The *Dry*,"— *i.e.* the Dry Canton—"of Moab." This district or canton—"The Field of Moab," or

Moab proper — has the precipices which border the Dead Sea on its western limit, a semicircular sweep of hills on the east, behind which lies the Arabian Desert; on the north it is defended by the tremendous chasm down which the river Arnon foams; while on the south the two ranges between which it lies run together, meet, and shut it in. It was a high table-land, dotted with cities, on which the grass grew sweet and strong; and it has been in all ages, as it is even now, a favourite haunt of pastoral tribes.

The prophets Isaiah and Jeremiah, who evidently knew Moab and the Moabites well, give us a graphic and artistic sketch of them. In their "burdens," or "dooms," the men of Moab "appear as high-spirited, wealthy, numerous, and even to a certain extent civilized, enjoying a wide reputation and popularity. With a metaphor which well expresses at once the pastoral wealth of the country and its commanding, almost regal, position, but which cannot be conveyed in a translation, Moab is depicted as the strong

sceptre, the beautiful staff, whose fracture
will be bewailed by all about him, and by all
who know him.   In his cities we discern 'a
great multitude of people' living in 'glory'
and in the enjoyment of great 'treasure;'
crowding the public squares, the housetops,
and the ascents and descents of the numerous high places and sanctuaries, where the
'priests and princes' of Chemosh, or Baal-
peor, minister to the anxious devotees.
Outside the towns lie the 'plentiful fields,'
luxuriant as the renowned Carmel, and the
vineyards and gardens of 'summer fruits;'
the harvest is being reaped and the 'hay
stored in abundance,' the vineyards and
presses are crowded with peasants gathering
and treading the grapes, the land resounds
with the joyful shouts of the vintagers." [1]

The Moabites, moreover, were of kin to
Israelites; for, while the men of Israel were
the sons of Abraham, the men of Moab were
descendants of his nephew Lot : and though
there was often war between the two nations,

[1] George Grove, in Smith's *Dictionary of the Bible*, art
"Moab."

and war as bitter as kinsmen's quarrels commonly are, at least in the intervals of peace
friendly and intimate relations were frequently
maintained between individual members or
families of the two races.

Here, then, in the pastoral canton of
Moab—which, though it plays a great part in
ancient history, is hardly so large as the
shire of Huntingdon, and is not so far from
Bethlehem as Huntingdon from London—
Elimelech might hope to find a good pasture
for his flocks and herds if only he were able
to purchase it, as no doubt he was, and
would receive the welcome which awaits the
" full," or wealthy, sojourner in almost every
land.

Was it *wrong* of him to abandon his native
land, in order to sojourn with Moab until the
famine was past? No doubt it was wrong.
Not that emigration is a sin, or even emigration to an alien, and sometimes hostile, land.
We, perhaps, are better pleased to hear of
Englishmen migrating to one of our English
colonies than to hear of them sailing to a
land in which the English name is, or may

be, held in suspicion and dislike. But who
would say that it was *wrong* for an English
family, on the compulsion of some strong
motive, to settle in France, or Spain, or
America ? What made it wrong for Elimelech
to migrate to Moab, wrong according to the
Old Testament standard, was that he was
abandoning his place among the elect people,
to sojourn among Heathen whose social life,
whose very worship, was unutterably licen-
tious and degrading. If it were right of *him*
to abandon his place, it would not have been
wrong for all Bethlehem, nay, for all Judah ;
and then how could the Divine purpose
concerning Israel have taken effect ? Elimelech was a wealthier man than many of his
neighbours ; and if *they* could bear the brunt
of famine rather than forsake the land of
their fathers and expose their children to the
seductions of Heathen license, why could not
he ? True, he is not directly blamed for his
error in the Book of Ruth, which is written
in the most considerate and generous tone
throughout ; but that the writer of the Book
thought him to blame, and held the calami-

ties which fell on him and his house to be a
judgment on his sin, there is scarcely room
to doubt.

What these calamities were we are told
in Chap. i. 3–5. Elimelech lost his life while
seeking a livelihood, and found a grave
where he had sought a home. And, apparently, this "judgment" fell on him at once,
judgment treading on the very heels of
offence. Before his sons were married he
was taken away from the evil to come. For
we can hardly doubt that it would have
seemed evil to him that his sons should
marry strange women, women of a race
of which God had said, " Thou shalt make
no covenant with them : and thou shalt not
make marriage with them ; thy daughter
thou shalt not give unto their son, nor shalt
thou take their daughter for thy son; for it
would turn away thy children from me, and
they will serve false gods." [1] The sin of these
young men in marrying strange women is
not expressly denounced as a sin in the
Story, any more than that of their father

[1] Deuteronomy vii. 2, ff.

in forsaking the land of promise, although it
is denounced in the Targum, which com-
mences verse 4 thus : *" They transgressed the
commandment of the Lord,* and took foreign
wives from among the daughters of Moab."
But no one can read the Old Testament
without feeling that they sinned against the
Law : for, to the Hebrews, marriage was
a religious covenant ; and St. Paul does but
utter an admitted and familiar truth when he
asks, " What fellowship has light with darkness, or Belial with God ? " The reason of
the law is given in the passage just cited
from Deuteronomy,—" they will turn away
thy children from me, and they will serve
false gods."

The daughters of Moab were specially
obnoxious to the faithful Israelites. They
appear to have been among the most fasci-
nating, and the most wanton and profligate,
women of antiquity. Their gods—Chemosh,
Moloch, Baal-peor—were incarnations of lust
and cruelty. They demanded human sacrifices. Children were cast into their burning arms. In their ritual sensuality was

accounted piety. True, Mahlon and Chilion were exceptionally fortunate in their wives. *They* were not turned to the service of false gods, though there was grave reason to fear that they might be; but, on the other hand, neither did they turn their wives to the service of the only true God. It was not till after her husband's death that Ruth learned to take shelter under the wings of the Lord God of Israel (Chap. ii. 12); and Orpah, as we are expressly told (Chap. i. 15), "went back to her people and *her gods.*"

Nevertheless, the home of Naomi in the Field of Moab seems to have been a very happy, although it was not by any means a prosperous, home. Gradually, as the years passed, the widow and sons of Elimelech appear to have lost all that they had, so that at her return to Bethlehem Naomi came back "empty." But, for once, love did not fly out of the window as poverty stepped in at the door; for Naomi prays (Chap. i. 8) that the Lord will deal kindly with Ruth and Orpah, because *they had dealt kindly with the dead and with her.* Orpah, probably, means

"*hind*," and *Ruth* "*rose*,"—pretty and pleasant names both, denoting grace and fragrant
beauty. Mahlon and Chilion mean "joy"
and "ornament." So that at the head of the
diminished household we have the lovely and
gracious Naomi ; and then "Joy" has for
wife the beautiful and fragrant "Rose," and
"Ornament" the graceful "Hind." The
very names are idyllic, and seem to indicate,
what the facts confirm, that the household
was a singularly pure and happy one,
characterized by a certain rustic grace and
refinement.

But "Death strikes with equal foot the
rustic cottage and the palaces of kings."
And after ten years, in which the members
of this notable family seem to have opposed
a constant face to the austere and threatening brow of Misfortune, and to have grown
the dearer to each other for the sorrows
and calamities they shared together, Mahlon
and Chilion, still young men, followed their
father to the grave, and Naomi was left a
childless widow. Songs of mirth were exchanged for songs of mourning. The three

men of the household had gone to their long home, and the three bereaved women were left to weep together and to comfort each other as best they might.

Thus far the Book of Ruth resembles that Symphony of Beethoven, in which the songs of birds, the cheerful hum of a holiday crowd, and all the pleasant voices of a rustic merry-making, are hushed by the crash of a sudden and threatening storm.

The fact that both Ruth and Orpah were minded to accompany the destitute Naomi, when she returned to her native city, confirms all that has been said of the pure and happy family life of the household into which they had been admitted. Mahlon and Chilion must have been men of worth and character, to win so sincere and stedfast an affection from these two daughters of Moab. And the gracious Naomi must have carried herself both wisely and graciously to these young wives, or she would not have inspired them with a love so devoted and self-sacrificing. And yet, when once they had breathed the pure atmosphere of a Hebrew home, it is no marvel that Ruth and Orpah were reluctant to lose it. To the men of Moab women were but toys to be played with while they retained their charm, and to be cast aside so soon as some brighter toy took the eye. But in ancient Israel, as happily also in modern England, the worship of God was, as a rule, conjoined with a pure domestic life, a life made pure and sweet by chastity and kindness, by respect for women, by love for children. No doubt Ruth and Orpah were profoundly impressed by the purity and fidelity which distinguished the Hebrew from the Moabitish home, and repaid it with tenderness and a grateful attachment to the family into which they had been welcomed. It speaks well for them that, after living with them for ten years and watching with motherly jealousy how they bore themselves to her sons, Naomi can thank them with impassioned sincerity and tenderness for their "kindness" to the dead and to her.

Their kindness to *her* is even more remarkable, perhaps, than their kindness to their husbands; for the ancient combine with modern authors to complain of the unhappy relations which obtain between the daughter- and the mother-in-law, and in laying the blame of it on the latter. " The mother-in-law has forgotten that *she* was ever a daughter-in-law," says an old German proverb; Terence laments that all mothers-in-law have ever hated their sons' wives; and Juvenal affirms that " domestic concord is impossible so long as the mother-in-law lives." And, no doubt, among selfish people, who confound jealousy with love, the relation is apt to be a source of irritation and discord; the mother is loth to relinquish her rights in her son, and the wife is forward to assert her rights in her husband: both are apt to forget that their common love for the same person should draw them together and make them of one heart and mind. But in lands where the home-life is pure and tender, and among persons of an unselfish and generous nature, even this relation becomes a very happy one. And, possibly, we may accept it as the weightiest testimony to the tenderness and purity of domestic life among the better Hebrews, that both the prophet Micah (Chap. vii. 6) and our Lord Himself (Luke xii. 53) imply that the tie between mother-in-law and daughter-in-law was as close and sacred as that between mother and daughter, or father and son; that both affirm it to be one of the last signs of utter social division and corruption when the daughter-in-law rises up against her mother-in-law. " Happy is the nation that is in such a case." For men labour, as well as fight, for hearth and altar as for nothing else; and when the hearth is itself an altar, when the home is bright and sacred with a Divine Presence and law, then indeed there is no place like home.

II.

THE RETURN TO BETHLEHEM

Chapter i. *verses* 6–22.

II.

THE RETURN TO BETHLEHEM.

Chapter i. verses 6–22.

THAN the scene depicted in these verses
there is hardly any more beautiful and
affecting in the whole range of the Old Testament Scriptures. All three actors in it
are admirable, and are admirably portrayed.
Even Orpah shews a love and a devotion
which command our respect, although her
love did not rise to the full heroic pitch;
while of Ruth and Naomi it is hard to say
which is the more admirable,—Naomi, in
putting from her her sole comfort and stay,
or Ruth, in leaving all that she had to
become the stay and comfort of Naomi's
declining years. The exquisite and pathetic
beauty of the scene has been recognized from

of old, and has inspired painter after painter, musician after musician : while Ruth's famous reply to Naomi's dissuasive entreaties takes high rank among the sentences which the world will not willingly let die.

It is not an easy, nor is it an altogether pleasant, task to break up this pathetic Story into its separate sentences, that we may analyse them and see what they mean and imply ; but it is a necessary task ; for only as we trace out the meaning of the separate sentences can we hope to reconstruct the Story with fuller knowledge, and permit it to make its due impression upon us.

Whether Elimelech and his wife felt that they were entering on a doubtful course when they left the Holy Land to sojourn with the Heathen of Moab, we have no means of knowing. But we have much reason to think that, during her ten years' sojourn in the Field of Moab, Naomi came to regard it as a sinful course. The loss, first of her husband, and then of her sons, came upon her as a Divine rebuke ; and as she laid her

sons, cut off in their prime, in an alien grave,
the thought and purpose of return, return to
God as well as to the land of God, seem to
have taken possession of her heart. This
purpose was probably strengthened both by
the hope that, in her poverty and bereavement, she would receive help and comfort
from her wealthy Hebrew kinsmen, and
still more by the happy tidings which now
reached her, that the famine was at an end,
that the valleys of Bethlehem were once
more covered over with corn and its hills
with flocks. In the fine Hebrew phrase,
" *The Lord had remembered His people, to give
them bread.*" The pious Hebrew saw God in
all things. What we call "the bounty of
Nature " was, for him, the immediate gift of
God. His bread came straight from Heaven,
though it came through the processes of
husbandry and the benignity of the seasons,
and shewed that God was thinking, and
thinking graciously, of him. And when the
fields yielded no food, and the flock was cut
off from the fold and the ox from the stall,

5

that was because God had "forgotten" him. Not that the pious Israelite conceived of God as losing sight of him in the vastness of His empire and the multiplicity of His cares. What he meant by God's forgetting him was that God was offended with him for his sins, was ceasing to be gracious to him, had purposely put him out of His mind, and was therefore refusing to make his fields and toils fruitful to him. He believed, what we too much forget, that Nature is instinct with a Divine Presence; that it rises into life and fruitfulness when that Presence is auspicious, and sinks into sterility and death when that Presence is clouded with sorrow and indignation at the sins of men. When the Lord "remembered" His people, *i.e.* when He saw with pleasure that they were doing righteousness and shewing mercy, then He gave them bread. When He turned away from their bold affronts against His righteous and loving Will, then famine and disaster stalked through the land.

In *this* sense God had forgotten Israel for

ten years. And, no doubt, the calamities which signified His displeasure with them produced their usual effect,—inducing humility and penitence. Now, therefore, He remembers them, and once more the land smiles with plenty. And now that He is once more gracious, may there not be grace and a blessing even for the impoverished and afflicted Naomi, if she too returns to Him and once more takes shelter under His wings? Perchance there may. At all events she will put Him to the proof. And so she starts on her homeward way.

But she does not start alone. Her two daughters-in-law resolve to accompany her. She, apparently, is not aware of their intention, and supposes they have only come to see her off and indulge in a last embrace, although *they* regarded themselves as already on the way to the land of Judah (verse 7). When, therefore, they reach the Ford of the Arnon, on the northern boundary of the Field of Moab, or, perhaps, when they reach the Fords of the Jordan, the eastern boundary of Judah, Naomi bids them return each to her mother's house, and prays, both that the Lord will deal kindly with them, as they have dealt with her dead and with her, and that He will grant that they may each find an " asylum " in the house of a new husband. As she clasps them in a parting embrace, they lift up their voices and weep. They protest, " Nay, but we will return with thee unto thy people." And, now, Naomi has the delicate, difficult task of breaking to them, as gently as she may, the sad secret that, if they go with her, they will find no welcome from her people, no kindness from any but herself.

If we would understand the scene, and especially the stress laid on these young widows finding new husbands, we must remember that in the East of antiquity, as in many Eastern lands to this day, the position of an unmarried woman, whether maid or widow, was a very unhappy and perilous one. Only in the house of a husband could a woman be sure of respect and protection.

Hence the Hebrews spoke of the husband's house as a woman's " *menuchah*," or " rest " —her secure and happy asylum from servitude, neglect, license. It was such an " asylum " of honour and freedom that Naomi desired for Orpah and Ruth. But, as she had to explain to them, such an " asylum," while it might be open to them in Moab, would be fast closed against them in Judah. In marrying them her sons had sinned against the Hebrew law. That sin was not likely to be repeated by Israelites living in their own land. Yet how is Naomi to tell them of this fatal separation between the two races ? how is she to make these loving women aware that, if they carry out their resolve to go with her, they must resign all hope of honour and regard ?

She discharges her difficult task with infinite delicacy. They, of course, had no thought of marrying any sons that might hereafter be born to the widowed Naomi. Such a thought could not possibly have entered their minds. Why, then, does Naomi

lay such emphasis on the utter unlikelihood
of her having sons, and of their waiting for
them even if she should have them? Simply
to convey to them that, if they went with
her, *they would have no hope but in herself.*
What she meant was: "I know and love
you: and, had I sons, I would take you
with me, that in their homes you might
find the asylum every woman needs and
craves. But I have none, nor am I likely to
have any, nor could you wait for them if I
had. And, outside my household, there is
no prospect for you; for the men of Israel
may not take to wife the daughters of Moab.
Alas, it is more bitter for me to tell you this
than for you to hear it. It is harder for me
than for you that we must part. But the
hand of the Lord is gone out against me. I
have no hope for the future. I must walk
my darkened path alone. But you, you may
still find an asylum with the people of your
own race. *Your* future may be bright. You
will at least have one another. Go, then,
and return each to her mother's house."

This, I apprehend, was what Naomi meant by the words which sound so strangely to us (verses 11–13): this was what Ruth and Orpah would understand her to mean. And if we cannot wonder that the prospect proved too cheerless and perilous for Orpah's love, let us all the more admire the constancy of her whom even this prospect could not terrify. Ruth risked everything which a woman holds dear rather than leave her "mother" to walk and suffer alone. And it may be doubted whether in all the crowded records of womanly heroism and self-sacrifice we anywhere meet a courage and devotion surpassing hers.

And yet, in this contest of self-sacrificing love, it is hard to tell whether the palm should be awarded to Ruth or to Naomi. Has not Naomi discharged her full duty of dissuasion in placing the discomforts and dangers of her lot before her daughter? She, at all events, thinks that she has not. When Orpah has kissed her and gone back, while Ruth is still "cleaving" to her, she renews her entreaties and dissuasions. "Thy sister-in-law has gone back to her people *and to her gods;* go thou also. It is not simply, or mainly, that we belong to different races : we worship different gods. It is *this* which really separates us, and makes it impossible that you should find an asylum in Judah. Return, then, after thy sister." When we consider how dark and solitary Naomi's path must have been had Ruth yielded to her entreaties, we cannot but feel that these two noble women were well matched, that it is hard to say in which of them love was the more generous and self-forgetting.

If, in the judgment of the world, Ruth carries off the palm, it is, in part, because we expect more of a mother in Israel than of a daughter of Moab : but it is still more, I think, in virtue of the exquisite and pathetic words in which her reply to the dissuasions of Naomi is couched. Her vow has stamped itself on the very heart of the world ; and that, not because of the beauty of its form simply, though even in our English Version it sounds like a sweet and noble music, but because it expresses, in a worthy form and once for all, the utter devotion of a genuine and self-conquering love. It is the spirit which informs and breathes through these melodious words that makes them so precious to us, and that also renders it impossible to utter any fitting comment on them. They shine most purely in their own light. *" Intreat me not to leave thee, nor to return from following after thee; for whither thou goest, I will go, and where thou lodgest, I will lodge. Thy people is my people, and thy God my God. Where thou diest, I will die, and there will I be buried.* JEHOVAH *do so to me, and more also, if aught but death part thee and me."* One wonders where the woman found breath to utter such words as these as she lay weeping on Naomi's breast, that her voice did not break into inarticulate sobs and sighs under the weight of so impassioned a tenderness.

I cannot pretend to interpret them, to dwell on them and bring out their beauty. Every heart must do that for itself. But

three points should be noted by all who study
them.   (1) That in these words Ruth meets
every dissuasive plea of Naomi.   Naomi
had no home, no asylum, to offer her ; and
Ruth replies, " Where thou lodgest, I will
lodge."   Naomi reminds her that she is
going among an alien people, who worship
another God; and Ruth replies. " Thy
people is my people, and thy God my God."
Naomi urges that there will be no bright-
ness, no *life*, in her life ; and Ruth replies
that she is content to die, so that she
may share Naomi's grave. (2) That Ruth
adopts Naomi's God *as yet* purely from love
of Naomi. And (3) that she shews how
instantly and entirely she adopts Naomi's
religion by sealing her vow with the Hebrew
oath and by calling on the God of the
Hebrews : " *Jehovah* do so to me, and more
also, if aught but death part thee and me."

When, from this impassioned invocation
of the Name of the Lord, Naomi perceives
that Ruth is " stedfastly minded " to go with
her, she ceases to dissuade her : and the two

noble women, united in an indissoluble bond
of love, go on their way side by side.

Thomas Fuller's comment on verse 19 is :
"Naomi was formerly *a woman of good quality
and fashion,* of good rank and repute ; otherwise her return in poverty had not so generally been taken notice of. Shrubs may be
grubbed to the ground, and none miss them ;
but every one marks the falling of a cedar.
Grovelling cottages may be levelled to the
earth, and none observe them ; but every
traveller takes notice of the fall of a steeple.
Let this comfort those to whom God hath
given small possessions. Should He visit
them with poverty, and take from them what
little they have, yet their grief and shame
would be the less ; they should not have so
many fingers pointing at them, so many eyes
staring on them, so many words spoken of
them ; they might lurk in obscurity : it must
be a Naomi, a person of eminency and
estate, whose poverty must move a whole
city." In these days we should hardly
think of calling Naomi "a woman of good

quality and fashion;" but Fuller's inference from the general excitement caused by her return is, on the whole, a fair one, though it is somewhat quaintly worded. She must have been a woman of substance and repute about whom all Bethlehem was moved. Their exclamation, "*This* Naomi!" expresses the general astonishment at the change which had passed upon her. No doubt the little hamlet had been all aflame with gossip when, ten years before, the rich sheep-master, Elimelech, had left it, and many pious brows had been shaken over his sin in going to sojourn among the Heathen. And, no doubt, on Naomi's return, many who would have shared that sin if they could, and many who had committed far worse sins than any of which she had been guilty, once more shook their heads in grave rebuke, and were forward to recognize the judgments of an offended God in the calamities which had befallen her. It may be feared that there was more blame than pity in the ejaculation, "*This* Naomi!"

Naomi confesses both the impoverishing change that had passed upon her and the sin of which she had become conscious, and is more than ever conscious now that she sees it reflected from the rebuking faces of her former neighbours. The passionate exclamation with which she meets their wonder and reproach is full of pathos: "Call me not Naomi, but call me *Mara* [bitter], for the Almighty hath dealt very *bitterly* with me! Life is no more pleasant to me, but full of bitterness. Call me, then, by a new name, answering to my new condition, a name as bitter as my afflictions." There is, too, a strange blending of sadness and generosity in her confession: "I went out full, and the Lord hath brought me home empty. . . . The Lord hath testified against me; the Almighty hath afflicted me." For while, like her neighbours, she feels the humbling contrast between her former wealth—wealth of happiness and of hope as well as of possessions—and her present poor and unfriended condition, she also feels

that it was *because* she went away when she
was full that she has been brought home
empty. She attributes her "emptiness" to
the Lord, but her going away to herself
alone. *That* was not the Lord's doing; it
was a sin against His will. Nor was it the
doing of Elimelech and her sons : at least,
she casts none of the blame of it on them,
although, in all probability, it was they who
decided to go, and she had but followed their
wishes or command. She takes the whole
blame on herself. She confesses that, in
leaving "the land of promise," she was
walking after her own will, not the will of
God. But, though she confesses her own
sin, she utters no reproach against the beloved dead. "I went because it was my
will to go ; and now God has taught me, by
all I have suffered and lost, that it was
wrong to go. He has justly emptied me
of all my possessions, all my hopes."

The whole city was moved at her return ;
but no one seems to have been moved by her
penitence and grief. She is left alone, save

for " Ruth *the Moabitess* " (verse 22), as the sacred historian once more calls her, to bring out the contrast between the tenderness of this Heathen outcast and the austerity of the pious Hebrews of Bethlehem.

Thus far, then, the Story is sad enough : it is a story of loss, of shame, of sore bereavement ; and but for the fidelity of Ruth we should leave Naomi—in her native place, too, and among her kin—alone, deeming herself forsaken of God and afflicted, because she saw herself abandoned and despised of men. Even the first Chapter of the Book, however, does not close without a hint of brighter days in store. Love and fidelity are always acceptable to God. And hence we might infer that the love and fidelity of Ruth would, in due time, meet with their reward. But we are not left to inference and conjecture. The last verse of the Chapter tells us that it was " *in the beginning of barley-harvest* " that Naomi and Ruth came to Bethlehem. And we know that before the harvest was over the mercy of God to these two loving women rejoiced over the judgments with which He had afflicted them. It was in the harvest-field that Ruth met Boaz, and with Boaz that " asylum " of honour and freedom which Naomi had thought it impossible for her to meet among the sons of Israel. The night of weeping is past; a morning of joy is about to break upon them. How, and how wonderfully, this new day dawned on their sad but faithful hearts, we shall see as we study the succeeding Chapters of the Book.

III.

IN THE HARVEST-FIELD.

Chapter ii. *verses* 1--23.

III.

IN THE HARVEST-FIELD.

Chapter ii. *verses* 1–23.

"WEEPING may endure for a night,
but joy cometh in the morning."
We have seen how dark Naomi's night was,
how she came back " empty " to the home
from which she went out "full." And in this
Chapter we are pathetically reminded of the
utter penury and destitution which were
implied in the word " empty." Once opulent and beloved, Naomi was reduced to
straits so sore that she was compelled to let
her beloved daughter go and glean among
the rude reapers, that she might bring home
a morsel of bread. Nay, so sore was the
need that, even as she ate the parched corn
in the harvest-field, Ruth set aside a portion
of it to take home with her for Naomi's use.

Nor was it simply the loss of husband and sons, of wealth and consideration, by which the spirit of Naomi was oppressed. To the pangs of hunger, and grief, and shame there was added the still keener torture of religious despair. To herself and her neighbours she seemed " smitten of God and afflicted." And hence she broke into the exceeding bitter cry, " *The Lord* hath testified against me, and *the Almighty* hath afflicted me."

The Lord *had* testified against her and afflicted her. But the judgments of God ever have a purpose of mercy; and we are now to see how His mercy shone through the cloud of judgment, turning night into day.

Among the kinsmen of Elimelech was a certain Boaz, a man who had distinguished himself in war, and who is therefore described, as Gideon and Jephthah are described, as "a valiant hero," *i.e.* a brave captain or commander, whose military exploits were well known to the men of his generation. It is unfortunate that our Version renders the Hebrew phrase "a mighty man of wealth;" for though Boaz was rich, and

was as able in peace as in war, the phrase
undoubtedly points to his valour and capacity
in the field of battle. His very name means
"son of strength;" and, no doubt, his
"strength," his vigour of body and of spirit,
had been displayed against the enemies of
Israel, *i.e.* the Philistines, with whom there
seems to have been almost constant war
while Eli was Judge. "None but the brave
deserve the fair;" and, considering the time
in which they lived, we cannot but be a little
glad, for Ruth's sake, that Boaz had proved
himself a brave soldier in the stricken field.

But there is a higher courage than that
which faces death without fear. This, too,
as we shall see, Boaz possessed. He had
"the courage of his convictions." When
once he saw a course of action to be just and
generous, he did not fear to take it, however
unusual it was, and though his neighbours
had much to say against it. Above all, he
was not ashamed of his *religious* convictions.
It was as natural to him to express them as
it was to breathe. As often as we see him
we see that "the law of the Lord is in his

heart," that it influenced the whole round and detail of his life.

How came it to pass, then, that a man so bold and generous and pious left Naomi unhelped and uncomforted in the time of her penury and grief? We cannot altogether tell. He may have been absent on military service when she returned from the Field of Moab, and have only got leave of absence, as soldiers then commonly did, during harvest. He may only just have heard the tale of Naomi's sorrows when he met Ruth in the harvest-field. And, indeed, his words to Ruth, "It hath been fully *shewn* me all that thou hast done," imply that he had only *heard* of what most of the other inhabitants of Bethlehem had seen, that he was absent when "all the city was moved" by the return of Naomi.

Moreover, the word rendered "kinsman" in verse 1 means, literally, "acquaintance;" and though the word "acquaintance" carried more to a Hebrew ear than it does to ours, it implies that Boaz was not a close kinsman of Naomi's husband: it signifies that, while not a near relative, Boaz was *known* to the family as belonging to it : they were acquainted with him as one of themselves. In brief, he was a kinsman, but a distant kinsman ; and, before he interfered, he might well wait to see what the nearer kindred would do. As they did exactly nothing, the opportunity of shewing mercy and doing kindness passed over to him.

Nay, by a special act of Providence—so at least the Sacred Narrative implies—this opportunity was brought to his very door. Ruth goes gleaning, and, as a stranger to Bethlehem and its vicinity, she might of course have lit on the fields of an unfriendly owner. But "*her lot met her* in the field of Boaz ;" *i.e.* she was guided to this field by the hand of Providence. Wandering at her will, going whithersoever she would, God was nevertheless with her and directed her steps.

We may be sure that it was not without some hesitation that the modest and gentle Ruth offered to glean after the reapers, and that it was not without much reluctance that

Naomi gave her consent. Then, as now, reapers were apt to be vicious and rude. All through this Chapter we can see that Ruth ran great risk of deadly insult. Boaz strictly enjoins his young men not to " molest," or maltreat, her. Naomi is overjoyed that she need not go into any other field than that of Boaz, lest, among strangers, she should be insulted or injured. So that we may be sure the cupboard was bare, and that Naomi and Ruth were hard pinched by hunger, before either the one or the other could resolve that the risk should be run. And we must take it as a fresh instance of Ruth's love and fidelity that she would run even this risk rather than sit still while Naomi was in want.

The Chapter gives us, incidentally, a graphic picture of an ancient harvest scene. The field is thick with waving barley. The reapers cut their way into it with sickles, grasping the ears till their arms are full. Behind them, the women gather up the armfuls and bind them into sheaves. Still farther in the rear follow the widow and the stranger, who, according to the Hebrew

law, have a right to glean after the reapers.
The Overseer is busily urging on the reapers,
and granting or refusing admission to the
gleaners. Vessels filled, probably, with the
rough local wine are at hand, that the heated
and thirsty labourers may refresh themselves
at need. The "house," with its barns,
threshing-floors, and various out-buildings,
stands in, or near, the field; and here the
weary may rest when the heat and burden of
the day prove too great for their strength.
Here, too, under the shade of some spreading
tree, men and women gather at meal-time,
and are supplied with parched corn, and with
bread, which they dip in a cool and strengthen-
ing mixture of vinegar and oil and water.
As the day advances, the Master of the
Estate comes to see how the work goes on.
With grave pious courtesy he salutes his
"young men" with the words, "Jehovah be
with you;" and they reply, "Jehovah bless
thee."[1] He is quick to notice the presence
of a stranger, and to inquire who she is and
whence she comes. He is careful to shield

---

[1] A somewhat similar scene is suggested in Psalm cxxix. 7, 8.

her from insult and wrong, and to help her
in her need.　His tone to his young men is
a fine blending of kindliness with authority;
he shews himself even more careful for their
good conduct than for their diligence in their
work.

It is a charming scene : and one does not
wonder that poets have sung of the beauty,
purity, and simplicity of rural life.　Nevertheless, one has only to go into country
villages, and to wander in the fields where
the reapers reap till the sun falls and all the
land is dark, to discover that rural life is not
so innocent and idyllic as it looks to the
poet's eye ; that it is marred by at least as
much ignorance, vice, and brutal coarseness
of speech, manner, and habit, as the life of
towns.　And even as we gaze on *this* fair
harvest scene, and listen to the pious greet-
ings of master and men, we are again and
again reminded of the cruel and deadly lusts
which lurk under its fair exterior, and can
only the more admire a man like Boaz and
a woman like Ruth who move untainted
through a scene by no means pure.

The very fact which would be likely to expose Ruth to the clownish jests and insults of the reapers, the fact that she was an alien, conspicuous perhaps by her foreign garb and ornaments, also drew upon her the attention of Boaz. Naturally, so soon as he sees her, he begins to ask of his Overseer who she is and from whence she came. The Overseer's reply shews that he had caught some touch of his master's generous and considerate spirit. He tells Boaz that Ruth is the Moabitish damsel who had come back with Naomi to Bethlehem; that, ignorant perhaps of her legal right to glean in any Hebrew field, she had begged his permission to "gather after the reapers;" and he is forward to commend her diligence. She has been hard at work from morning till now, and had only once rested for a few moments in the shed, or "house," set apart for the weary.

Boaz, struck perhaps by the beauty of Ruth and the modesty of her demeanour, and knowing that she is of kin to him, multiplies marks of favour and kindness upon her. She

is to remain on his estate, following the
reapers from field to field, till the harvest
is over. She need fear no rudeness or insult,
for he has strictly charged the young men
not to "molest," or offend, her. She is to
drink freely from the vessels prepared for the
reapers, although, as a gleaner, she could
have no claim to share with them.

In her humility, Ruth, who had done so
much for Naomi, and made so many sacrifices, expects no grace or help from others.
Even the slight kindness of Boaz overwhelms
her with gratitude. She flings herself at his
feet and pours out her thanks for the kindly
notice he has taken of an alien and a
stranger.

And, as might have been expected, the
generous heart of Boaz opens all the wider
as he listens to her thanks, and learns how
unassuming she is, how grateful even for the
easy kindness he has shewn her. He knows
who she is, and what she has done. And the
piety, as well as the generosity, of the man
comes out in his reply. "You have left all,"
he says, "in your love for Naomi,—father,

mother, and the land of your nativity. The
Lord recompense you for this good deed. As
you have come to take refuge under the wings
of Israel's God, may He grant you a full
reward." Obviously Boaz had the history of
his great ancestor in his mind. Like Ruth,
Abraham had left all, and gone out into a
strange country. And to him God had said,
"*I* am thy great reward." May the blessing
of faithful Abraham come on faithful Ruth
—this is the wish and prayer of Boaz. He
speaks, not as a Hebrew landowner to a
Moabitish vagabond and beggar, but, rather,
as a Hebrew judge and prophet,—as a prophet who knew that even the stranger who
works righteousness and shews kindness is
acceptable to God.

The blessing of Boaz fell on the heart of
Ruth like showers on the mown grass.
Hitherto she had known only sorrow and
shame. No Israelite had recognized her,
or helped her, or shewn either any appreciation of her noble love for her mother, or any
wish to welcome her to the faith and privilege of Israel. To all but Boaz she was

simply "*the Moabitess*,"—a stranger to the
Covenant, an alien from the Commonwealth.
But now the valiant soldier whom all Bethlehem praised, who sat as judge and teacher
among his people, blesses her for her goodness, and assures her of the protection and
goodwill of the God of Israel. " Thou hast
comforted me," she gratefully replies ; "thou
hast spoken to my very heart, in thus blessing
me, the alien, and in naming the Name of
thy God upon me."

Ruth utters no reproach against the men
of Bethlehem for leaving her in her unpro-
vided loneliness and need ; but the very
passion of her gratitude for his friendly
recognition must have made Boaz aware
of the utter isolation in which she had
lived, of the unsympathetic and suspicious
element through which she had sadly moved.
And his heart warms to her more and more.
Here are a virtue, a tenderness, a fidelity,
such as he had not found, no, not in Israel;
and yet no man seems conscious of it : it
meets with no appreciation, enlists no sympathy, wins no response. The noble love

noble deeds, and those who do them; and, probably, this brave soldier felt that even his courage was as nothing to that of the gentle woman who stood before him. He, therefore, will help her all he can. As she has come to glean in his fields, he will take care that her gleanings be ample, and that her wants be satisfied. As the reapers gather for their meal, he bids Ruth sit with them. Knowing that they will take their tone from him, he himself hands her the parched corn. When the meal is over, he bids her, instead of following the reapers afar off, glean among the sheaves,—nay, bids the reapers pull out a few ears from those they gather in their arms and let them fall where she will find them. Above all, he charges them not to "shame" her, not to jest or romp in their rude country fashion so as to put her to the blush. In any harvest field a woman, and especially a comely woman, to whom such extraordinary favour was shewn by the "master," would only too surely become a mark for evil tongues. And we can, therefore, well understand why Boaz, who

shewed his true courtesy by resolving to
help Ruth in her own way, laid so stringent
a rein on the young men's lips. Happily,
too, the Overseer was her friend, or, despite
the strict injunction of Boaz, Ruth might
have suffered much and deeply from the men
who cut the barley and the women who bound
it into sheaves.

Amid this shower of favours Ruth did not
cease to be herself. When Boaz hands her
an abundance of parched corn, she eats till
she is satisfied—so generous is the supply;
but she thinks of Naomi's hunger as she
satisfies her own, and lays aside a portion of
the food. Nor does she stint her labour
because, by the kindness of Boaz, it is now
more productive. She works on till evening,
and works to such good purpose that, when
she beats out her gleanings, she has upwards
of fifty pounds of barley to carry home.

When Naomi sees how much Ruth has
gleaned she is amazed, and cries, "Where
hast thou been? In whose field canst thou
have gleaned?" But here once more we
are made to feel that we are with those in

whom piety is an active and ruling power. Any woman, however selfish or godless, might have been as surprised and glad as Naomi was at this unexpected turn of fortune. But she, before even her question can be answered, and moved simply by the manifest happiness of Ruth in the abundance of her gleanings, "blesses" the man who has given her this happiness. For *this* she does not need to know who he is. Whoever had been kind and bountiful to Ruth must have meant to shew that he appreciated her virtues and felt for her misfortunes. And therefore Naomi exclaims, " Blessed be he, whoever he may be, who has taken friendly note of thee." It had been hard for her to send Ruth out to such work. The man who had treated her beloved daughter so kindly that she came home loaded with a weight of barley, and bright and happy in the issue of her toils, has done a good deed, for which she invokes on him the benediction of God.

When the blessing has been pronounced, Ruth tells the story of the day, and names Boaz as the man who had befriended her.

7

She, apparently, did not know how much the sound of this name would convey to Naomi's ears,—knew nothing probably either of the kinsmen of Elimelech or of the obligations which kinship imposed among the Hebrews. But Naomi sees the full significance of her kinsman's kindness at a glance, and breaks into a transport of religious gratitude. She explains, "The man is akin to us, one of our *goelim*" (a term the significance of which I reserve till we reach the next Chapter), and pours forth a song of praise : "Blessed be he of the Lord, who hath not left off His kindness to the living and to the dead."

If we would enter into the force of this outburst of praise, we must remember that Naomi had lost her faith—not in God, indeed, but in the goodwill of God for her. She had thought that He was turned to be her foe, and the foe of the husband and sons who had been snatched from her by a premature death. They were dead because they had sinned in forsaking the land of the Covenant. She was bereaved, forsaken, "empty," because she had shared their sin. So, at least, she had conceived. But now, in the wonderful Providence which had led Ruth to find a friend in her valiant and wealthy kinsman, she descries a proof that God had not wholly abandoned her, that He had not left off His kindness whether to her or to the beloved dead. No one who has witnessed such a revulsion from spiritual despair to renewed hope in the Divine goodness and compassion will marvel at the ecstasy which breathes in Naomi's words. Rather, he will be sure that it would be long before she could recover her composure, and listen to what Ruth had still to tell; he will feel that in this brief exclamation of praise we have, compressed into a single sentence, the substance of many heartfelt thanksgivings.

When we consider how potent our kindness may be in quickening the sense of God's kindness and compassion in a neighbour's heart, and how potent, therefore, our lack of kindness and compassion may be, in inducing or confirming a neighbour's despair, we may well tremble at the responsibility which, at any moment, may fall upon us. It was not till Naomi arrived in Bethlehem, and saw her neighbours indifferent and apathetic, however curious and inquisitive they were, that she concluded herself to be shut out from the mercy of God. It was only when Boaz shewed a little kindness to her daughter—such a kindness as we may shew a neighbour any day—that she felt the door of mercy was once more thrown open to her. Let us, then, be kindly affectioned one to another. We may not be able to do much,—Boaz did but give a few handfuls of barley and speak a few considerate words,—and yet what we do may suffice to lift the weight from some heavily burdened heart. Our kindness may make way for the kindness of God. Our little may help Him to do much.

IV.

IN THE THRESHING-FLOOR.

Chapter iii. *verses* 1-18.

IV.

IN THE THRESHING-FLOOR.

Chapter iii. *verses* 1–18.

IT is somewhat difficult to handle the main incident of this Chapter. Not that there is any, even the faintest, touch of impurity in the Story itself. If, as we read it, we think of Ruth as guilty of an immodest boldness, or of Boaz as in any way lacking in manly honour and virtue, that can only be because we judge these ancient worthies by the standard of modern conventions, or because we ourselves are wanting in true delicacy and refinement. If we would do them justice, it is above all things requisite that we should carry our thoughts back through more than thirty centuries, and bear in mind the patriarchal simplicity of the manners and customs of that antique world in which they

lived.   An age in which the wealthy owner
of a large and fertile estate would himself
winnow barley, and sleep among the heaps
of winnowed corn in an open threshing-floor,
is, obviously, an age as different from this as
it is remote from it.   And Ruth, in creeping
softly to the resting-place of Boaz and nest-
ling under the corner of his long robe, was
simply making a legal claim in the approved
manner of the time.   No doubt the custom
was a hazardous one; and we are expressly
told that the heart of Boaz was " cheerful "
with food and wine when Ruth came to him,
to indicate both the risk she ran and the
virtue of the man who was able to master
both inclination and opportunity, even when
they combined their forces in a single
moment of temptation, rather than betray
the confidence reposed in him.   The very
words which he addressed to her are reported,
moreover, that we may catch their simple
piety, the fatherly tenderness of the tone in
which he spake to his " daughter," the pure
devotion with which he invoked on her the
blessing of God; and so be saved from any

misconception whether of her conduct or of his.

There are but two words in the Chapter which call for detailed explanation ; and in explaining these perhaps all may be said that the reader needs to enable him to peruse this section of the Story with an intelligent apprehension of its meaning. In the Hebrew these two words are *menuchah* and *goel :* *menuchah* means "rest," or, rather, "a place, or asylum, of rest ;" and *goel* means "kins- man," or "redeemer," or "avenger," accord- ing to the connection in which it is found.

I. Let us take the word *Menuchah* first. Naomi said to Ruth (verse 1), "My daughter, shall I not seek *a place* [or *an asylum*] *of rest* for thee, that it may be well with thee?" What she meant by that question we learn from other passages of Holy Writ. For, in the Old Testament Scriptures, the word *menuchah* is used to designate the asylum of honour, freedom, and peace which the Hebrew woman found in the house of her husband. The position of an unmarried woman in the ancient Oriental world was, as I have already remarked,[1] an unhappy one, so unhappy that, in some Oriental tribes, the birth of a girl brought no joy with it, but grief and lamentation; and even among the Hebrews the daughters counted for little; it was the sons, who could work for them and fight for them, in whom the family and the nation rejoiced. Only in the house of a husband was a woman sure of safety, respect, honour. And hence the Hebrews spake of the husband's home as the woman's *menuchah*, or place of rest, her secure and happy asylum from servitude, neglect, and license. In like manner they regarded a secure and hereditary possession of land as the *menuchah*, or rest, of a nation. Thus Moses said to the children of Israel, when they wandered in the Wilderness, " Ye have not yet come unto *the rest* [*menuchah*] which the Lord your God giveth you : " by which he meant that they had no secure possession, no asylum of repose and freedom, no settled and well-defended inheritance, in the Desert; *that* was not their rest, but only the way to their rest. King Solomon was

[1] See page 68.

the first Hebrew chieftain who could bless God for the gift of a complete "rest" to his people. But as, in his reign, every man sat under his own vine and under his own fig-tree, none daring to make him afraid, he could thankfully acknowledge that the whole land had, at last, become the secure and tranquil inheritance of the Hebrew race. And hence, at the opening of the Temple, in his sublime dedicatory prayer, he said: "Blessed be the Lord who hath given *a rest* [*menuchah*] unto His people Israel, according to all that He promised." The Prophets rose to a still higher conception and use of the word. For them, God Himself, God alone, was the true rest, or *menuchah*, of men. And hence they predicted that when God came, in the person of the Messiah, the golden days of Paradise would return, and the whole world would enter into its true *menuchah*, its final and glorious "rest." When the Messiah came, when Christ dwelt among men, He invited the weary and heavy-laden to come to Him, on the express ground that He was their *rest* : that in and with Him they would

find such an asylum of freedom and honourable repose as the Hebrew wife found in her
husband's home; such a rest as the Hebrew
race found in the promised land when it was
wholly their own; nay, such a rest as the
Prophets had taught them to look and hope
for only in God.[1]

This is the history of the word which
Naomi uses in verse 1. When, on her way
home from the Field of Moab, she was fain to
bid her daughters-in-law farewell, she had
prayed that, in return for their kindness to
the dead and to her, " the Lord would grant
them each to find *an asylum* in the house of "
a new husband.[2] When, despite her entreaties and commands, they refused to leave
her, she had had the hard task of warning
them that no such asylum of rest would be
open to them in the land of Israel; that, if
they *would* go with her, they must give up
all the hopes which women hold most dear,
since the Hebrew law torbade the men of
Israel to marry the daughters of Moab.[3]

---

[1] See Appendix A, on Christ the Menuchah of the World.
[2] Chap. i. 9.　　　　[3] Chap. i. 11–13.

The prospect was too dark for Orpah's love to encounter; but Ruth clave unto Naomi, despite the darkness of her future lot. And, now, Naomi sees that the time is come in which the fidelity of Ruth may receive a reward beyond the reach of hope. Ruth is known " in all the Gate, " *i.e.* in all the city, of Bethlehem as "a good and brave woman,"[1] a woman distinguished by an heroic love and virtue. She has been recognized and blessed by Boaz himself as an Israelite indeed, as having " come to take shelter under the wings of the Lord God of Israel."[2] So that now Naomi sets herself, with courage and hope, to find a *menuchah*, an asylum of rest and honour, for the daughter who had clung to her with a love so rare. She knew, or suspected, perhaps, that Boaz looked with kindness, with respect and admiration, on Ruth. Perhaps, too, she was aware of the two considerations which held him back from seeking a wife in Ruth. These considerations were, as we learn from this Chapter, first, that there was a nearer kinsman than him-

[1] Chap. iii. 11.   [2] Chap. ii. 12.

self, who had a prior legal claim on Ruth;
and, secondly, that he was very much older
than Ruth, and hesitated to place himself in
the way of a more suitable and equal match.[1]
The tone in which he addresses Ruth,—"my
daughter,"—and the fact that he had observed
she did not respond to the advances of any
of the " young men, whether poor or rich,"
indicate that he was many years her senior,
and had waited to see whether she would not
select some man younger than himself before
he offered her a *menuchah*, or resting-place,
in his house.[2]

It was, I suppose, this hesitation on the
part of Boaz, and perhaps some glimpse of
the generous and kindly motive that prompted
it, which induced Naomi to resort to a deci-
sive and somewhat dangerous expedient,
although an expedient fully warranted by
the law and custom of the time.

What the legal claim which stood in the
way of Boaz was, and how the expedient of
Naomi drove him to take immediate action,
we shall better understand when we have

---

[1] Chap. iii. 13.   [2] Chap. iii. 10.

looked at the second of the two notable words of this Chapter.

II. This word is *Goel.* Like the word *menuchah*, it has a history, and a history that runs on and up into the Hebrew conception of the Messiah. According to its derivation, *goel* means "*one who unlooses*"—unlooses that which has been bound, and restores it to its original position. The *goel* did his duty, for example, if he redeemed a promissory note by paying it and handing it back to the man who had given it; or if he redeemed a piece of land by paying off the liens upon it and restoring it to its original owner; or if he redeemed a captive by paying his ransom and setting him free. So that the fundamental idea of a *goel* was that of a man who *redeemed*, or set loose, that which had in any way been bound.

This general conception was specialized in two different ways. (1) In virtue of an ancient custom in Israel, a custom sanctioned by the law of Moses, when a man died without issue, his brother, or, if he had no brother, his nearest kinsman, was bound

to marry his widow. This singular custom
was based on a fine principle. Whatever
the defects of their political economy, the
ancient Hebrews firmly grasped a conviction
which it were well that our modern statesmen held and acted on far more stedfastly
than they do. They heartily believed that
the true strength, wealth, and glory of a
nation lay, not in the breadth of its possessions, nor in the victorious conduct of its
wars, nor in the fortunes amassed by its
citizens, but in its *men*, and in their manliness
and virtue. And hence they would not lose
a single man, if they could help it; and,
above all, they would not suffer a single
family to become extinct: for they knew
that it is the families of a land, holding the
ground held by their ancestors for many
generations and trained in the habits of their
pious fathers, which are the very heart and
substance of the national life.

For myself, I wish we all held this conviction closer to our hearts. I never hear of
the thousands who emigrate from our shores
without a feeling of shame and regret that

we are carelessly losing many of our most industrious and skilful citizens because, in this wealthy England of ours, they can earn no sufficient livelihood. A time may come when we shall only too bitterly rue what we have lost in losing our *men* ; and, so far from taking any pride in hearing of the swarms which we annually throw off, I can but feel with how little wisdom we are ruled when the enormous wealth of the country cannot be so distributed as to ensure for every man born into our midst a fair field and a due reward for his industry.

Among the many laws by which the Hebrew legislators sought to preserve their families from extinction was the law of the *goelim*, the law which made it incumbent on the nearest kinsman to take a childless widow to wife, and ordained that any son born of this marriage should inherit the name and possessions of the first husband. This kinsman was called the *goel*, because, " by raising up seed to his brother," he *redeemed* his brother's name and inheritance from being blotted out. It is easy to under-

stand how in process of time this title came
to be applied both to Jehovah and to Jesus.
Jehovah was the *Redeemer* of Israel; for,
again and again, He interposed to save them
from captivity, or to ransom them when they
had been carried away captive, and to preserve them a name and a place in the earth.
Jesus is the *Redeemer* of the whole world;
for when we were captive to divers lusts and
groaning under the oppressions of Evil, the
Son of Man proved Himself our true kinsman
by paying a ransom for us and setting us free
from our intolerable bonds.[1]

(2) It is easy, moreover, to understand
how the kinsman who redeemed had a dark
and miserable counterpart in the kinsman
who avenged. For the very man who was
bound by the ties of kinship to keep his
brother's name alive, was also bound by the
self-same ties to avenge his brother if he
were slain or wronged. Thus it came to
pass that in the Bible the word "*goel*" is
used both for the kinsman-redeemer and the
kinsman-avenger, or " the avenger of blood."

[1] See Appendix B, on Christ the true Goel of Men.

These, then, are the two special meanings of the word *goel* : it means " one who redeems ; " it also means " one who avenges." But it is only in the first and happier of these two senses that it is used in the Book of Ruth. Boaz was among the *goelim* of Naomi and Ruth. He was not THE *goel*, for there was a nearer kinsman than he ; but he was A *goel*, and if this nearer kinsman should refuse to do his duty, then Boaz might step in and do it for him.

Mark, then, how the case stands. On the one side we have the two noble women, Naomi and Ruth, both widows and both childless ; on the other side we have the two men, Boaz and the unnamed kinsman, the latter of whom is bound, according to the Hebrew law, to take Naomi, or, if she should refuse, to take Ruth to wife, in order that the family of Elimelech may not perish out of the land. Of the women, Naomi has the first claim. How is she to shew that she waives her legal claim in favour of Ruth ? Of the men, the unnamed kinsman has the first right to redeem How is Naomi to indicate that she would prefer Boaz to this nearer kinsman? She achieves both points at a stroke by sending *Ruth* to make the claim instead of making it herself, and by sending her to make it of *Boaz* instead of the nearer kinsman. By sending Ruth instead of going herself, she shewed that she waived her own prior claim; and by sending her to Boaz, she shewed that she wished Boaz, rather than the next of kin, to play the part of *goel*.

This is, I believe, the true secret motive and reason of Ruth's hazardous adventure in the threshing-floor of Boaz. Happily, the adventure, hazardous as it was, ran to a happy close. Ruth puts off her widow's weeds, arrays herself in holiday attire, to shew that the days of her mourning are past. She creeps, unseen, to the feet of Boaz, makes her claim in the usual form, thus constraining him to see her righted or himself to be put to shame. And Boaz is charmed to have the duty of the *goel* thrust upon him. He says to her, " Blessed be thou of the Lord, my daughter, *for thy latter*

*kindness is better than thy former, inasmuch as
thou didst not go after the young men, whether
poor or rich.*" By which he meant, I suppose,
that Ruth had shewn even a nobler fidelity
and love in claiming his services as *goel* than
in leaving her native land to follow and
comfort Naomi. Had she been set on her
own pleasure or advancement, with her
strange foreign beauty she might easily, it
would seem, have won to herself any of the
young unmarried men of Bethlehem, and
have gained a suitable and wealthy mate.
But, on Naomi's bidding, she had carefully
observed the law of Israel, the law which
bade her, as a childless widow, claim alliance
with her husband's kinsman. And in thus
sacrificing the natural preference of a young
and attractive woman, she had shewn even a
finer kindness to Naomi and her family, and
a nobler devotion to the law and God of the
Hebrews, than in leaving Moab for Bethlehem.

But Boaz does not simply laud her fidelity
and piety. He promises, he swears, that,
should the nearer kinsman refuse the duty

and honour, he himself will redeem her dead
husband's name and inheritance. Probably
Boaz found it hard to utter the words,
" There is a nearer *goel* than I ; " for,
obviously, by this time, as his allusion to
"the young men" indicates, he was deeply
attached to his fair young kinswoman. And
it illustrates the nobility of his character, his
honour and integrity, that he should propose
to give this " nearer kinsman " his legal due,
although to give it might cost him no small
sacrifice. We may be sure, I think, that
there was a good deal of quiet heroism in the
words of Boaz : " Truly I am a *goel ;* but
there is a nearer *goel* than I. Tarry here to-
night, and it shall be in the morning that if
he will redeem thee, well ; let him redeem :
but if he will not redeem thee, then, as the
Lord liveth, I will redeem thee."

In the morning, at break of day, before
there was light enough for "a man to
recognize his friend," they "rose up," that
Ruth might be home before any one was
stirring, lest any breath of suspicion should
blow on the woman whom all the city pro-

nounced to be as good as she was brave.
Still further to divert suspicion, Boaz bids
Ruth take off her shawl and hold it out while
he pours barley into it. When it is full, he
lifts the load on to her head, and Ruth goes
homeward, bearing her burden with a joyful
heart. And now, should any early neighbour meet her, he will but think that she has
been to fetch away her gleanings from the
field of Boaz : he will only see what he has
often seen before, a woman stepping lightly
along beneath a load of grain.

But so much stress is laid (verses 15 and
17) on the number of measures which Boaz
gave Ruth,—*six*, and Ruth is so expressly
told to take them to her mother-in-law, and
numbers are so significantly used in the
Bible, that we can hardly doubt that this
emphasized *six* has a symbolical meaning
which Naomi would be quick to read. If
there were any such meaning in it, as probably to Hebrews there would be, it would
be this : " The number *six* is the symbol of
labour and service, and is followed by *seven*,
the symbol of rest : for did not God make

the heavens and the earth in six days, and
rest from His labours on the seventh day?
Was not the land of Israel diligently tilled
for six years, and was not the seventh a
sabbatical year, or year of rest?" Naomi,
then, would probably find in the *six* measures
of barley a hint that Ruth's term of labour
and service had come to an end, and that she
was about to find, what Naomi had desired
for her, a *rest* (*menuchah*) in the house of a
husband.

Naomi seems to have read the symbol
thus; for, in the last verse of the Chapter,
she bids Ruth "stay at home," as the
Hebrew bride had to do until her affianced
husband came to fetch her. In past years,
when Elimelech and Boaz were friends and
companions as well as kinsmen, Naomi had
learned enough of the character of Boaz to
be sure that he would not "let the grass
grow under his feet," that he "would not
rest" till he had finished the matter of
Ruth's redemption and found her a "rest."

V.

IN THE GATE.

Chapter iv. *verses* 1-22.

V.

IN THE GATE.

Chapter iv. verses 1–22.

THE gates of ancient cities played many parts: they were guard-houses; they were markets; they were courts of justice; they were places for public deliberation and audience. Necessarily, therefore, they were massively built, with recessed chambers, or divans, in the sides, and often with chambers also above the arch. Here the inhabitants of the city were wont to assemble, either for the transaction of business or to hear and tell the news. Here the judges sat, and administered justice to all comers. Here even kings came to give audience to other kings, or to their ambassadors. So that the Gate played a great part, not only in the defence, but also in the public economy, of the city. Some faint resemblance to these ancient Gates may be found in the structures called " Bars," in London and Southampton, though these modern gates are much smaller than their ancient prototypes; and some faint reminiscence of their character as seats of judicial and royal authority in the titles Sublime *Porte*, or the Ottoman *Porte—porte* meaning *gate*, — by which the Government of Turkey is still designated.

The scene of Chapter iv. is the Gate of Bethlehem. We have already followed Boaz to the Harvest-Field and the Threshing-Floor; we have found in his bearing many illustrations of the simple and primitive customs of the antique time in which he lived. And as we now study this Chapter— a veritable cabinet of antiquities—and follow him to the Gate, and mark how he prosecutes a legal suit, we shall once more be impressed by the simplicity of the ancient Hebrew manners, a simplicity, however, quite compatible with a certain dignified and stately formality.

As we are to " assist " at a legal suit, it

will be well for us to acquaint ourselves, at the very outset, with the law to which an appeal is to be made. This law is the law of the *Goelim,*—the law which governs all acts of exchange and redemption. So far as we are at present concerned with it, this law demanded that the nearest kinsman of a childless widow should marry her, even though he himself were already married : and that the eldest son born of this marriage should, in due time, enter on the inheritance and perpetuate the name of his mother's *first* husband.[1] The law was designed to prevent the extinction of any Hebrew family and the alienation of any family estate. All male blood-relations of the deceased man were reckoned as among his *goelim,* or redeemers ;

[1] This singular, and, if judged by modern standards, immoral, law of Levirate marriage, like other of the laws of Moses—*e.g.* the law of divorce—which have been called in question, was a concession to "the hardness of their hearts" for whom he legislated ; and, so far from being a license to immorality, it was really a limitation of the current immoralities of the time. In ages long anterior to his, a wife, being *bought* from her parents, became the property of her husband, and too valuable a property to be given up at his death. With other property she descended to his heirs, commonly his brothers, any one of whom might possess her, in some tribes going even to the shameful excess of all possessing her in common. Michaelis, in his *Commentaries*

but the nearest of all was THE *goel*, and was the first who was bound to redeem his kinsman's name and inheritance. If, however, he refused to redeem, then the next kinsman succeeded to his right and duty; but he himself, for his refusal, was put to an open shame. But let us have the very statute itself before us. It is recorded in Deut. xxv. 5-10, and runs thus :—

If kinsmen dwell together, and one of them die, and have no child, the wife of the dead shall not marry outside [*i.e.* outside the family circle], *unto a stranger; her husband's kinsman shall go in unto her, and take her to wife, and perform the duty of a husband's kinsman unto her. And it shall be that the first-born whom she beareth shall stand upon the name* [*i.e.* take the

---

on the Laws of Moses (Book iii. Chap. v. Art. 98), has well brought out the process and advance by which this hateful custom drew into a legalized system of Levirate marriages. This system obtained among the Canaanitish tribes for centuries before the time of Moses, as is proved by the shocking story recorded in Genesis xxxviii. All that the great legislator of the Hebrews is responsible for is, that he set still straiter limits to the prevailing custom, including among the duties of the Goel that he, and he only, should "raise up the name of the dead upon his inheritance, that the name of the dead might not be cut off from among his brethren."

place, or arise in the place] *of the kinsman who is dead, that his name be not wiped out of Israel. And if the man like not to take his kinsman's wife, then let his kinsman's wife go up to the gate, unto the elders, and say, My husband's kinsman refuseth to raise up unto his kinsman a name in Israel; he will not do the duty of my husband's kinsman. Then the elders of the city shall call him, and speak unto him; and if he stand to it, and say, I like not to take her; then shall his kinsman's wife come unto him in the presence of the elders, and loose his shoe from off his foot, and spit in his face,[1] and shall*

---

[1] Michaelis will not hear of such a rendering of the Mosaic statute. He admits, indeed, that the Hebrew of Deuteronomy xxv. 9 may signify that the wronged and slighted widow had a right to spit in the kinsman's face. " But, then," he argues, "that act in a public court is so indecent, that if any other interpretation is admissible, this one ought not to be adopted. Now there are two others. (1) *She shall spit before his face.* The Arabs, at this day, when they wish to affront any one, spit, and cry *Fi;* even people of rank do so, just as the common people do with us." And no one who remembers how terribly, during the Civil War in America, the ladies of Baltimore and other Southern cities punished the Northern soldiers by simply spitting as often as they passed them in the streets, will doubt that even this rendering of the phrase describes what might be regarded as a sufficiently cruel indignity. Accordingly, I see that Dr. Benisch, in his Jewish School and Family Bible, renders the phrase, "and spit *before* his face." Michaelis, however

*answer and say, So let it be done unto the man
who will not build up his kinsman's house. And
his name shall be called in Israel, House of the
Shoe taken off* [*i.e.* any one might call him
" Baresole," without committing a legal
offence; his family would be stigmatized
as the family of a shoeless or barefooted

---

finds, and prefers, a second admissible interpretation of it. He
argues (2) that the Hebrew verb may mean *to revile, bilem
evomere,* and judges the phrase to mean that the slighted widow
had a right to revile the kinsman in court as much as she
pleased. With unusual humour and liveliness, this learned
commentator proceeds to remark that the punishment pre-
scribed by the Mosaic law was, after all, not so very severe,
since most men would rather have it known that they had
refused a woman than that they themselves had been refused ;
and adds : "To be once in his lifetime solemnly abused in
a public court by a woman is, at any rate, much easier to be
borne than the same treatment from a man, or extra-judicially ;
and if, besides, the cause is known, and that the court allows her
this liberty, in order to give free vent to her passion, because
the man will not marry her according to her wish, the more
violent the emotions of her rage are, the more flattering to him
must they prove ; and he will go out of court with more pride
than if she had excused him from marrying her with much cool-
ness, or without any emotion at all." All this, however, evidently
savours too much of modern times and modes of thought. The
plainest and most obvious meaning of the Hebrew phrase is
that of our Authorized Version ; and if we remember the simplicity and directness of ancient customs, and that much which
we now esteem delicate and becoming is an outgrowth of
modern civilization and refinement, we shall not scruple to read
it, "and she shall spit *in* his face."

vagabond,—*shoeless* "fellow" being equivalent to "*miserable* fellow," since it was only
in extreme penury and misery that the
Hebrews went barefoot].

This is the statute to which Boaz is about
to appeal; and the one provision of it which
still calls for explanation is that symbolic
act, the taking off of the shoe. The custom
was even thus early a very ancient one, as
we are reminded in this Chapter (verse 7),
and was observed in all cases of redemption
and exchange: in fact, it was the legal form
for confirming or binding legal or commercial
transactions. And this custom had its origin
in the fact that when a man took possession
of landed property, he did it by planting his
shoe on the soil: he asserted his right to it
by treading on the land he had bought.
Thus the shoe symbolized a possession or an
estate which a man actually held, and which
he could tread with his feet at will. Naturally and easily, therefore, the taking off of
the shoe and offering it to another came to
signify that a man renounced his own legal

claim to a possession and transferred it to the neighbour to whom he gave his shoe: with the shoe he gave the right to tread and till the land. This singular custom was not peculiar to the Jews; it also obtained anciently among the Germans. But among the Hebrews of the earlier times it grew into common use as a symbol of exchange, and was employed as a sign of the transfer of rights of any kind, and not only to denote the transfer of land: in short, it seems to have been as common as signing a deed or handing over a warrant is with us. And if we bear this fact in mind, we often get a new light on even the most familiar passages. Thus, for example, the Prodigal Son, in our Lord's parable, has shoes put on his feet, to denote that he is reinstated in the inheritance he had left.

Of course a custom so common was not of itself ignominious. But to the Hebrew there was as wide a difference between taking off his own shoe and having it taken off by another, as there is with us between lifting

off one's own hat and having it knocked off
by another. And in the case of the kinsman
who refused to do a *goel's* duty by his
brother's widow, the shoe was *taken off*, before the Elders, by the woman whom he had
refused to marry. He was thus publicly
and ceremoniously branded as one who had
broken the law, as having failed in the sacred
and imperative duties of kinship, as having
preferred his private interests and aims to
the welfare of the Commonwealth. And
this public disgrace was enhanced by the
indignity of being spat upon by the
woman he had wronged, and having his
whole family saddled with the nickname,
"House of the Shoeless," or "Baresole's
Kin" — which exposed them to general
ridicule and contempt.

The severe law was not enforced by Boaz
in all its severity. But, in order to make
his own marriage with Ruth lawful and legal,
he was obliged to appeal to it, and, in part,
to put it in force. His mode of action shews
how primitive the time was, how simple the

social organization. Obviously there was as yet no king in Israel, no accessible judge even, before whom he might carry his suit. And so, very early in the morning, Boaz hurries from the threshing-floor that he may seat himself in the Gate in time to catch those who, like himself, had slept outside the walls, and will be returning into the city, and those who may leave the city for the fields. He has not long taken his seat before the *goel*, the unnamed kinsman, passes by. Boaz calls on him to sit down,—using a legal form of summons from which his kinsman would understand that he had some legal business to transact with him.

We translate the summons, " *Ho, So-and-so,*" or, " *Ho, Such-an-one,* turn aside, sit down here." But it is difficult, if not impossible, so to translate the Hebrew form as to convey its full significance. In the Original we have two Hebrew words, *Peloni Almoni*, and these two words, apparently, embody one of those legal obliquities of which most ancient systems of law retain some trace;

as, for example, in those fictitious personages,
John Doe and Richard Roe of the English
action for ejectment, who have only recently
been abolished, and in the custom which, till
a few years since, obtained in the German
courts of suing, not in one's own proper
name, but in some common and familiar
name, such as *Hans.*

The ancient Hebrew form of procedure
was of this oblique kind. Instead of sum-
moning even his near kinsman by his personal name, Boaz cried, " *Peloni Almoni*, turn
aside, and sit down,"—the words meaning
literally " *such* " and " *nameless ;* " the effect
of using this antique form being, so far as
we can now recover it, very much as if he
had summoned an anonymous person before
the Elders instead of giving him his proper
name ; just as a few years ago certain fictitious personages, John Doe and Richard Roe,
might have been, and were, summoned into
an English court. What the origin of the
form was, whether it denoted that only a
friendly suit was to be tried, or whether it

was intended to cover errors of misdescription, or whether it grew out of the solemn Eastern courtesy which would shrink from naming a man when threatening him with vexation or harm, it is impossible to say : but, in any case, we have here, in this phrase, an old legal fossil, a remnant of a still more ancient legal form in one of the most ancient systems of jurisprudence.[1]

Peloni Almoni, in the person of the unnamed kinsman of Boaz, responds to the summons. And now, his legal adversary or

---

[1] It is curious to observe how long these "survivals" last. That the phrase "*Almoni Peloni*" should be not only still in use, but in common use here in England, seems incredible. Nevertheless that it is in common use in the English synagogues is beyond doubt. In his instructive and entertaining *Sketches of Anglo-Jewish History*, Mr. Picciotto incidentally informs us that any *anonymous* donor to the Synagogue funds is habitually styled "Almoni Peloni." He tells the following curious story of Sampson de Rebuel Abudiente, the very able Jew from whom the well-known Culling-Eardley family descend. In 1754, having previously acquired an immense fortune by speculating in stocks during the panic caused by the Pretender's march on London, Sampson professed himself a Christian, assumed the name of Gideon, and brought up his children in the Christian faith. But, like most Jews who have assumed Christianity, he never ceased to be a Jew in heart and faith. When he died, his executors forwarded a copy of his will to the authorities of the Spanish and Portuguese congregation, with a request that orders

respondent being secured, Boaz sits and watches the citizens as they pass in and out, asking now this and now that grave elder to sit down, until he has ten, the legal number, of the best-reputed men of Bethlehem to act at once as judges and witnesses of his procedure. In accordance with Oriental custom, many other citizens, seeing these grave elders assembled, and understanding that the wealthy and pious Boaz had some business of grave importance to transact, would add themselves, unbidden yet not unwelcome, to

---

might be given for the interment of the deceased. This strange clause was found in that document: " To my executors,— £1000 to be paid by them, and applied to and for the use of the Portuguese Synagogue in Bevis Marks, London, in case I should be buried in the Jews' burying-ground at Mile End, in the *carreira* [regular row of graves], with the right of a *guebir* [member], and an *Escaba* [or prayer for the dead] said every *Kippan*." The reply of the Portuguese elders was brief and dignified, and to the effect that orders had been given to the keeper of the burying-ground at Mile End to let the grave be opened according to the desire of the deceased, and that his remains would be treated as those of any other member. Then Phineas Cornes Serra, a gentleman belonging to one of the first families of the community, came forward and stated that a certain sum offered annually by him in the name of "Pelon-- Almoni,"—*as anonymous donors were designated,*—was in reality contributed by the late Sampson Gideon, who had thus regularly kept up his payments as a member of the synagogue.

the company, that they too might hear and see what was going on.

Boaz opens the proceedings by formally announcing to his kinsman that Naomi has sold, or is about to sell, the field, the parcel of land, which formerly belonged to their common kinsman Elimelech. Naomi may either have sold this land to supply her necessities, though, if that were so, one hardly sees how she should have come to extreme want in the lapse of a single year; or, more probably (comp. verse 5), she may have put it up for sale for the express purpose of putting the law in motion and compelling her kinsman to redeem it. In either case the kinsman was legally bound both to redeem the estate and to marry Naomi, or, should she waive her claim or be past child-bearing, to marry Ruth. Each of these two women was a childless widow, and each had a claim on the estate. Should neither of them have a child, the family of Elimelech would become extinct, " his name would be put out of Israel." Here clearly, then, was a case in which the *goel* was bound to come forward and do his duty. And, indeed, the *goel* of Naomi admits the claim ; nay, more, so long as he thinks it is only the redemption of Elimelech's land that is in question, he is willing to satisfy the claim. To the appeal and inquiry of Boaz, " Wilt thou redeem ? " he formally replies, " I will redeem it."

Now Boaz had set his heart on marrying Ruth, and therefore he must have heard his kinsman's reply with some dismay. But one resource is left him. His kinsman may not admit that he is bound to marry Ruth, or he may not care to marry her, even if he admit the obligation. And hence Boaz now rejoins, " But, if you redeem the land of Elimelech, you must also take Ruth *the Moabitess* to wife, and raise up the name of the dead man on his inheritance. Are you prepared to do this also ? " The kinsman is not prepared to assume *this* function of the *goel*. And, in an ordinary case, he would have been in no little embarrassment between his reluctance to marry his kinsman's widow and his fear

lest, should he refuse, she should inflict the
disgraceful penalty of his refusal upon him.
But Boaz has made the way easy for him.
He has brought neither Naomi nor Ruth with
him, so that his kinsman has no indignity
to fear. For the present, at least, his shoe
will not be pulled off, nor will the slighted
and injured woman spit in his face. And,
moreover, Boaz has expressed his perfect
willingness to discharge all the duties of the
goel should his kinsman decline them. His
motive in thus sparing his kinsman is not
simply, I suppose, either a kindly consideration for a man closely related to him or his
love for Ruth, but also the conviction that
an Israelite, caring only for the letter of the
law and not for its spirit, might honestly
doubt whether he were bound to marry his
"brother's" widow *when that widow was a
daughter of Moab.* True, Ruth had come to
put her trust under the shadow of Jehovah's
wings. True, she was known as a good and
brave woman in all the city of Bethlehem.
But, none the less, she was by birth an alien,

one of the Heathen women, with whom the sons of Israel were forbidden to intermarry. The law was doubtful: if the appeal to it were pushed too far he might defeat his own end.

We need not think over hardly, therefore, even of this anonymous kinsman. He may have been, probably he was, a just man according to his lights. Walking by the strict requirements of the law of Israel, he may have honestly doubted whether he were bound to marry Mahlon's *Moabitish* widow. Undoubtedly it was a sin against the Law for Mahlon to have married her while she was a Heathen, even if it were not a sin to take her to wife now that she was a proselyte. Could, then, the widow of an illegal marriage claim quite the same rights with a widow of a legal marriage, even though she afterwards became a proselyte to the Hebrew faith? And if he was not bound to marry her, would it be prudent to marry her? Evidently he thinks it would not be prudent. He declines to redeem, on such terms, the inheritance of his dead kinsman, "*lest I mar mine own in-heritance.*" By which he meant, I think, that his doubt as to the right conferred on Ruth by the Hebrew law was reinforced by a Hebrew superstition. For, in Israel, marriage with the daughter of an alien race was held to be "unlucky," even when it was lawful. Many such marriages had proved unhappy and disastrous. And, by expressly calling Ruth *the Moabitess* in his challenge, Boaz seems to have touched his kinsman's superstitious fears. No doubt, the calamities which had befallen Elimelech and Naomi were popularly attributed to their sojourn in the Field of Moab. No doubt, the popular voice of Bethlehem affirmed that Chilion and Mahlon had been cut off before their time because they had married "strange women." Here, then, was one Hebrew family in imminent danger of extinction solely because of such a marriage as was now proposed. The *goel* fears a similar fate. He fears that, should he marry Ruth, he may "injure his own inheritance,"—fears that he too may die

before his time, and his name be put out of
Israel. He, therefore, will run no such risk:
let Boaz run it, if he will.

This, I believe, was his real reason for
refusing to discharge the duty of the *goel*.
And it is a curious comment on his narrow,
selfish ambition that, of this man who was
bent on preserving his name and fame, who
would run no risk of having his name cut off
from the gate of his place, neither Israel nor
the world knows even so much as the mere
name. He is unnamed in the very Book
which recounts his story; we know him
simply as the "anonymous kinsman:" while
Boaz, who had no such selfish ambition, who
held that in every nation they who trust God
and work righteousness are acceptable with
Him, lives for ever on the sacred page, and
is enrolled, together with Ruth, in the
pedigree of Him whose Name is above every
name.

The anonymous kinsman refuses to redeem
Ruth and her inheritance; and, as a symbol
and attestation that he cedes all right to the

inheritance, he draws off his shoe and hands it to Boaz, transferring to *him* the legal right to plant his foot on the parcel of land left by Elimelech.

With profound and solemn emotion Boaz calls on the Elders and the circle of bystanders to observe and remember this legal transfer of rights and duties, expressing himself, however, with legal fulness and precision: "Ye are witnesses this day that I have acquired all that was Elimelech's, and all that was Chilion's and Mahlon's of the hand of Naomi. Moreover, Ruth the Moabitess, the wife of Mahlon, have I acquired to be my wife, to raise up the name of the dead upon his inheritance, that the name of the dead be not cut off from among his brethren and from the gate of his place. Ye are witnesses this day." They reply: "We are witnesses,"[1]—thus completing the legal transaction,—and break out into a profusion of good wishes which amply verify the state-

[1] It is probable that in the appeal of Boaz and the response of the Elders we have another "survival" of an ancient system of jurisprudence.

ment of Boaz concerning Ruth in the previous Chapter: "All the gate of my people doth know that thou art a good and brave woman." They lift her to the level of the most famous women of Israel by praying that she may be like Rachel and Leah, the mothers of the twelve tribes. And though the words, "The Lord make the woman that cometh into thy house like Rachel and like Leah, which two did build the house of Israel," may probably have already become the usual formula of congratulation and benediction when an Israelitish marriage was announced, yet the fact that this sacred formula was conceded to Ruth *the Moabitess* shews that, at last, the inhabitants of Bethlehem had learned to value her at her true worth. They would not have uttered this prayer if they had not come to esteem her, for her love and piety, as an Israelite indeed.

Boaz, being now the recognised *goel* of Ruth, marries her; and in due time a son is given to them. And now the shadows, which lay so thick on the opening incidents

of the Story, clear off, and both Naomi and
Ruth receive a full reward for their rare and
heroic love.   It is one of the many fine points
of the Story that its concluding sentences
are almost wholly devoted, not to the young
and happy wife and mother, but to Naomi,
who had suffered so many calamities, and
who, by the piety and resignation with which
she bore them, had drawn Ruth from the
idolatries of Moab.   It is Naomi, not Ruth,
whom " the women her neighbours " con-
gratulate on the birth of Ruth's son.   In him
they see Naomi's *goel*—Ruth already had
hers in Boaz; and they pray that, as he
grows up, he may restore her to her former
happiness and be the stay and gladness of
her old age.   But though they speak to
Naomi, and pray for her, they do not utterly
forget the singular virtue of Ruth.   In the
words, " Thy daughter-in-law, *who loveth
thee, who is better to thee than seven sons*," they
pronounce on her an eulogy such as few
" strange " women could have heard from
Hebrew lips.   It is because the boy is Ruth's

son that he is Naomi's *goel;* for how can he
fail to love and cherish the woman whom his
mother has loved with a love even passing
that of women?

And so the Story closes, not simply leaving
these two brave and noble women happy in
each other, and in Boaz, and in Obed his
son, but weaving for them an immortal
crown of honour in that it marks their
intimate connection with David, the " darling
of Israel," and with Him who was at once
David's Son and Lord. " Boaz begat Obed,
and Obed begat Jesse, and Jesse begat
David;" and of David, as concerning the
flesh, came Jesus the Christ, the Light of
the Gentiles and the Glory of the people of
Israel.

It is not every story of faithful love and
piety which mounts to so happy a close,
at least in this world. But before we complain, as though our virtue had been passed
over by our God, it will be well for us to ask
ourselves whether our virtue can compare
with that of Ruth. It will also be well for
us to remember, what Ruth did not know,

that godliness has the promise of the life to come, as well as of that which now is, and to rest in the conviction that the longer the promise tarries the richer and sweeter will be its fulfilment. Through the tender mercy of God we most of us get quite as much happiness as is good for us even here, quite as much as, and far more than, we have deserved ; but, through that same tender and abounding Mercy, we may all get a blessedness far larger than we have deserved hereafter, and shall get it, if only we follow those who, through faith and patience, now inherit the promises.

APPENDICES.

ON CHRIST AS THE MENUCHAH OF THE WORLD.

ON CHRIST AS THE TRUE GOEL OF MEN.

APPENDIX A.

ON CHRIST AS THE MENUCHAH OF THE WORLD.

ST. MATTHEW xi. 28-30.[1]

" WORDS of so sweet breath composed " but rarely
fell even from the lips on which sat the law of
kindness. In their Divine quickening melody we have
a strain which might well create a soul within the very
ribs of Death, which *has* given life to many a soul dead
in trespasses and sins.   Nowhere do we find a more
pathetic revelation of the will of God as a saving, life-
giving Will. We are conscious of a certain tender and
moving beauty in the very sound of the words ; and
when we pause to consider them, even in their first and
most obvious meaning, we become aware of a power
in them which attracts and calms our hearts: but only
as we deliberately study them, and set them in their
proper framework of circumstance and occasion, do

[1] At the request of the Society I very gladly append to this
Commentary a brief homiletic exposition of the most spiritual
and Johannine passage to be found in the Gospel according to
St. Matthew.

we sound their depths of meaning, and feel that they
are as full of truth as of grace.

If, for instance, we ask, What was the occasion
which prompted Jesus to utter them? St. Luke's
answer[1] to the question instantly places them in a new
and pathetic light. For he tells us that, while our Lord
was lamenting over the unrepentant cities of Galilee,
the Seventy returned from their mission with joy, to
report the immense and unexpected success of their
labours. Everywhere they had been welcomed by the
poor and simple. Their message, "Repent, for the
kingdom of heaven is at hand!" had proved a word of
power. Moved by compassion for the multitude, who
were as sheep without a shepherd, torn and bitten by
the wolves, Christ had sent them forth to call the
wandering sheep to Him, to *lead* them to Him, the
true Shepherd and Bishop of souls. And now, as He
listens to the happy tidings they bring Him, His heart
expands, and He turns, from lamenting the unbelief of
the most favoured of men, to address a gracious and
persuasive invitation to the untaught and rude. He
hears that *some*, that *many*, are coming to Him, and
He longs that *all* should come. He opens His arms,
as it were, to the whole world, and cries, "Ho, all ye
poor simple souls, despised and oppressed by 'wise'
rabbi and 'prudent' priest, smitten and fleeced by the
hirelings who should feed and defend you, come unto
Me, and your wanderings and miseries shall have an
end; ye shall find rest unto your souls."

The occasion which prompted these gracious words
sheds new meaning into them, then, and new pathos.

[1] St. Luke x. 13–22.

But this occasion moved our Lord to speak to God as well as to men ; and we must consider the thanksgiving He addresses to His Father if we would apprehend the full meaning and beauty of the invitation He extends to the weary and the heavy-laden. He speaks to God, indeed, *before* He speaks to men. His first emotion on hearing the happy tidings brought Him by the Seventy is one of profound and joyful gratitude. In " answer," or response, to their report (see Matt. xi. 25, 26) He lifts up his eyes to heaven, and says: " I thank thee, O Father, Lord of heaven and earth, that, hiding these things from the wise and prudent, Thou hast revealed them unto babes. Even so, Father, for so it seemed good in Thy sight." Now, of course, we are not to understand our Lord as rejoicing that the things of the kingdom had been concealed from the learned rabbi and the wise scribe. He had no pleasure in the spiritual blindness of any man. Glad as He was to hear that the simple and unlettered had received the gospel of the Seventy, He would have been still more profoundly glad had the wise and the prudent received it also. And yet we *are* to understand Him as recognizing the will of God in the unbelief of the wise, no less than in the faith of the simple, and as making that Will His own. It *is* an ordinance of Heaven that, while the things of the Spirit are freely disclosed to the simple and childlike heart, they should be concealed from the proud and confident heart. Who are the men that to this very day set themselves most strongly against the revelation of the fatherly goodwill of God ? Are they not "the wise," and " the prudent," the men who dabble in science and philosophy, and

the men who are much occupied with the affairs of life
and keep a keen eye on what they deem "the main
chance ? "

It is a rule, then, that self-confident wisdom rejects
the Revelation which childlike simplicity accepts. This
rule, or law, Christ here recognizes and states: nay,
He adopts, and even rejoices in it, since it expresses
the will of God.   He who is "the Amen" utters His
"So be it" to this canon, or ordinance, of Heaven,—
"*Yea*, Father, since so it seemeth good in Thy sight."
Why should He not?   The law is at once just and
merciful.   Is it not just, if, when God holds out His
hand to lead men to truth and righteousness, they
refuse to take it, that they should be left to wander on
unguided and unrestrained?   Must God drag men,
unwilling, into the way of salvation?   *That* is impossible ; for salvation is *in the will*, and consists, indeed
in a voluntary, a cheerful, and unforced, adoption of
the Divine Will.   The law is just, then: and is it not
as merciful as it is just?   When men are left to walk
in ways of their own choosing, they sooner or later
discover that they have missed the way of peace ;
they fall into unforeseen perils and harms ; they learn
their need of a Guide to whom all the mysteries of Time
and Change and Death lie open as the day: they seize
the Hand they once refused.   And what can be more
merciful than that men should be *constrained*, by the
pain and loss and shame which come from walking
unguided through life, to accept the guidance of Him
to the tender invitations of whose love they long
refused to listen ?

It *is* the will of God, then, that the knowledge in

which eternal life consists should come only to the simple, childlike heart. This simple and childlike heart it is the very office of true wisdom to induce ; but if any are rendered proud and self-confident by the very wisdom which ought to make them docile and humble, it is the righteous will of God that this living and saving knowledge should be "hidden" from them. It *is* hidden from them—hidden by their own self-confidence and pride.

This law, this determination that the truth shall only be found by wise simplicity and trust, our Lord proceeds still more emphatically to express (verse 27). He affirms that as only the Father knows the Son, so also only the Son knows the Father, and he to whom the Son *wills* to reveal Him. His words seem at first to narrow and obscure our hopes, whether for ourselves or for the world. In express terms we are taught that we lie absolutely at the mercy of the wills of the Father and of the Son, or, rather, at the mercy of Their *will*, since They have but one and the selfsame will. And as we listen we feel as though our souls were being fettered in the bonds of an inexorable necessity, an eternal and changeless decree. "What are *we ?*" we cry ; "and what can we do but stand and wait, if we thus utterly depend on a Will other than our own?" Rightly viewed, however, it is this very subjection to a higher Will than our own in which lie our strength and comfort. For this higher Will is also a better and a kinder Will. And, oh, how gloriously does the light rush back upon our thoughts, sweeping away every shadow of despair and suffusing our souls and the whole story of Time with the bright hues of an immortal hope, as Christ continues and closes His discourse with the invitation : " Come unto Me, all ye that labour and are heavy laden, and I will give you rest." For these final words shew us what that Will is on which we depend,—that it is a saving and redeeming Will, a Will bent on giving life and rest to the toilworn and burdened sons of men, to all who feel the weight and curse of sin. Said I not truly, then, that these words are of so sweet breath composed, and ring out so true a melody of " the everlasting chime," that they might well create a soul within the very ribs of Death ? Do they not contain, when we read them in their connection, a most pathetic revelation of the sovereign will of God as a saving Will, a Will *set* for the redemption of the world ?

But, now that we have placed them in their proper framework of circumstance and occasion, let us look a little more closely at the words themselves, that we may still more deeply enter into their wealth of meaning and grace.

Who are those whom Christ calls to Himself, beseeching them that, by a free movement of the soul, they rise from their bondage to sorrow and care, change the direction of their aim, and turn toward Him as their Refuge, Asylum, Rest ? They are all who " labour " as at a yoke, and all who—in this more miserable than the ordinary beast of draught—are also laden with a heavy burden. But who may these be ? what is the spiritual condition set forth under this dolorous image of an ox tugging wearily at a galling yoke, and, at the same time, crouching under the

weight of an intolerable burden ? If we go to our own
hearts for an answer to this question, we shall not be
long kept waiting for a reply. For they only too feel-
ingly persuade us that what we have here set forth, to
the very life, is the miserable lot of the transgressor,
who, while still attempting to meet the severe demands
of duty, is borne down by an intolerable sense of guilt.
The Law is the yoke; and the burden is our con-
sciousness of having disobeyed that law. When men
sin, they mean to be free. When, in order to gratify
the lusts and desires of their hearts, they shake off the
fetters and restraints of law, they flatter themselves
that they have slipped from every yoke and flung off
every burden. " Let us have done with these formal
and vexatious restraints," is the thought of their hearts :
"let us be free for once to take our own way and follow
our own will, to be merry unchecked, to enjoy our life
a little before we lose all our power of enjoyment."
This is their aim—to be free, merry, glad. But they
soon discover that none are so miserable as those who
put pleasure before duty, none so cruelly enslaved as
those who break all bounds of law. Their sins find
them out, breeding consequences, conducting to issues,
which they did not anticipate, and which fill them with
shame, fear, and self-loathing. The law they have
broken avenges itself upon them ; they receive the
due reward of their deeds. And *now* it is far harder
for them than before to restrain their lawless and
sensual desires, since use doth breed a habit in a man,
and habit soon becomes second nature. *Now* they
are tormented by an incessant craving for indulgence ;
and they are the more tempted to yield to it by the

hope that, in fresh indulgence, they may lose, at least for a moment, the intolerable sense of shame and guilt which hangs upon them like a weight. More unhappy than the goad-driven ox, they are laden with a burden, while yet they tug hopelessly at a yoke.

To all who are in this strait of misery, to all who feel the burden of sin, to all who have sunk into bondage by their very endeavour to be free, to all who are fevered with the unrest which springs from conflicting aims and desires, Christ cries : " Come unto Me, and I will give you rest."

But what is the "*rest*" He promises us? and *how* may we secure it?

The Hebrew word which our Lord doubtless used, the word for "rest," has an instructive history : it would be charged with sacred associations to those who heard it fall from his lips. For this word " *menuchah*," as we have seen,[1] is used in many weighty sentences in the Old Testament Scriptures. It is used to designate the asylum of honour and freedom which a Hebrew found in the home of her husband, her secure refuge from servitude, insolence, neglect. It is also used to denote the asylum of freedom and repose on which the Hebrew race entered when it gained full possession of the promised land, when, in the days of Solomon, every man might sit under his vine or his fig-tree, none daring to make him afraid. It was used by the Prophets in a still higher sense : with them *God* was the true *menuchah*, or rest, of His people, nay, of the whole world: to them it was revealed that only when the Immanuel came, the God-with-us, would the golden days of Paradise return, and the world enter into its final and glorious rest. So that those who first listened to our Saviour's gracious Invitation, those on whose weary and fevered spirits His promise of "rest" first fell, would understand that He was offering them an asylum of repose, honour, freedom, such as the Hebrew wife found in her husband's house, such as the Hebrew race found in the sacred land when it was wholly their own, such as the Hebrew Prophets had found in God in the moments of their loftiest inspiration. Nay, more, in proportion as they were familiar with the prophetic writings—which they daily read in school and synagogue—they would understand that Jesus of Nazareth was claiming to be the Anointed One of God, the promised Immanuel, the Lord of that sacred kingdom, that golden age, in which, redeemed from its confusion and strifes, the world should rise to its golden close and enter into an everlasting peace.

And *we* must understand Him as offering us no less a "rest" than this. He calls us from the noise, from the contentions and rivalries, from the vulgar ambitions and feverish unrest of life, from shame and remorse, from the fear of change and the fear of evil, into a secure and happy asylum in which we may dwell in honour and freedom, unalarmed by the loud uproars of the world, unfretted by its cares and vexations, untainted by its pollutions, unstained by its guilt. He summons us to " God, who is our home," to God as revealed in Him who is our peace. " Come unto Me," He cries ; " let there be a free, glad movement of your will toward Me ; claim Me for your Redeemer and Helper, and you shall find yourselves in a happy and

inviolable Rest, secure from all the shocks of change
from all the wiles and assaults of evil !

But *how* can this be ? Is it possible that this supreme
good—rest, a free and honourable rest for our weary
and fretted spirits—is open to us all ?   And if it be,
how may we possess ourselves of it ?

To this question Christ replies, " *Come unto Me,*
and I will give you rest."   And by coming to Him, He
meant, of course, that we should make a spiritual approach toward Him ; that we should trust in Him :
that we should heartily believe in that Revelation of
the Divine Love and Mercy which He came to make.
So long as our spirits are galled and oppressed by a
sense of guilt, so long as we lie under the heavy and
weary weight of unforgiven sins, rest is impossible to
us.   The very first thing we have to do, therefore, if
we would enter into the rest of Christ, is to exercise
faith in the atonement He has wrought, in the demonstration He has made of God's willingness to save us
from our sins, if only we confess and renounce them,
and to infuse into us the power of that endless life
which is prolific in all the fruits of righteousness and
charity.

By His " Come unto Me," again, He means not
simply that we are to acquiesce in, to accept, His
revelation of the forgiving and redeeming will of God,
but also that we are to strenuously adopt and obey that
pure and gracious Will.   We enter into rest, not by
leaning indolently against the Cross and warbling
dainty hymns of praise, but by manfully taking up the
Cross, and shewing ourselves to be of one spirit with
Him who gave Himself, the Just for the unjust, that

He might bring us to God. The faith that saves is not only the faith which trusts in what Christ has done for us : it is also the faith which works by love, to produce in us a love like His own. If, as we listen to the invitation, "Come unto Me, all ye that labour and are heavy laden, and I will give you rest," our first thought is, "Thank God, we have done with yokes and burdens, with obligations and restraints ; we may lie down and take our rest, and leave all to Christ," we simply shew that, in our impatience, we have wholly mistaken His meaning. For to the promise of rest, and in order that it may be fulfilled, He Himself immediately goes on to say, " Take *My yoke* upon you, and *My burden*, and learn of Me." From which it is obvious that, so far from having escaped obligation and restraint by our faith in Him, we still have much to learn, much to do, much to bear ; so far from having done with yokes and burdens, we are invited to wear a new yoke, to assume a new burden. And it is for this call to new endeavours and new endurances that we ought to be thankful, rather than for an imaginary and impossible enfranchisement from obligations and restraints, and for which we are thankful the very moment we pause and reflect. There is no *rest* in indolence, but the cruellest unrest. There is no freedom in lawlessness, but the most terrible bondage. We rise into our true *menuchah* and true rest only when all our faculties are fully and happily engaged, and yet are not strained and fevered with anxiety. Did the Hebrew bride, when she found her " rest " in her husband's home, sink into listless indolence ? On the contrary, new happy duties and responsibilities were laid upon her; and in the faithful discharge of these she rose to her true dignity and honour and peace. When the children of Israel entered into their "rest," when the promised land was all their own, did they fall into an inglorious ease? On the contrary, they were never so active as in the age of David and Solomon; they reared their noblest buildings, engaged in their widest commerce, raised their most abundant harvests, wrote their finest chronicles and poems. And if we truly respond to the calls of Christ, we shall not find our "rest" in an indolent and inglorious ease, but in the new order and energy of our life, in doing all we do as unto Him, in more abundant labours for the good of others, in bearing the inevitable sorrows and losses of life with a more constant spirit, and in that sincere and cordial trust in the Providence and purposes of God which can alone arm us against the stings and frets of care. It is not *work*, but *worry*, that kills. It is not the duties and labours we have to discharge which fever and perturb our spirits; but our ambitions, our rivalries, our anxieties for the present and for the future, for ourselves and for our children. We waste and are consumed in the fire of an inward restlessness, not because we have so much to do, but because we do not carry to all our labours a composed and trustful spirit. Did we but come to Christ, and learn of Him to live in a constant affiance and communion with the Father who careth for us, our very labour would become a rest, and our duty our delight. *He* was as poor as any of us. He was dependent for daily bread on the casual charity of His friends; and His

friends were few and not rich in this world's goods.
He was as busily, as exhaustively, occupied as any of
us. And yet He was redeemed from all care, from all
fear, and out of the abundance of His peace gave peace
to as many as drew near to Him. Who ever found
Him apprehensive of what to-morrow might bring
forth? Who ever heard *Him* complain that His burden
was too heavy or His work too hard?

Christ, then, has a right to say to us, and to as
many as long for a tranquil heart, " Learn of *Me*:
learn of Me, that you may enter into My rest." And
in His grace He does say it ; nay, in large measure He
explains to us, by the very terms of His invitation,
the secret of that "rest" which He asks us to share
with Him. For He virtually says : " Come to Me ;
learn of Me ; for I, too, am under the yoke. *I* keep
and magnify the law which you have to obey. But I
am meek and lowly of heart, not haughty and self-
assertive ; and therefore the yoke does not gall Me. I
love the law I keep : how, then, should it be a burden
to Me? If you love it, it will be but an easy yoke and
a light burden to you. Obey the pure and gracious
Will of God with a meek and lowly heart, and you
shall find rest to your souls." And, beyond a doubt, if
we heartily respond to His call, if we do love the Will
we have to obey, though to our weakness it must
always seem a yoke, the yoke will not gall us ; we
shall find, at least, that rest which comes from having
the ruling aim and desire of our soul satisfied.

If any ask, "How is it, then, that, though we believe
in Christ, *we* are still weary and heavy laden, still
toiling under a weight of cares and apprehensions

which grows as we advance, still restless with anxieties
about our children, our future, our spiritual condition
and prospects?" we can now answer them with the
very words of Christ. We need not say, in general
terms, "Your faith is weak, inconstant, wavering,"
although that is only too true both of us and of them .
we can also point out exactly what it is that they have
failed to learn, and need to learn, of Him. He was
meek and lowly of heart.   That is why the yoke sat so
lightly on Him. But are we? are they? Who does
not see that many of our most biting cares, if not all of
them, spring from our self-love, our self-assertion, our
high thoughts of ourselves, and of what is due to us,
of "what we may fairly expect"? Instead of being
"meek," we are quick and sudden to resent slights
and wrongs, and even to imagine them. Instead of
being "lowly of heart," we are full of ambitions to
excel or surpass our neighbours, to lay up a greater
store, to make a greater show, to get before or above
them, and compel them to minister to our vanity,
greed, reputation, comfort. Alas, this conception of
ourselves as in some way better than our neighbours
is native and habitual to us, and often discloses itself
in the very heat and resentment with which we dis-
claim it. And how can we enter into "rest," the rest
of Christ, while we hold this high opinion of ourselves
and our deserts, while our hearts are torn by these
selfish and vulgar ambitions? He who was the Lord
of all became the Servant of all. If *we* are still more
conscious of our "rights" than of our duties, of our
"claims" than of our obligations, we still need to
learn of Him who was meek and lowly of heart the

very rudiments of that sacred and Divine Rest in which His pure Spirit found an asylum from the clamours and rivalries and conflicts of the world. *This* secret of the Lord is not with those who are wise and prudent, strong or great, in their own conceits ; but with those who are of a meek, humble, and childlike heart ; who live in a constant intercourse with the great Lord and Lover of Souls, and who learn of Him to chasten their desires, to moderate their aims, to purify and raise their wills, to look for rest in labour, for freedom in obedience, for honour in service.

Christ, then, is the true Menuchah of the world : for in proportion as men believe in Him He takes away their sins, and gives them to share in His own ineffable and unbroken peace.

APPENDIX B.

ON CHRIST AS THE TRUE GOEL OF MEN.

RUTH ii. 20.

IT may be worth while to define the functions of the Hebrew *goël* more exactly, and to shew more in detail how in the Lord Jesus Christ we have the Divine "Substance" which cast that prophetic "shadow" before.

We learn from the Pentateuch that the main functions of the Goel were three, or, rather, that there were three tragic contingencies in which the legal Redeemer and Avenger was bound to interpose—each of which was, in the very nature of things, of much more frequent occurrence than the case recorded in the Book of Ruth. 1. If any Hebrew had fallen into such penury as that he was compelled to part with his ancestral estate, the Goel was bound to purchase it, and, after certain conditions had been observed, to restore it to his impoverished kinsman. 2. If any Hebrew had been taken captive, or had sold himself for a slave, the Goel was bound to pay the price of his redemption, to unloose and set him free.   3. If any Hebrew had suffered grievous wrong, or had been slain, the Goel was bound to exact compensation for the wrong, or to avenge his murder.   A brief examination of these three functions of the Goel will open up to us their moral and prophetic significance, and perchance constrain us to say, with a keener accent of conviction and gratitude, " The man Christ Jesus is near of Kin to us, our nearest Kinsman, the true Goel of the whole race."

1. *The Forfeited Inheritance.* — If an Israelite, weighed down by penury, had sold his estate, or any part of it, any one of his near kinsmen who was able to do so was enjoined to purchase it, that it might not remain in the hands of the stranger or the alien.   For a time, till the year of Jubilee, the estate was his ; but when the silver trumpets announced that the year of Jubilee had come, it reverted to its original owner. Even before then the vendor might at any moment redeem or reclaim it, if he were able to pay back the purchase money, or an equitable proportion of it, should his kinsman have already enjoyed the use and produce of the land for a term of years : but in any case it returned to him in the year of Jubilee.   The object and good policy of this statute are obvious. Moses was statesman enough to know that the yeomen who live on and farm their own land are the strength and backbone of a country : he set himself, therefore, to preserve their number unimpaired.   Hence he made it legally impossible for them to cede the land itself ; all they could sell was the use and the fruits of it for a limited term of years—a fact which was duly

considered, no doubt, in the price for which it was sold.   In fifty years, at the farthest, every plot of land reverted to the family to which it originally belonged : and thus, for many centuries at least, the country was parcelled out mainly among those small proprietors who are found to be the most thrifty and expert tillers of the soil, and whose patriotism is commonly more stedfast and more ardent than that of any other class.

The political sagacity of this enactment is obvious enough, then ; nor are its prophetic meaning and reference far to seek.   For of whom can the Israelite, sunk in penury and alienating his original inheritance, be the type but of fallen man ? God made him upright, clothed him with glory and honour, set him over all the works of His hands.   And he, violating the conditions of loyalty and obedience on which it was held, alienated the broad and fair inheritance, leaving himself heir only to shame and want and death.   All things were his ; but, by his sin, he put them all into the hands of the Stranger and the Adversary ; so that, for his sake, and through his sin, the whole creation, of which under God he was lord, has been brought under the sorrowful and obscuring shadows of vanity and corruption.   And who can the Goel be but that Divine Kinsman—bone of our bone and flesh of our flesh— who has redeemed and restored the inheritance we had forfeited ?   " All things are ours " already—made ours by His grace—if we are His, even the sorrows and imperfections of earth and time : and when the trumpet shall sound and the great Jubilee is come, even the creation also, our original inheritance, shall be delivered from all the shadows of imperfection, out of that bondage to vanity and corruption to which we have subjected it, into the glorious liberty of the sons of God.

2. *The Forfeited Liberty.*—To discharge a debt, or to save himself from the last extremities of want, a Hebrew might sell *himself* either to a stranger or a fellow-citizen. If he sold himself to an Israelite, he was treated, not as a slave, but as a hired servant, and became free even from those light bonds so soon as the year of Jubilee arrived. But if he sold himself to a stranger, a foreigner, he became a slave ; and in that case any "one of his brethren" was permitted to interpose, and to pay the price of his redemption. Here, again, it is easy to see why the Mosaic law enjoined and limited the interposition of the Goel. If the man were in the hands of an Israelite, he lost none of his rights and privileges ; he was still a member of the Divine Commonwealth, of the Holy Congregation. There was no need, therefore, to interpose on his behalf. But if his master were a foreigner, a Heathen, he might, and probably would, be withdrawn from the Commonwealth, and lose his standing as one of the chosen people. And if Moses would not suffer a single yeoman to be lost, much less would he suffer a single *man* to be lost to Israel. For the Hebrew who became a slave to a Heathen, therefore, the Goel was to interpose.

Here, too, the prophetic intention of the enactment is as plain and obvious as its political intention. For we men were "sold under sin," led captive at the will, not of a brother and an equal, but of an alien and adverse spirit. Our freedom was gone : we were in a cruel bondage. We could neither break our bonds in sunder nor ransom ourselves with a price. We had lost our place and standing in the Congregation, among the sons, of God. And Christ has proved Himself our Goel by " giving Himself a ransom for all," by redeeming us, " not with corruptible things, as silver and gold," but with His own " precious blood, as of a lamb without blemish and without spot."

3. *The Forfeited Life.*—" The avenger of blood," of whom we so often read in our English Version, is in Hebrew simply " the Goel," the kinsman-redeemer, who, in virtue of his kinsmanship, becomes an avenger of wrongs. If a murder were done in Israel, the pursuit and execution of the murderer devolved on the next of kin. If the kinsmen of the murdered man were not at hand, no stranger had the right of arrest, and still less the right to revenge. Unmolested, the homicide betook himself to the nearest city of refuge, where he found a secure asylum until he could be brought before the judges of the land. To us this may seem to be, as indeed it was, but a rude form of justice. Its very rudeness, however, adapted it to those rude times. Judges were few ; their circuits were rarely and slowly travelled, and were often interrupted for long and indefinite periods. And if, on the one hand, *the Goel* might avenge a murder, not waiting for session and legal verdict ; on the other hand, none but the next of kin could thus take the law into his own hands : and, always, the cities of refuge were open to all. In those rude and early times, perhaps no more equitable arrangement could have been made. It did not foster, or enjoin, revenge ; it defined and

limited it, bringing within narrow legal bounds the wide unlimited revengefulness of the natural Eastern man. It was better that the Goel, breathing out threatenings and slaughter, should chase the flying felon along the road that led to the sacred city, or even that he should thrust him through with a dart, than that a blood-feud should be permitted to spring up between family and family, clan and clan, such as was common among the neighbouring tribes.

And even the Lamb of God has a certain " wrath ;" even in Him who was meek and lowly of heart we may find that which answers to the avenging function of the Hebrew Goel. Christ came to destroy as well as to redeem ; to destroy, that He might redeem. He followed after that great enemy of our souls of whom the Hebrew " shedder of blood " was a type, and smote him that " was a murderer from the beginning." To avenge the world for all that it had suffered at the hands of the powers of evil, to redeem it from its bitter thraldom to them, He " despoiled the principalities and powers of evil, and made a show of them openly, triumphing over them in His cross."

There is one feature of the Goel which comes out very markedly, whatever the function he had to discharge. Whether redeeming an alienated inheritance, restoring liberty to a captive, or hunting down a homicide, he is in each case a kinsman, one of the nearest kin. *Kinship with the redeemed,* in short, *is an invariable law and condition of redemption.* And this law holds of the Divine Goel. " Forasmuch as we were partakers of flesh and blood, Christ also Himself took part in the same." None but a man could be the

Goel of men. No alien, no stranger, could interpose for us ; only " the Man who is near of kin to us, our nearest Kinsman." Hence the Son of God became the Son of Man.

In thus speaking of the redemption wrought for us and for all men by our Divine Kinsman, it must not for a moment be supposed that we are playing with mere fancies and figures of speech. Under this manifold and most appropriate image we have presented to us the supreme facts in the moral history of the world, the truths which have most profoundly entered into our spiritual experience. No poor Hebrew who had been compelled to part with the fields he had inherited from his fathers suffered a loss comparable with ours, when, by sin, we had lost the righteousness, the right relation to God and man, in which we were originally placed by the Father of our spirits. No Hebrew sold, or selling himself, for a slave to a hard and alien master, ever endured a bondage half so bitter and shameful as that into which we fell when, sold under sin, we sank into bondage to our own lusts. No deliverance wrought by a Hebrew Goel is worthy to be compared with that by which Christ has made it possible for us to subdue our evil passions and lusts, and to possess ourselves of a righteousness more stable and more perfect than that which we had cast away. If we are conscious that this happy change has passed in us ; if we know and feel that we are no longer mastered and coerced by the lusts which war against the soul, that Christ has conferred on us, not simply the pardon of our sins, but also the liberty of a growing obedience to the righteous will of God ; if we can look abroad with an unpresumptuous eye, and say, "All things are ours, and work together for our good;"— then, with a fervour and a triumph infinitely transcending that of Naomi, we may exclaim, "This Man is near of kin to us, our nearest Kinsman. Blessed be He of the Lord, who hath not left off His kindness to the living and to the dead!"

FINIS.

The Book of Ruth

by

Thomas Fuller

Klock & Klock Christian Publishers, Inc.
2527 Girard Avenue North
Minneapolis, Minnesota 55411

Originally published by
William Tegg
London, 1868

ISBN: 0-86524-140-6

Printed by Klock & Klock in the U.S.A.
1982 Reprint

EDITOR'S PREFACE.

THIS volume contains Dr. Thomas Fuller's *Comment on Ruth*, and *Notes upon Jonah*. The former, though not published by the author till 1654, was in reality one of his earliest compositions; having been delivered by him in the shape of Lectures, at St. Benet's, Cambridge, as far back as 1630–1, when he was but a stripling, of two or three and twenty. In issuing it in a printed form, Fuller does not seem to have altered its style, or rooted out the frequent allusions to the current topics of twenty years previously. Between the delivery of the Lectures, and their publication as a Comment, the government of England had undergone a radical change; and it is one amongst many proofs of Cromwell's wise moderation, that Fuller could thus openly retain the fervent expressions of his youthful loyalty; as where he recounts amongst special mercies the preservation of Charles on his trip to Spain, &c. There was a certain amount of courage in printing such a passage as the following, which, however palatable to the heads of church and state when originally delivered, might easily have given offence to a powerful party under the Protectorate :—With regard to " some who leap from the loom to the pulpit,—I must confess, an ass's head was good food in a famine; coarse meat is dainty when no better can be had. But now," &c. That there was in Fuller's day the same difficulty as in ours in dealing with the poor so as to damage neither justice nor charity, is evident from the following aspiration, in which we, of two centuries later, can heartily join: "Would all poor and impotent were well placed in a hospital; all poor and able well disposed in a workhouse; and the common stocks of towns so laid out as they thereby might be employed!" Just below this quotation occurs proof of the antiquity and respectability of a word which is now regarded as close upon the confines of "slang," and as suited chiefly for records of foot and boat races, &c. :— "After a *spurt* in their calling for some few hours, they relapse again to laziness."

Though the *Comment on Ruth* is written with ease, and is full of ingenious thought, we can well suppose that the young clergyman, just entering on his preferment, would, in delivering Lectures in a University town, carefully avoid any approach to punning, and repress that fondness for alliteration which soon afterwards became a special characteristic of his style. But the *Notes upon Jonah*, though published only three years after the *Ruth*, carry on their very face marks of the five and twenty years which had intervened between the composition of the two works. They extend no farther than to verse 7 of the first chapter of Jonah, and have the appearance, here and there, of being jottings for pulpit use, which (like the *Comment*) Fuller published simply in defence against the pirates who preyed on the renown of the popular divine. But, fragments as these *Notes* are, we can trace everywhere in them the original engraving, the inimitably inwoven water-marks, of the genuine paper of the Fullerian bank of ready wit and sterling piety. How thoroughly autographic is the following !— " Away then with the Anabaptist, who would set all men *at odds* by making them *even !* " And the very next sentence is like unto it :—" For a commonwealth to *want a chief*, it is the *chief of all wants.*"

But it is not so much for its wit and humour, or its apt illustrations from every day life, that we commend this volume to the reader : it is chiefly valuable for its even tenor of genuine devotion and of common-sense exposition of Scripture. It will, we feel sure, be hailed by every lover of Fuller, as a fit addition to the series of reprints which are now bringing his scarce and valuable works within the reach of all, and so refurbishing the lustre of his great name. As in former volumes of this series, I have modernized the spelling, and added a few short notes where explanation seemed needful.

WILLIAM NICHOLS.

6, Stratheden Villas, Hackney,
1868.

CONTENTS.

A COMMENT ON RUTH.

PAGE

CHAPTER I... 5

CHAPTER II... 105

NOTES UPON JONAH................... 179

A COMMENT ON RUTH.

CHAPTER I. VERSE 1.

Now it came to pass in the days when the judges
ruled, that there was a famine in the land.

BEFORE we enter into these words, something
must be premised, concerning the name, matter,
end, author of this book.

It hath the name from Ruth, the most remarkable person in it, to whom God vouchsafed His
grace, not only to write her name in the Book of
Life in heaven, but also to prefix her name before
a Book of Life in earth.

The matter may be divided into these two
parts : the first chapter showeth, that "many are
the troubles of the righteous;" and the three
last do show, that "God delivereth them out of
all." One of the *ends* is, to show the pedigree of
our Saviour; otherwise genealogers had been at
a loss, for four or five descents, in the deducing
thereof. Another end is, under the conversion

of Ruth the Moabitess, to typify the calling of the
Gentiles, that, as He took of the blood of a Gentile
into His body, so He should shed the blood out of
His body for the Gentiles; that there might be
one Shepherd, and one sheepfold.

The author's name (probably Samuel) is concealed, neither is it needful it should be known:
for, even as a man that hath a piece of gold that
he knows to be weight, and sees it stamped with
the king's image, careth not to know the name
of that man who minted or coined it; so we,
seeing this book to have the superscription of
Cæsar, the stamp of the Holy Spirit, need not to
be curious to know who was the penman thereof.

And now to the words.

*Now it came to pass in the days when the judges
ruled, that there was a famine in the land.*

Observe in the words,—what? A famine:—
where? In the land:—when? "In the time that
the judges judged;" the time being set down for
the better certainty of the history.

QUESTION.

Is this the land whereof it is said, Gen. xlix. 20,
"Asher his bread shall be fat, and afford dainties
for a king;" which is called, Deut. viii. 7, "a
good land of wheat and barley, vineyards and
fig-trees, oil, olive, and honey;" which is com-
mended, Ezek. xx. 6, to be "a land flowing with

milk and honey, the glory of all lands?" How cometh it to pass, that thy rivers of oil are now dammed up? thy streams of wine drained dry? that there is no bread found in Bethlehem, "the house of bread?"

ANSWER.

Israel hath sinned. "A fruitfnl land maketh He barren, for the sin of the people that dwell therein." The people's *hard hearts* were rebellious to God, and the *hard earth* proved unprofitable to them : their flinty eyes would afford no tears to bemoan their sins, and the churlish heavens would afford no moisture to water their earth : man proved unfaithful to God his Maker; the earth proved unfruitful to man her manurer.

OBSERVATION.

Famine is a heavy punishment, wherewith God afflicteth His people for their sins. That it is a heavy punishment appeareth, because David (2 Sam. xxiv. 14) chose the pestilence before it: for even as Zebah and Zalmunna (Judges viii. 21) chose rather to fall by the hand of Gideon than by the hand of Jether his son, because the child's want of strength would cause their abundance of pain; so better it is to be speedily dispatched by a violent disease, than to have one's life in a famine prolonged by a lingering torture. That it is inflicted for their sins is showed, Lev. xxvi. 19; Deut. xxviii. 23; 1 Kings viii. 37 : and these sins

most especially procure famine :—First. Idolatry.
(1 Kings xvii. 1; 2 Kings iv. 38.) Secondly.
Abuse of plenty. The prodigal child, (Luke xv.,)
from the keeping of harlots, was brought to the
keeping of hogs. It is just with God to make
men want that to supply their necessity, which
they have misspended in their nicety. Thirdly.
Shedding of innocent blood. (2 Sam. xxi. 1.)
Fourthly. Oppression of the poor. (Amos iv. 6.)
And no wonder, if men, to grind the faces of poor
people, make money, to which God gave no
natural fruit, to bring forth a monstrous increase,
—if God cause the earth, which naturally should
be fruitful, to become barren and afford no profit.

USE I.

It may serve to confute such, that when God
doth scourge them with famine, (as blind Balaam
fell a beating of his dumb beast, when he himself
was in fault,) they vent their spite in cursing and
railing on the poor creatures; whereas, indeed,
were the matter well weighed, they might say of
all creatures as Judah did of Tamar his daughter-
in-law, "They are ' more righteous than ' we:"
for locusts, mildew, blasting, immoderate drought
and moisture, are the means by which—man's sin
is the cause, for which—famine is inflicted. And
yet in prosperity we are commonly like hogs
feeding on the mast, not minding his hand that
shaketh it down; in adversity, like dogs

biting the stone, not marking the hand that threw it.

If any desire to prevent or remove a famine, let us prevent and remove the causes thereof.

First. Let us practise that precept, 1 John v. 21 : " Babes, keep yourselves from idols."

Secondly. Let us be heartily thankful to God for our plenty, who, by the seasonable weeping of the heavens, hath caused the plentiful laughter of the earth, and hath sent the former rain to perform the part of a midwife, to deliver the infant corn out of the womb of the parched earth ; and the latter rain to do the duty of a nurse, to swell and battle * the grain. Let us not seethe the kid in the mother's milk : let not our wanton palates spoil wholesome meat, before it cometh to the just maturity : neither let us cast away any good food, but, after our Saviour's example, let us cause the fragments to be basketted up, that nothing may be lost.

Thirdly. Let us pray with David, (Psalm li. 14,) " Deliver us from bloodguiltiness, O Lord : " and let us seek that the hoary hairs may not go down to the grave in peace of such as have shed innocent blood ; (lest the personal offence of a private man, remaining unpunished, become the national sin of a kingdom ;) but upon the king, and upon his seed, and upon his house, and upon his throne shall be peace for ever from the Lord.

* [" Fatten," or " fill out."—Ed.]

Lastly. Let us be pitiful, and liberal to relieve the distresses of the poor; for why should our dead tables groan under the weight of needless feast upon them, whilst God's living temples groan under the want of necessary food within them? The Athenian women had a custom to make a picture of Famine every year, and to drive it out of their city with these words : " Out, Famine ; in, Food ! Out, Penury ; in, Plenty ! " But let us say in word, and second it in deed, " Out, Sin ; in, Sanctity ! Out, Profaneness ; in, Piety : " and then we shall see, that as long as our King reigneth, there shall be no famine in our land.

But however God shall dispose of us for outward blessings, I pray God keep us from that soul famine, mentioned Amos viii. 12, that we living under the northern heavens should wander to the east, and " run to and fro to seek the word of the Lord," and should " not find it ; " but may the light of the Gospel remain with us on earth as long as the faithful witness endureth in heaven.

And a certain man of Bethlehem-Judah went to sojourn in the country of Moab.

These words contain a journey or removal; wherein observe : Who went ? " A certain man." Whence ? From Bethlehem-Judah. Whither ? " To sojourn in Moab." We shall have a fitter occasion to speak of the party removing hereafter.

I begin with the place from whence he went, Bethlehem-Judah.

This was the place nigh to which Rachel, as she was travelling, fell into travail, and ended her journey to heaven in the midst of her journey on earth. There was another of the same name in Zebulun; (Josh. xix. 15 ;) and therefore " Judah " is added for difference and distinction.

OBSERVATION.

The Holy Spirit descends to our capacity, and in Scripture doth multiply words to make the matter the plainer. Let this teach the sons of Levi, when they deliver one doubtful and ambiguous doctrine, which may admit of several constructions, so that there is danger lest that people may mistake their meaning, to demur a while on such a point, and not to be niggardly of their words, till they have blotted all doubt and difficulty out of it. Herein they shall follow God for their pattern, who, lest Bethlehem in my text should be confounded with Bethlehem in Zebulun, addeth for distinction " Bethlehem-Judah."

Went to sojourn in Moab.

The prodigal child complained, " How many hired servants of my father have bread enough, and I die for hunger ! " (Luke xv. 17.) So here we see that the uncircumcised Moabites, God's slaves and vassals, had store of plenty, whilst Israel, God's children, (but His prodigal children,

which by their sins had displeased their Heavenly
Father,) were pinched with penury.

Hence we gather, God oftentimes denies outward blessings to His children, whenas He vouch-
safeth them to the wicked. The wicked man's
eyes start out with fatness ; David's bones scarce
cleave to his flesh : Ahab hath an ivory house ;
the godly wander in "dens and caves of the
earth : " the rich glutton fareth deliciously every
day ; whilst the godly (Psalm cvii. 5) were "hungry
and thirsty, their soul fainted in them : " he was
clothed in purple and fine linen ; whilst the
godly wander up and down "in sheep-skins ; "
and well may they wear their skins without them,
that carry their innocency within them. And the
reason thereof is, because judgment begins at the
house of the Lord, whilst the wicked have their
portion in this world.

Let us " not judge according to outward appearance, but judge righteous judgment," lest otherwise we condemn the generation of God's children,
if we account outward blessings the signs of God's
favour, or calamities the arguments of His displeasure. Neither let the afflicted Christian faint under
God's heavy hand ; but let him know to his comfort, God therefore is angry in this world, that He
may not be angry in the world to come ; and

mercifully inflicteth temporal punishment, that He
may not justly confound with eternal torment.

But here ariseth a question, Whether Elimelech
did well to go from Bethlehem-Judah into the land
of Moab? For the better satisfaction whereof,
we will suppose a plain and honest neighbour thus
dissuading him from his departure.

DISSUASION.

" Give me leave, neighbour Elimelech, to say unto thee, as the angel did to Hagar, 'Whence comest
thou? and whither goest thou?' Wilt thou leave
that place where God's worship is truly professed,
and go into an idolatrous country? Woe is thee,
that must dwell in Moab, and be an inhabitant
amongst the worshippers of Melchom! Indeed, our
father Abraham came out of Ur of the Chaldees, an
idolatrous country, to come into the land of Canaan;
but why shouldst thou go out of the land of Canaan
into an idolatrous country, where thou shalt have
neither priest, nor prophet, nor passover? Yea,
what most is to be feared, your frequent conversing
with the people of the country will at length bring
you into a love and liking of their superstitions,
and so draw God's anger against you. Wherefore, reverse your intent of removing, lest, while
thou seekest to store thy body, thou starvest thy
soul: rather venture the breaking of the casket
than the losing of the jewel; and go not from
Bethlehem-Judah unto the land of Moab."

ANSWER.

To this Elimelech might answer : " Your dissuasion doth somewhat move me, but not remove my resolution. I do not forsake my country, but am forced from it. God hath withholden the wine and the winepress ; and if I stay, I am likely to starve. I conceive it therefore to be my bounden duty to provide the best means for my family ; and following the examples of Isaac's going into Gerah, and Jacob's going down into Egypt in the time of famine, I intend to remove to Moab. And though I shall be divided from the visible congregation of Israel, yet shall I with my family still remain the lively members of God's true church. For, first, I intend to carry with me the five books of Moses, (they will be no great burden, being comprised in so small a volume,) and, according to my poor ability, out of them will I instruct my family ; whilst my dear wife Naomi, and dutiful children, Mahlon and Chilion, will be diligent to hear and practise what I propound unto them. I confess, we shall have no outward sacrifices, (because I am not of the tribe of Levi,) yet may we offer unto God prayers and praises, which God no doubt will as graciously accept as of a bullock that hath horns and hoofs. Thus hope I to have a little church in mine own house ; and I know, where two or three are met together in the name of God, there He ' will be in the midst of them.' Whereas you object I should be in danger of being defiled with their idolatry, I will be by God's grace so much the more wary, watchful, and vigilant over my ways. We see the flesh of fishes remaineth fresh, though they always swim in the brackish waters; and I hope that the same God who preserved righteous Lot in the wicked city of Sodom, who protected faithful Joseph in the vicious court of Pharaoh, will also keep me unspotted in the midst of Moab, whither I intend speedily to go, not to live, but to lodge; not to dwell, but to sojourn; not to make it my habitation for ever, but my harbour for a season, till God shall visit His people with plenty, when I purpose to return with the speediest conveniency."

Thus we see Elimelech putting the dangers of his removal in one scale, the benefits thereof in another: the beam of his judgment is justly weighed down to go from Bethlehem-Judah into the land of Moab.

OBSERVATION.

It is lawful for men to leave their native soil, and to travel into a foreign country; as,

1. For merchants; provided always that, while they seek to make gainful adventures for their estates, they make not "shipwreck of a good conscience."

2. For ambassadors, that are sent to see the practices and negociations in foreign courts.

3. For private persons, that travel with an in-

tent to accomplish themselves with a better sufficiency to serve their king and country.

But unlawful it is for such to travel, which,
Dinah like, go only to see the customs of several
countries, and make themselves the lackeys to
their own humorous curiosity. Hence cometh it
to pass, when they return, it is justly questionable,
whether their clothes be disguised with more
foolish fashions, or bodies disabled with more
loathsome diseases, or souls defiled with more notorious vices; having learned jealousy from the
Italian, pride from the Spaniard, lasciviousness
from the French, drunkenness from the Dutch.
And yet what need they go so far to learn so bad a
lesson, when (God knows) we have too many
schools where it is taught here at home ?

Now if any do demand of me my opinion concerning our brethren which of late left this kingdom to advance a plantation in New England;
surely I think, as St. Paul said concerning vir-
gins, he had "received no commandment from
the Lord;" so I cannot find any just warrant to
encourage men to undertake this removal; but
think rather the counsel best that king Joash pre-
scribed to Amaziah, " Tarry at home." Yet as for
those that are already gone, far be it from us to
conceive them to be such to whom we may not say,
"God speed," as it is in 2 John verse 10 : but let
us pity them, and pray for them; for sure they

have no need of our mocks, which I am afraid have too much of their own miseries. I conclude therefore of the two Englands, what our Saviour saith of the two wines, Luke v. 39: "No man having tasted of the old presently desireth the new: for he saith, The old is better."

He, and his wife, and his two sons.

VERSE 2.

And the name of the man was Elimelech, and the name of his wife Naomi, and the name of his two sons Mahlon and Chilion, Ephrathites of Bethlehem-Judah. And they came into the country of Moab, and continued there.

These words contain, First, The principal party that undertook the journey. Secondly, His company, described by their relations,—his wife and children; and by their names,—Naomi, Mahlon, and Chilion. Thirdly, The success of his journey. When he came into the land of Moab, he " continued there."

Now whereas Elimelech took his wife and children along with him, from his practice we gather this observation.

OBSERVATION.

It is the part of a kind husband, and of a careful father, not only to provide for himself, but also for his whole family. Gen. ii. 24: "A man shall cleave to his wife, and they two shall be one flesh."

Eph. v. 25 : " Husbands, love your wives ;...for no man as yet hated his own flesh." 1 Tim. v. 8: " If any one provideth not for his own family, he denieth the faith, and is worse than an infidel."   This made Abraham to take with him at his removal his meek Sarah ; Isaac, his wise Rebecca ; Jacob, his fair Rachel and fruitful Leah ; and Joseph (Matt. ii.) took with him Mary, his espoused wife, and our Saviour, his supposed son.   And when Pharaoh (Exod. x. 10, 11) offered Moses with all the men of Israel to go out of Egypt, but on condition they should leave their wives and children behind them, Moses refused the proffer : he would either have them all go out, or else he would not go out at all.

USE.

It confuteth such cruel husbands and careless parents, who, if so be, with Job's messengers, they only can escape alone, they care not though they leave their wives and children to shift for themselves ; like the ostrich, (Job xxxix. 14,) " who leaveth her eggs in the sand," and so forsakes them. Surely the two kine which drew the ark of God out of the land of the Philistines to Beth-shemesh, (1 Sam. vi. 12,) shall rise up at the day of judgment and condemn such cruel parents : for it is said of them, that, as they " went along the highway," they did pitifully " low," by that querulous ditty, as nature afforded them utterance, witnessing and expressing their affection to their calves shut up at home. O, that there should be such humanity (as I may term it) in beasts, and such beastliness in many men! Remember this, you that sit drinking and bezzling [x] wine abroad, whilst your family are glad of water at home; and think thus with yourselves : " To what end is this needless waste ? Might it not have been sold for many a penny, and have been bestowed on my poor wife and children ? "

OBSERVATION.

Secondly. Whereas we find Naomi and her sons going with Elimelech, we gather it is the duty of a dear wife, and of dutiful children, to go along with their husbands and parents, when on just cause they remove into a foreign country. It was an unmanly and cowardly speech of Barak to Deborah, (Judges iv. 8,) " If thou wilt go with me, then will I go : but if thou wilt not go with me, then will I not go :" but it would be a gracious resolution of a grave matron and her children, " Husband, if you be pleased to depart, I will be ready to accompany you. Father, if you be minded to remove, I will attend upon you. But if you be disposed to stay, I will not stir from the place

* [" Drinking wastefully and riotously." A twin word to *guzzling*. —Ed.]

where you abide." Otherwise, if the wife refuseth
to go along with her husband, what Abraham said
to the servant in another case, (Gen. xxiv.8,) is
true in this respect : " But if the woman will not
be willing to follow thee, then thou shalt be clear
from thine oath." If the wife be so peevish and
perverse that she will not go along with her husband, who propoundeth lawful means unto her to
relieve her wants ; then is he acquitted from the
oath he made her in marriage, when he plighted
his troth unto her, in sickness and in health, to
maintain her.

QUESTION.

But methinks I hear the widows and orphans
crying unto me, as the soldiers to John Baptist,
" But what shall we do?" (Luke iii. 14.) "It is
true," saith the widow, " that kind husbands are
to provide for their wives ; but, alas ! we have no
Elimelechs to carry us into a foreign country in
the time of famine." " Indeed," saith the orphan,
" it is the father's duty to provide for his children ; but my parents are dead long ago ; I have
not, as Samuel had, a mother Hannah every year
to bring me a new coat. What shall we do in
this our distress ? "

ANSWER.

Use the best means you can ; and, for the rest,
rely on God's providence, who is said, Psalm x. 20,
to " help the fatherless and poor to their right ; "

Psalm lxviii. 5, to be " a Father to the fatherless, and to defend the cause of the widow; even God in His holy habitation ;" who will deal with thee as he did with David : " When my mother and father forsook me, the Lord cared for me."

So much for Elimelech's company described by their relations. We should come now to speak of their names; where we might take occasion to speak of the antiquity and use of names, but that hereafter we shall have better conveniency to treat thereof, in those words, " Call me not Naomi, but call me Marah." We come therefore to the success of Elimelech's journey.

And they came into the country of Moab, and they continued there.

The meaning is, that the Moabites afforded them harbour without any molestation.

OBSERVATION.

From whence the observation is this : We ought to be hospital [hospitable] and courteous to receive strangers. First. Because God in several places of Scripture enjoineth it. (Exod. xxiii. 9 ; Levit. xix. 33.) Secondly. Because God apprehendeth all courtesy done to a stranger as bestowed on Himself: " He that receiveth you receiveth Me," &c. "I was a stranger, and ye harboured Me." (Matt. xxv.) And then if we entertain strangers, it may be said of

us, not only as it is of Lot and Abraham, Heb.
xiii. 2, that we "entertained angels," but that we
entertained God Himself "unawares." Thirdly.
Because, if spiritually considered, we ourselves are
strangers : with the patriarchs, (Heb. xi.) we have
here no abiding city, but seek one from above,
"whose Builder and Maker is God." "I beseech
you as strangers and pilgrims." (1 Peter ii. 11.)
Lastly. Because of the uncertainty of our own
estates; for thou knowest not what evil shall be
upon the earth : it may be, we that now relieve
strangers, hereafter ourselves, being strangers,
may be relieved by others.

USE.

Let us not therefore abuse strangers, and make
a prey of them, making an advantage of their
unskilfulness in the language, and being unac-
quainted with the fashions of the land; like Laban,
that deceived his nephew Jacob in placing Leah
for Rachel, and, to cloak his cheating, pleaded it
was the custom of the country. Wherefore rather
let us be courteous unto them, lest the barbarians
condemn us, who so courteously entreated St.
Paul, with his shipwrecked companions; and the
Moabites in my text, who suffered Elimelech,
when he came into the land, to continue there.

VERSES 3, 4, 5.

*And Elimelech Naomi's husband died; and she
was left, and her two sons, &c.*

In these words we have two marriages ushered
and followed by funerals. I will begin there,
where one day all must make an end,—at death.

And Elimelech Naomi's husband died.

I have seldom seen a tree thrive that hath been
transplanted when it was old. The same may be
seen in Elimelech: his aged body brooks not the
foreign air; though he could avoid the arrows of
Famine in Israel, yet he could not shun the darts of
Death in Moab: he that lived in a place of penury,
must die in a land of plenty. Let none condemn Elimelech's removal as unlawful, because of his sudden death; for those actions are not ungodly which
are unsuccessful, nor those pious which are prosperous; seeing the lawfulness of an action is not
to be gathered from the joyfulness of the event,
but from the justness of the cause, for which it is
undertaken.

OBSERVATION I.

Hence we observe, that God can easily frustrate
our fairest hopes, and defeat our most probable
projects, in making those places most dangerous
which we account most safe and secure; causing

death to meet us there, where we think furthest to fly from it.

We see that no outward plenty can privilege us from death: the sand of our life runneth as fast, though the hour-glass be set in the sunshine of prosperity, as in the gloomy shade of affliction.

And she was left, and her two sons.

Here we see how mercifully God dealt with Naomi, in that He quenched not all the sparks of her comfort at once; but though He took away the stock, He left her the stems; though He deprived her as it were of the use of her own legs, by taking away her husband, yet He left her a staff in each of her hands, her two sons to support her. Indeed, afterwards He took them away; but first He provided her a gracious daughter-in-law. Whence we learn, God poureth not all His afflictions at once, but ever leaveth a little comfort; otherwise we should not only be pressed down, but crushed to powder, under the weight of His heavy hand.

And they took them wives of the women of Moab, &c.

Here we see the fashion of the world. Mankind had long ago decayed, if those breaches which are daily made by death, were not daily made up by marriage. But here ariseth a question,—Whether these matches were lawful? for answer whereof, we will suppose Naomi dissuading her sons on this manner.

DISSUASION.

" What, my sons? and what, the sons of my womb? and what, the sons of my desire? Give not your strength to strange women, and your ways to that that destroyed men. It is not for you, O Mahlon and Chilion, it is not for you to marry Moabites; nor for the sons of an Israelite to marry the daughters of the uncircumcised. Remember, my sons, what God saith by the mouth of Moses: (Deut. vii. 3:) 'Thou shalt not make marriages with them; thy daughter shalt thou not give to his son, nor take his daughter to thy son. For they will turn away thy son from following Me, to serve strange gods: so will the anger of the Lord be kindled against thee, to destroy thee suddenly.' Take heed therefore lest, long looking on these women, you at length be made blind; lest they suck out your souls with kisses, and, snake-like, sting you with embraces. Curb your affections until you come into Canaan, where you shall find a variety of wives, who, as they come not short of these for the beauties of their bodies, so they far go beyond them for the sanctity of their souls."

ANSWER.

To this dissuasion thus might her children answer: "We thank you, dear mother, for your carefulness over our good; but we must entreat you not to interpret it undutifulness, if upon good reason we dissent from your judgment herein. In the place by you cited, marriages are forbidden with such strange women as are of a stubborn, obstinate, and refractory nature, such as are likely to seduce their husbands; whereas you see the mild, towardly, and tractable disposition of these women we mean to make our wives. We hope to plant these wild branches in God's vineyard, to bring these straggling sheep to His fold, to make them proselytes to our religion. Besides, this marriage will be advantageous for us: thereby we shall endear ourselves into the Moabites' affections; they will use us the more courteously, when we have married one of their own kindred."

But methinks my tongue refuseth to be any longer the advocate of an unlawful deed, and my mouth denieth to be the orator of an unjust action. When I have said what I can for the defence of their marriage, I shall make but a plaster too narrow for the sore: the breach is so broad, I cannot stop it, though I may dam it up with untempered mortar. Nothing can be brought for the defence of these matches; something may be said for the excuse of them, but that fetched not from piety, but from policy; not certain, but conjectural. Yet here may we see the power and providence of God, who made so good use of these men's defaults, as hereby to bring Ruth, first to be a retainer to the family of Faith, and afterwards a joyful mother in Israel. This is that good Chymic that can distil good out of evil, light out of darkness, order out of confusion, and make the crooked actions of men tend to His own glory in a straight line, and His children's good.

I speak not this to defend any man's folly in doing of evil, but to admire God's wisdom, who can bring good out of evil : and surely He that will turn evil to good, will turn good to the best.

And they dwelled there about ten years.

Here we have the term of Naomi's living in Moab, and the family's lasting in Israel,—"ten years." We read of a famine for three years, 2 Sam. xxi. ; of three years and a half, 1 Kings xvii. ; of seven years, Gen. xlii., as also 2 Kings viii. : but this ten years' famine longer than any. Seven years which Jacob served for Rachel, seemed to him but a short time ; but surely those ten years seemed to the afflicted Israelites, and to the banished Naomi, as so many millions of years.

OBSERVATION.

God doth not presently remove His rod from the back of His children, but sometimes scourgeth them with long-lasting afflictions. The reason is, because we go on and persist so long in our sins. And yet herein even Mercy exalteth herself against judgment: for if God should suffer the fire of His fury to burn so long as the fuel of our sins doth last, "Lord, who were able to abide?" Were the days of our suffering apportioned to the days of our living, no flesh would be saved; but "for the elect's sake those days" are "shortened."

USE.

Bear with patience light afflictions, when God afflicteth His children with long-lasting punishments. Mutter not for a burning fever of a fortnight. What is this to the woman that had a running issue for twelve years? Murmur not for a twelvemonth's quartan ague: 'tis nothing to the woman that was bowed for eighteen years; nor seven years' consumption, to the man that lay thirty-eight years lame at the pool of Bethesda.

And Mahlon and Chilion died also both of them.

It was but even now that old Elimelech was gone to bed: see, his sons would not sit long up after

the father. Only here is the difference : he, like
ripe fruit, fell down of his own accord; they, like
green apples, were cudgelled off the tree.

OBSERVATION.

Even young men in the prime of their age are
subject to death. The sons of Jacob, when they
came to the table of Joseph, sat down, the eldest
according to his age, and the youngest according
to his youth : but Death observes not this method;
she takes not men in seniority, but sometimes
sends them first to the burial that came last from
the birth, and those that came last from the
womb, first to their winding-sheet. There were
as many lambs and kids sacrificed in the Old
Testament, as goats and old sheep; but surely
more there be that die in infancy and in youth,
than of those that attain to old age.

USE.

"Remember thy Creator in the days of thy
youth." You whose joints are knit with sturdy
sinews, whose veins are full of blood, whose
arteries are flushed with spirits, whose bones are
fraught with marrow; Obadiah-like, serve God
from your youth; put not the day of death far
from you; think not your strength to be armour
of proof against the darts of Death, when you see
the corslet of Mahlon and Chilion shot through in
the left. So "Mahlon and Chilion died both of
them."

And the woman was left of her two sons and of
her husband.

Before, we had the particular losses of Naomi;
now, we have them all reckoned up in the total
sum. "A threefold cable," saith Solomon, "is
not easily broken;" and yet we see Naomi's threefold cable of comfort, twisted of her husband and
her two sons, broken by death. Of the two sexes
the woman is the weaker; of women, old women
are most feeble; of old women, widows most
woful; of widows, those that are poor, their
plight most pitiful; of poor widows, those that
want children, their case most doleful; of widows
that want children, those that once had them
and after lost them, their estate most desolate;
of widows that have had children, those that are
strangers in a foreign country, their condition
most comfortless. Yet all these met together in
Naomi, as in the centre of sorrow, to make the
measure of her misery " pressed down, shaken together, running over." I conclude therefore, many
men have had affliction,—none like Job; many
women have had tribulation,—none like Naomi.

VERSE 6.

Then she arose with her daughters in law, that she
might return from the country of Moab : for she

had heard in the country of Moab how that the Lord had visited His people in giving them bread.

These words contain two general parts.

1. God's visiting His people with plenty.

2. Naomi's visiting of her people with her person.

I begin with the first in the order of the words.

Then she arose with her daughters in law, &c.

OBSERVATION.

We must tarry no longer in an idolatrous land, when God offereth us an occasion to return into our own country: for so long as we tarry in an idolatrous land on a just cause, so long we are in our vocation and in God's protection: but when God openeth us a gap to return, and we will not through it, we are neither in our calling nor God's keeping, but must stand on our own adventures; and who knows not how slenderly we shall be kept, when we are left to our own custody? Let not therefore Joseph, with his wife and son, tarry any longer in the land of Egypt, when he is dead that sought the life of the child.

Examples we have of those which, in the days of Queen Mary, fled beyond the seas; though they were not in a paganish, only in a foreign country: Mr. Scorey, Cox, Whitehead, Grindal, Horne, Sandys, Elmore, Gwest, Jewel. If fear lent them feet to run when they went away, joy gave them wings to fly when they came home again. Let none therefore pretend in needless excuses to linger in the land of Egypt, when they may return into the honey-flowing land of Canaan.

For she had heard in the country of Moab.

I suppose when any messenger arrived in Moab out of the land of Canaan, Naomi did presently repair unto him, and load him with questions concerning the estate of her country: " How do the Jews my countrymen? How fareth it with the Bethlehemites my neighbours? with Boaz my kinsman? What is the rate of corn? What the price of oil? What the value of wine? If there be no performance for the present, what promise is there for the future? Though things be bad now, what hope is there but they will be better hereafter? " Alas! he answers little; and from his silence and sorrowful looks Naomi gathers a denial. But as Elijah sending his servant towards the sea, to see what signs there were of rain; for six several times together he returned this answer, " There is nothing; " (1 Kings xviii. 43;) but at the seventh time he

brought him the tidings of a cloud rising out of
the sea : so, though for nine years Naomi had no
news but of want and scarcity, yet the tenth year
there came a man (probably he was a good man
that brought these good tidings) who brought
her word that the valleys began to laugh and
sing with plenty. And so, though the hope that
was deferred was the fainting of the heart, yet
when it came, it was the " tree of life." Perchance because the covetous Jews had made nine
parts great for their own profit, and the tenth
small to cozen God of His portion, God, quite
contrary, gave them nine years of scarcity and
want, and at length made the tenth of store and
plenty.

OBSERVATION.

The fame of remarkable accidents will fly into
foreign countries : for, if it be bad news, the
wicked will be sure to tell it in the gates of Gath,
and publish it in the streets of Askelon : if it be
good, the godly will proclaim it in the courts of
Zion, and disperse it within the walls of Jerusalem. Whether good or bad, if it be of moment
and importance, it will not be covered nor concealed.

QUESTION.

Is it lawful for us to listen, hearken, and inquire after matters of foreign countries ?

ANSWER.

Though I would not have men to be like the Athenians, " to hear or tell some new thing ;" yet it is both lawful and laudable for them to inquire after foreign affairs, whereby they express the desire that they have of the welfare of their distant brethren, the members of the same mystical body. Example, Nehemiah i. 2. And yet would I have men, though they lend their ears, not to bestow their belief on every groundless report which is blazed abroad.

1. Because fame is often untrue, relating (2 Sam. xiii. 30) that " all the king's sons" are killed, when only Amnon is slain.

2. Because many there be which, with the soldiers, Matt. xxviii., do nothing but invent and disperse lies to gull over-credulous people : and as many a benighted traveller hath wandered out of his way, whilst he followed for his lanthorn the meteor of foolish fire ; so many a man hath been deceived by embracing of lying relations, instead of true news. Yet in case that Cushi and Ahimaaz confirm the same thing, that variety of messengers from divers places, of sundry sides and several factions, all agree in material and substantial points ; we ought not to be like unbelieving Thomas, to trust no more than our eyes have seen, but may rely on the truth of such relations ;

and ought accordingly to be affected with sorrow if the news be bad, or joy if the tidings tend to the church's good and God's glory.

That God had visited His people.

This was the privilege of the people of the Jews, that they were styled " God's people ;" but now Ammi is made Lo-Ammi, and Ruhamah, Lo-Ruhamah ; and we, the Gentiles, are placed in their room.   Let us therefore remember the words of St. Paul, Rom. i. 20, 21 : " Be not high-minded, but fear : for if God spared not the natural branches of the olive, fear that He will not spare thee also."

O that He would be pleased to cast His eye of pity upon the poor Jews, which for fifteen hundred years and upwards have wandered without law, without lord, without land ; and, as once they were, so once again to make them His people !

In giving them bread.

By " bread " is meant all sustenance necessary for the maintaining of our lives, whereof bread is the chiefest.   As the temple of Dagon principally leaned on two pillars, and fell to the ground when Samson took them away ; so the buildings of our bodies chiefly rely on bread and water for outward sustenance, which being taken away, [they] cannot but presently decay. Let others therefore wish those dishes which curiosity hath invented, rather to increase than satisfy hunger, which are more delightsome to the eye than pleasing to the palate, yet more pleasing to the palate than wholesome to the stomach ; let us pray, " Give us this day our daily bread."

Bread is a dish in every course : without this can be no feast, with this can be no famine.

OBSERVATION.

God's punishments, though they last sometimes long, yet always they end at last : and yet sometimes, for the manifestation of His power, and trial of His children's patience, He suffers them to be brought into great extremities. Abraham's hand shall be heaved up to slay Isaac, before the angel shall catch hold of it : Lazarus shall be three days dead, before Christ will raise him ; the ship ready to sink, before our Saviour will awake : Peter must be drenched in the water, before our Saviour will keep him from drowning : St. Paul must be in the lion's mouth, before he shall be delivered out of it : the famine must last ten years, before God will give them bread.

An example hereof we have in our neighbouring churches of Germany, which long have been afflicted under the tyranny of their oppressors ; and now at length a sun is risen out of the north, and after a long night the morning beginneth the day. And thou, Swethland,* shalt not be counted the meanest amongst the kingdoms of Europe; for out of thee did a prince arise, who hath delivered the distressed Protestants; who at his first landing seemed to his enemies an object fitter of their scorn than opposition.† They thought our youthful David too unequal a match to cope with their general, who had been a man of war from his youth. But as verity consisteth not in the plurality of voices, so victory standeth not in the multitude of soldiers; but God so ordered it, that he that had the best cause had the best success. I dare boldly say, that all the Protestant princes and states of Germany will be ready truly to say of him what Tertullus spake flatteringly of Felix, Acts xxiv. 2: "Seeing that by thee we enjoy great quietness, and that very worthy deeds are done unto this nation by thy providence, we always accept it, and in all places, most noble prince, with all thankfulness." But let us turn our praises of him into prayers for him, that he who hath conquered his foes may subdue himself, not to be puffed up with his good success. So let all Thine enemies perish, O Lord; but let all them that love Thee be as the sun when he goeth forth in his might. And as ever I have

---

* [Sweden.—ED.] † [The reference is to Gustavus Adolphus, who, after landing in Pomerania (in 1630) with only 8,000 soldiers, was gaining a series of brilliant victories over the Imperial troops at the very time when t ese Lectures on Ruth were probably delivered.—ED.]

earnestly desired, so now do I steadfastly hope to
see the day, when our Naomi (our worthy Naomi,
more fruitful in miseries than in children, and in
virtue than in both) shall arise, to return out of
the land of Holland, with her prince and progeny,
when she shall hear in the land of Holland that
God hath visited the Palatinate, and given them
rest.*

VERSES 7, 8.

*And she went out of the place where she was, and
her two daughters-in-law with her; and they
went on the way to return into the land of Judah.
And Naomi said to her daughters-in-law, Go, return each of you to her mother.*

These words contain the continuation of
Naomi's return; wherein we may observe,—

First. The company that went with her,—
" her two daughters-in-law."

Secondly. The discourse she had with this company; consisting of a precept, in the text, " Go,
return each of you to her mother;" and of a
prayer, in the words following.

Now, whereas her daughters-in-law did not take
their farewell of Naomi at the threshold of their
house, but went part of the way with her, we
gather,—

---

* [By "our Naomi" was intended Elizabeth, daughter of James I.,
Princess Palatine, and Queen of Bohemia, who, at the date of these
Lectures, and for many years subsequently, enjoyed a comfortable asylum
at the Hague.—Ed.]

OBSERVATION.

That all offices of kindnesses and courtesies ought to be betwixt the mother-in-law and the daughter-in-law; I mean, her son's wife. And yet look into the world, and ye shall commonly find enmity betwixt them; as saith Terence *in Hecyrâ*, "*Neque declinatam mulierem reperias ab aliarum ingenio; itâ adeò uno omnes animo socrus oderunt nurus.*" And their fallings out chiefly proceed from these two causes:—

First. They contend which should have the greatest right and interest in the man, who is son to the one, husband to the other. Judah and Israel contested (2 Sam. xix. 43) which should have most part in king David; the former claiming it because he was bone of their bone; the latter pleaded they had eleven [ten] parts in him, to Judah's single share. Thus mother-in-laws and daughter-in-laws use to fall out. The mother, because her son is flesh of her flesh, and bone of her bone, pleads it is right that he should side and second with her: the daughter-in-law, because he is her husband, and therefore one flesh, challengeth that he should rather take her part: so betwixt them they fill the family with all discord.

Secondly. They fall out about the managing of the matters in the household, after whose mind they should be ordered.

But as St. James said in another case, "Beloved, these things ought not to be so;" both these brawls may be easily ended. The first may be taken up by the wisdom and discretion of the son-in-law, who ought so indifferently to poise his affections betwixt them both, with such dutifulness and respect to the one, such love and kindness to the other, that neither may have just cause to complain. And the second controversy may thus be decided : if the mother hath the state [estate] still in her hands, good reason it is she should rule the affairs, and that the daughter-in-law should wait till her mother-in-law's natural death hath paved the succession to the governing of the family. But if the old woman hath resigned her estate, and confined herself to a yearly pension, then ought she not to intermeddle with those matters from which she had willingly sequestered herself. Were this observed, there would not so many daughters-in-law rejoice, when the day of mourning for their mother-in-law is come ; some whereof say, as the wicked said of David, "O, when will she die, and her name perish ?"

Now to come to the discourse she had with them: *Go, return, &c.*

Where ariseth a question, Whether Naomi did well, in persuading her daughters to go back unto Moab ? For the satisfaction whereof, I will set down, First, What may be said against; Secondly, What may be brought for her defence.

ACCUSATION.

"Why, Naomi, why didst thou quench the zeal of thy daughters, which proffered themselves so willingly to go with thee? O, rein them not backward with dissuasions, but rather spur them forward with exhortations; and strive to bring them out of an idolatrous land, to a place where God's worship is purely professed. Say unto them, 'Hearken, O daughters, and consider; incline your ears; forget also your country, and your own mother's house: so shall the Lord your God have pleasure in you. True it is, ye have a mother in Moab; but what of that? Care not for your mother, but care for your Maker: care not for her that conceived you, but care for Him that created you. Tarry not with them, no, not so much as to express your last love in performing their funerals; rather let the dead bury their dead: those that are dead spiritually, let them bury such as die naturally; and come, go ye along with me to the land of Canaan.' Thus, Naomi, oughtest thou to have said, and then hadst performed the part, done the duty, of a mother. If, whilst thou hadst travelled with them on the way, thou hadst travailed with them till God had been formed in them; then shouldst thou shine as a double sun in heaven for saving of two souls: whereas now thou art in a manner accessory to their ghostly murder, in sending them back to an idolatrous country."

DEFENCE.

To this accusation Naomi might justly answer,
" It is my heart's desire and prayer to God, that I
may be an instrument of my daughter-in-laws'
conversion; but the wisdom of the serpent, as
well as the innocency of the dove, is to be
used in all our actions, lest we draw needless
danger upon ourselves. True it is, my daughters-
in-law proffer to go with me; but here is the question, whether this is done out of courtesy and
compliment, or out of singleness and sincerity.
Now, should they through my persuasions go into
the land of Canaan, and there live in want and
penury, they will be ready to rail on me another
day : 'We may thank Naomi for all this; we had
plentiful provisions in our own country, but she
must have us hither; she by her restless impor-
tunity must wring a constrained consent from us
to come into Canaan; all these miseries are
befallen upon us through her default.' Yea, I am
afraid that, finding want, they again will return
into their own country, to my shame, the scandal
of our religion, and the deeper punishment of
their own souls. Wherefore without their minds
would I do nothing, that their going might not be
as it were of necessity, but willingly. To which
end I will put them to the touchstone, to see
whether their forwardness be faithful or feigned,

sound or seeming, cordial or counterfeit: I will weigh them both in the balance, hoping that neither shall be found too light."

Upon these grounds learned men have acquitted Naomi from any fault in managing this matter, she doing it only with an intent to try them.

Whence we may observe, that Pagans that proffer themselves to become converts, are not without proof presently to be received into the church.

And here we may take occasion to digress a little, to show how Christians ought to behave themselves in the converting of infidels.

First. They must strive, in their mutual conversing with them, to season them with a good opinion of their honesty and upright dealing: otherwise their doctrine will never be embraced, whose manners are justly misliked.

Secondly. Having possessed them with his good esteem, they ought, as occasion is offered, to instruct them in the rudiments of Christian religion; and to begin with such as are plain and evident by the light of nature, and so in due time to proceed to matters of greater difficulty.

Lastly. They are to pray to God to give His increase to their planting and watering: for, as Athanasius saith, "It is a Divine work to persuade men's souls to believe."

But as for the using of tortures and of torments, thereby to force them, we have no such custom, nor as yet the churches of God: for, though none come to Christ but such as His Father draws by the violence of His effectual grace, yet ought not men to drive or drag any to the profession of the faith. Yet notwithstanding, if after long patience and forbearing with them, and long instructing them in the points of religion; if still these Pagans continue refractory and obstinate, then surely the civil magistrate, who hath the lawful dominion over them, may severely, though not cruelly, with Josiah, compel them to come to church, and to perform the outward formalities of God's worship.

Go then, ye bloody Jesuits, boast of those many millions of Americans whom you have converted, who were not converted by the sword of the mouth, gained by hearing the Gospel, but compelled by the mouth of the sword, forced by feeling your cruelty. Witness those seventy thousand, which, without any catechizing in the points of religion, were at once driven to the font, like so many horses to a watering trough. Indeed, I find my Saviour (John ii. 15) driving the merchants out of the temple with a whip of cords; but never before did I read of any which against their wills drave or instructed * Pagans to the font to be baptized.

* [Evidently a misprint,—perhaps instead of *dragged*.—ED.]

Each to her mother's house.

Here we see, widows, if poor, are to be maintained by their parents, if they be able. These widows (1 Tim. v. 16) were not to be burdensome to the church, but to be relieved by their own country.* Let parents therefore take heed how they bestow their daughters in marriage: for if they match them to unthrifts and prodigals, will it not be bitterness in the end? The burden will fall heavy on their backs, when their poor daughters with their children must be sent again to their fathers to maintain them.

House.

Widows are to contain themselves within the "house"; not like the harlot, Prov. vii. 12, always "in the streets;" but like meek Sarah in the tent: whereby they shall sooner gain the love and esteem of others. For let base and beggarly fellows buy that rascal ware which is hung out at the doors and windows of shops and stalls, whilst men of quality and fashion will go into the shop, to cheapen the worth of those merchandise as are therein kept secret and concealed. And so surely all discreet and grave men will have the highest esteem, and bear the best affection to such women

* [Probably a slip of the pen for *kindred*.—ED.]

which do not gad abroad to be seen, but, with
Ruth and Orpah, being widows, keep themselves
in their mother's house.

VERSES 8, 9.

The Lord show favour unto you, as ye have done
with the dead, and with me.
The Lord grant you that you may find rest, either
of you in the house of her husband.

Naomi being ready to take her leave of her
daughters, fain she would leave them something,
for which they might be the better after her
departure. But gold and silver she had none, yet
such as she had she freely gave unto them,—hearty
prayers. Whence we learn, it is the best expression of a grateful mind, to pray to God for the
welfare of those at whose hands we have received
greater courtesies than we can requite.

As ye have done.

Hence we learn, God, in the rewarding of the
good deeds of His servants, dealeth with them
accordingly as they have done with others. Yet
far be it from us to suppose, that in our stained
and imperfect works there is any meritorious
virtue, which deserveth that God should proportion a reward unto them: but this freely proceed-

eth from God's favour; who, to encourage us in well-doing, will not suffer a cup of cold water to pass without its reward. Do we desire, then, to have dutiful children and faithful servants hereafter? Let us be dutiful to our parents, faithful to our masters. On the other side, hath God afflicted us with Zibahs to our servants, and with Absaloms to our sons? Let us reflect our eyes on that which is past, and call ourselves to account, whether we formerly have not been unfaithful to our masters, undutiful to our parents : no doubt, we may then take up the confession of Adoni-bezek: "As I have dealt with others, so the Lord hath done to me."

With the dead.

QUESTION.

Here ariseth a question, How can one show favour to the dead, who, being past sense, are not capable of kindness or cruelty?

ANSWER.

The Papists (who leave the souls of most men departing from hence, like Absalom's body, hanging betwixt heaven and hell) expound it, that these women did fast and pray for the souls of their deceased husbands, that they might be delivered from torments, and in due time brought to happiness in heaven. For the confutation of which erroneous exposition, I need say no more than that the Scripture makes no mention of any such middle place, wherein the souls of the godly should be detained before they go into heaven ; and in matters of faith every Christian may safely say, " Except I see in the Bible the print thereof, or can feel it deduced out of it by undeniable consequence, I will not believe it."

It is strange to see what impertinent places are produced by Bellarmine, to prove praying for the dead ; as James v. 16 : " Confess your faults one to another, and pray one for another, that ye may be healed. The effectual fervent prayer of a righteous man availeth much." Then he endeavoureth to prove, that the dead pray for the living, from the parable of Dives, Luke xvi. 27 : "I pray thee therefore, father," &c. : where Dives was charitably solicitous for the good of his surviving brethren. But let the first place in St. James be perused by impartial judgments, and it obligeth mutually the dead saints to confess to us, as well as we to them ; which being impossible, directeth us to confine the words only to reciprocal confessing and praying to and for the living.

Some will say, Bellarmine having sufficiently proved purgatory before, (which necessarily infereth prayers for the dead,) he might be the briefer in that subject. It is confessed, many arguments are alleged by him to that intent, though to small purpose; as Psalm lxvi. 12: " We went through fire and through water: but Thou broughtest us out into a wealthy place." We answer: First. The living there speak *de præterito*, " We went;" not *de futuro*, " We shall go." Secondly. It was literally meant of the children of Israel: they went " through the fire," when envassalled to work in the Egyptian brick-kilns; and "through water," when miraculously they passed through the Red Sea. Again, they went through fire, when, preserved from the stinging of the fiery, they beheld the brazen, serpent. Thirdly. If from " fire" in this text any can kindle a purgatory, others will quench it from the word " water," seeing no Papists ever fancied a watered purgatory.

They urge the place, Matth. v. 26: " Thou shalt by no means come out from thence, till thou hast paid the uttermost farthing;" importing, say they, a possibility on satisfaction to be freed thence, that is, from hell fire.

Answer: " Until " there is not taken terminatively, but extensively; equivalent to " never" or " not at all;" paralleled to that place, Psalm lvii. 1: " In the shadow of Thy wings will I make my refuge, until these calamities be over-past." What, would David depart from God, after his deliverance? Would he use Him as travellers a bush,—come under it in a storm, and leave it in

fair weather? No, surely; David would trust in
God until that time, and at that time, and in
that time, and after that time, and at all times.
Parallel also to that place of Matthew i. 25:
" And knew her not till she had brought forth her
firstborn son:" it being the constant tradition
of antiquity, according to the proportion of faith,
and embraced by the Papists themselves, that
Christ's mother lived and died a spotless virgin.

Much stress he layeth on that passage of the
apostle, 1 Corinth. iii. 15: " He himself shall be
saved, yet so as by fire." This place, saith
Bellarmine, is *locus utilissimus et difficillimus,*
" most profitable and most hard."

We answer, First, in general. Seeing by the
Jesuit's confession it is so hard a place, it is utterly
improbable that purgatory (being of so high
concernment to every soul as Papists would persuade us) can be therein intended: for all matters
necessary for men to know and believe, wherein
the safety of every single soul is interested, (such
as purgatory is pretended to be,) is by the confession of all divines expressed in plain and pregnant
texts of Scripture; for want whereof, Bellarmine
is fain to shroud and shelter himself under the
most obscure places, alleging a text most dark
and difficult, by his own confession.

Secondly. That " fire" there meant by St. Paul,
is affliction in this life. As for such fathers who

expounded it *de igne conflagrationis,* of that " fire " which should burn up all things at the end of the world ; it makes nothing for the patronizing of purgatory, in the Popish notion thereof.

Come we now to find an office, and make an inquiry, how many things a dying godly man leaves behind him in this world. His soul is sent before him; and " from henceforth blessed are the dead that die in the Lord." (Rev. xiv. 13.) He leaveth behind him,

First, his *body ;* to which we must be kind, by burial and lamentation.

Secondly, his *estate;* to which we must be kind, by careful and faithful administration.

Thirdly, his *children, friends, or kindred;* to to whom we must be kind, by love and affection.

Fourthly, his *faults and failings;* to which we must be kind, by silence and suppression.*

Fifthly, his *memory and virtues ;* to which we must be kind, by congratulation, commemoration, and imitation.*

Of these in order : for, although these words, " Ye have been kind to the dead," are capable of this sound sense, "You have been kind to your husbands, who now are dead, whilst they were living ;"

---

* [Prior might almost have had these passages in his eye when he wrote:
> " Be to her virtues very *kind ;*
> Be to her faults a little blind."—ED.]

yet, because more seemeth imported therein, we will prosecute the aforesaid particulars.

I say, First, his *body;* to which there is due burial and lamentation.

Burial; and that according to the quality and condition wherein he lived. We read of king Hezekiah, 2 Chron. xxxii. 33, "They buried him in the chiefest" (in the Hebrew, "in the highest") ["of the] sepulchres of the sons of David." It must be allowed, that the sepulchre of David his father was higher than his; and next David, Hezekiah's. O that height might be but measured by true holiness! There was an officer amongst the Greeks, whose place it was to measure monuments according to the standard of the men's merits therein interred. Such officers, if used in England, would pare off great parcels from some tombs, more proportioned to the party's wealth than virtues. But nothing could be abated of Hezekiah's monument, all the dimensions whereof were due to his devotion.

And *lamentation.* Surely, of all the godly that ever departed this life, God's servants had the least cause to bewail the death of St. Stephen. For, first, whereas there is a threefold degree of certainty of salvation; first, that of hope, which, as the least and lowest, scarce deserveth to be styled certainty; secondly, that of evidence, whereby the person clearly in his soul apprehendeth

God's favour; thirdly, that of vision, peculiar to this Stephen alone, antedating his happiness with his bodily eyes, being in heaven before he was in heaven; so that, as many gates in his wounded body stood open to let out his soul, he beheld alive the heavens opened to receive it.

And yet we read, Acts viii. 2, "And devout men carried Stephen to his burial, and made great lamentation over him." Observe, it was not said they made great lamentation *for* him, but " *over* him." They knew him [to be] in a happy condition : it was themselves they bemoaned in his death, the sight of his corpse sharpening their sorrow, that the infant church had lost one of her best swaddling-clothes.

Secondly, his *estate ;* to which we must be kind, by careful and faithful administration. Heb. ix. 17 : " For a testament is of force after men are dead." Gal. iii. 15 : " Though it be but a man's covenant," or "testament," " yet if it be confirmed, no man disannulleth, or addeth thereto." *No man :* he must either be less than man in knowledge,—a mere beast; or more than man in malice,—a mere devil. By "testament" I understand not only the very words thereof, but also what appeareth to be the testator's will to the conscience of the executor. How many in this kind are cruel to the dead ! so that some of the legacies bequeathed by them have had a thumb or a toe, yea, some an arm or a leg, cut off from them. Many legacies which came sound forth from the testator, before they could get through the executors, have been more lame and maimed than the cripples in the hospital to whom they have been bequeathed.

Thirdly, his *children*, or (because Mahlon and Chilion had none of them) his *kindred or friends*; to whom the living must be kind, with love and affection. Remember the character of the good wife, Proverbs xxxi. 12 : " She will do her husband good, and not evil, all the days of her life." We have many wives only negatively good, pleasing and praising themselves in this, that they do their husbands no hurt. This will not do the deed; they must be positively profitable. Nor is it said, " all the days of his life," but, " all the days of her life. " What if he dieth? her obligation to him is not cassated or nulled, (as many wives generally conceive,) but still continueth " all the days of her life." True it is, she is set free so far, as she may marry again in a competent time, without the least shadow of sin; yet so as still obliged to do good all her lifetime to the friends, to the children (if any) of her dead husband; and he, if surviving her, reciprocally engaged to do the like.

Fourthly, the best men leave *faults and failings* behind them; to these the living must be kind, by silence and suppression.

First : of those of whom thou canst say no good, say nothing.

Secondly : of those of whom thou canst say some good, say no bad.

David is a most excellent instance hereof, 2 Sam. i. 24. Who could more, or more justly, have inveighed against Saul than David ? " O ye daughters of Israel, rejoice for the death of so great a tyrant, who killed Ahimelech the high priest, and fourscore more of God's priests, whose souls were as clear from treason as the white linen ephods they wore were from spots. Twice I had him at my mercy, once in the cave, once when asleep ; yet he (notwithstanding all his fair promises to the contrary) was the more cruel to me for my kindness to him." No such matter ; David conceals what was bad, remembereth what was good in Saul, at leastwise what would make his memory acceptable with the weaker sex ; namely, his making of gallantry fashionable amongst them : " Ye daughters of Israel, weep over Saul, who clothed you in scarlet, with other delights, who put on ornaments of gold upon your apparel."

Fifthly, *memory* of his *virtues :* to which three things are due, to make thee kind thereunto.

First, *congratulation.* I will touch this string but tenderly ; not so much because fearing mine own fingers, (as if the lesson should be false I play thereon,) but expecting other men's ears as

ill-disposed with prejudice. It is no Popery, nor
superstition, to praise God for the happy condition
of His servants departed ; the ancient patriarchs,
the inspired prophets, the holy apostles, the
patient martyrs, the religious confessors. When
the tribe of Reuben, Gad, and half Manasses,
erected the altar *El* at the passage over
Jordan, it startled all the rest of the tribes, as if
under it they had hatched some superstitious
design; whereas indeed the altar was not intended for sacrifice, but was merely an altar of
memorial, to evidence to posterity that these two
tribes and a half, though divided from the rest by
the river of Jordan, were conjoined with them in
the worship of the same God. In like manner,
when some ministers thank God for the departure
of His servants, some people are so weak, and
some so wilful, to condemn such for passages of
Popery, as if superstitious prayers were made for
their departure : whereas, indeed, such congratulation, on the contrary, speaks our confidence on
their present bliss and happiness, and continueth
the church militant with the church triumphant,
as the completing one entire catholic church of
Jesus Christ.

Secondly, *commemoration* is due to the memories
of the deceased. Hence the ancient custom of fune-
ral orations, continued in our modern practice, both
to the honour of the dead, and profit of the living.

Thirdly, *imitation* of their virtues. It hath been a great question amongst such who desire to express themselves thankful to their dead ancestors, of what metal or matter to make their monuments, so as they may be most lasting and permanent. Wise men have generally decried silver and brass; not so much because too costly, (such may be the worth and wealth of the executors and party deceased,) but too tempting to sacrilege to demolish them. Brass is generally subject to the same mischief, and marble touch * and alabaster are generally used for that purpose; but the monument less subject to casualty is, to imitate the virtues of our dead friends : in other tombs the dead are preserved; in these they may be said to remain alive.

When we see a child very like to the father and mother thereof, we use to say, "Thy father will never be dead as long as thou livest." Thus it is the best remembrance of our dead progenitors to follow their virtues. St. Paul cannot look upon Timothy, but presently calls to mind his mother Eunice, and his grandmother Lois, though the latter no doubt [was] long since departed.

The Lord grant that you may find rest, each of you in the house of her husband.

Here we may observe, first, that it is the part of

* [An inferior kind of black marble.—Ed.]

pious parents to pray to God for the good success of their children, especially in the matter of their marriage: example in Abraham, Gen. xxiv. 7. Secondly, hence we may gather, that the life of married persons meeting together in the fear of God, is "rest."

OBJECTION.

How then cometh it to pass that many men and women may take up the words of Rebecca, "Seeing it is so, why am I thus?" (Gen. xxv. 22.) If the married life be "rest," how cometh it to prove my purgatory, my hell, my cause of restless torment? Men and women were joined in marriage (Gen. ii.) to the end to be a mutual help one to the other; but many prove such helpers as the king of Ashur [Assyria] did to Ahaz, of whom it is said, He "distressed him, but helped him not." (2 Chron. xxviii. 20.)

ANSWER.

Who can hinder it, if men of their girdles and garters make halters to hang themselves? If those things which should be for their strength and ornament, be through their own default turned to their utter undoing; the estate of marriage is not herein to be blamed, but the folly of such who out of some sinister ends undertake it. Happily [haply] some choose their wives like as our grand-

mother Eve did the apple, because they are pleasant to the eyes to be looked upon : others, out of a
love of their wealth, saying of their wives what the
Shechemites did of the sons of Jacob, " Shall not
all their herds and cattle be ours ? " Whereas,
if grace and piety were principally respected in
their choice, (other outward accommodations in
their due distance not neglected,) they would find
the truth of our observation, that a married life
is " rest." For, though some petty brawls may
happen amongst the most sanctified couple, which
may move their anger, yet shall it not remove their
love, if one with Christian discretion beareth with
the infirmities of the other. Joab made this com-
pact with his brother Abishai, 2 Sam. x. 11 : "If the
Aramite be stronger than I, thou shalt help me :
but if the Ammonites be too strong for thee, I will
come and succour thee." Thus ought man and
wife to make a bargain, with their best counsel
to, and prayers for, each other, to assist themselves mutually against their sundry weaknesses
and infirmities, which otherwise would turn their
" rest " of their life into unquietness.

VERSES 9, 10, 11, 12, 13.

*And when she kissed them, they lifted up their voices,
and wept.*

*And they said unto her, Surely we will return with
thee unto thy people.*

But Naomi said, Turn again, my daughters: for what cause will you go with me? Are there any more sons in my womb, that they may be your husbands?

Turn again, my daughters, go your way; for I am too old to have a husband. If I should say, I have hope; and if I had a husband this night; yea, if I had born sons;

Would you tarry for them while they were of age? Would you be deferred for them from taking of husbands? Nay, my daughters; for it grieveth me much for your sakes that the hand of the Lord is gone out against me.

And when she kissed them.

Kisses was the ordinary salutation of the Jews at the meeting of acquaintance, men with men, women with women, men with women; provided that then they were of near kindred, to avoid all suspicion of unchastity.

And they lifted up their voices, and wept.

The observation here may be the same which the Jews collected; (John xi.;) which, when they saw our Saviour weep for Lazarus, they said, " Behold how He loved him ! " So these tears in this place were the expression of their affection. Sorrow, like the river of Jordan, (1 Chron. xii. 15,) in the first month did overflow the banks, and streamed water down their cheeks.

But Naomi said, Turn again, my daughters, &c.

In these words, she dissuadeth her daughters-in-law from returning with her. The strength of her reason, contained in three verses, may thus be set down, as if she had said : " Happily, [haply,] daughters, you have heard that it is the custom in the land of Canaan for childless widows to marry their deceased husbands' brothers. But if your return be grounded hereon, know that you build your hopes on a false foundation, it being impossible for me, by the course of nature, to have any more sons. Who will look that water should flow from a dry fountain, grapes grow on a withered vine, fruit flourish on a dead fig-tree ? Though Sarah at ninety was made a mother; though Aaron's rod did bud and blossom when it was dry ; I myself should be a miracle, if I should expect such a miracle : and therefore know, that there are no more sons in my womb."

DOCTRINE.

Now whereas Naomi dealeth thus plainly with her daughters, not feeding them with false hopes, it teacheth us this : We ought not to gull our friends with the promises of those things that neither will nor can come to pass. Otherwise we

shall both wrong our friends, who, the higher
they are mounted upon the hill of seeming hopes,
at length the deeper they will be cast into the dale
of real despair : and also we shall wrong ourselves ; when Time, the mother of Truth, shall
unmask us, we shall prove ourselves to be no
better than liars and cheaters.

USE.

Let us labour to be Nathanaels, true Israelites,
" in whom there is no guile : " and as John Baptist,
when as the Pharisees asked him whether he was
the Christ or no, he " confessed, and denied not,"
and said plainly, " I am not the Christ ; " (John
i. 20 ;) so if we neither mean to do, nor know
that such things can be done which our friends
request of us, let us confess, deny not, and say
plainly, that their suits cannot, shall not be
granted ; and by such downright dealing we shall
at last get more favour from them than they who
flatter them with their tongue.   Let not the
physician, when he reads in the urinal those dis-
mal symptoms which are the ushers of death, still
promise life and health unto his patient ; but
plainly tell him that there is *mors in ollâ ;* that so
he may fly unto the Physician of the Soul, for a
better life, when this shall fade.   Let not the law-
yer, when he knows the case is desperate, feed his

client with false hopes to recover it, that so from him he may be fed with money; but rather let him advise him to "agree with his adversary, while he is in the way;" that, though he cannot get the conquest, yet he may have the easier composition.

For I am too old to have a husband.

Here ariseth a question.

QUESTION.

Is there any age so old, wherein a man or woman may not marry?

ANSWER.

Naomi's meaning was not simply and absolutely that she was too old to marry, but she was too old to have a husband, and by a husband to have children, and that those children should grow up, and make fit husbands for Orpah and Ruth. Yet, by the way, I would advise such who are stricken in years, especially if impotency be added unto age, and that it may stand with their conveniency, to refrain from all thoughts of a second marriage, and to expect that happy day when death shall solemnize the nuptial betwixt their soul and their Saviour. For when Barzillai hath counted eighty years, he hath even had enough of the pleasure and vanity of the world; let him retire himself to a private life, and not envy his

son Chimham to succeed to those delights, of
which his age hath made his father uncapable.
Yet if any ancient persons, for their mutual
comfort and society, (which is not the least end
for which marriage was ordained,) are disposed to
match themselves herein, they are blameless;
especially if they have a care to observe a corre-
spondency of age with those to whom they link
themselves.   Otherwise, as our Saviour noteth,
when the old cloth was joined to the new, it made
no good medley, but the rent was made the worse;
so when the spring of youth is wedded to the
winter of age, no true comfort can arise from
such unequal yokes, but much jealousy and suspicion are caused from the same.

Would ye tarry for them?

That is, "You would not tarry for them; or if
you should tarry for them, you should wrong
yourselves, and do unadvisedly; because in the
mean time, refraining from the using of God's
ordinance, you expose yourselves to the devil, to
tempt you to incontinency." Therefore St. Paul's
counsel is good which he prescribes in 1 Tim. v. 14:
"I will therefore that the younger women," &c.

While they were of age.

Note from hence, that children are not to be
married in their non-age, before they are arrived

at years of discretion : Tamar (Gen. xxxviii.) is to
wait till Shelah be grown up. Those persons are
therefore to be blamed, who out of by-respects
match their children in their infancy. Whence
it cometh to pass that as their age doth increase,
their mind doth alter : so what formerly they did
like, afterwards they do loathe, such marriages
proving commonly most insuccessful.

Nay, my daughters ; for it grieveth me much for
your sakes.

As if she had said, " It grieveth me much that
you are already plunged into poverty ; but it
would add more to my sorrow, if you should
increase your calamities by returning home with
me. For mine own part, my misery troubleth me
not so much, because the sun of my life is ready
to set, and it mattereth not though the ship be
scanted of victuals, when it is hard by the
harbour. All my care is for you, who are young
women, and stand upon your own preferment :
it grieveth me much for your sakes."

DOCTRINE.

See here, such is the ingenuous nature of God's
children, that they sorrow more for others that
are inwrapped with them in a common calamity,
than for themselves. Example in Elias, 1 Kings
xvii. 20. But then it goeth nearest to their heart,

when others are not only afflicted with them, but also for them; when they themselves are the principal malefactors, for whose defaults others are punished, as in David. (2 Sam. xxiv. 17.)

It may confute the devilish nature of such who, being in trouble, care not though they pawn their dearest friends in their stead, so be it they themselves may escape. And it may also serve to comfort those that are in distress, when God only layeth His punishments on them alone, and doth not involve others together with them. Art thou afflicted with poverty? Comfort thyself, that though thou beest poor, yet thou hast undone none by suretiship for thee. Art thou in sickness? Be glad that thy disease is not infectious, and that thou hast not derived the contagion to others. Doth God punish thee for thy sin with a personal punishment? Be glad that thou bearest the weight of thine own offence, and that thou art not the Jonah, for whose private sin a whole ship of passengers is endangered to be cast away; for then their case would grieve thee more than thine own calamity.

That the hand of the Lord.

Naomi here taketh especial notice, that her losses proceeded from no other by-causes, but from the hand of God. As David therefore asked the widow of Tekoah, (2 Sam. xiv. 19,) "Is not the hand of Joab with thee in all this?" so, when any affliction befalleth us, let us presently have recourse unto God, and say, "Is not the hand of the Lord the principal cause hereof?" —and not with the priests of the Philistines say, "It was a chance that happened us."

Is gone out against me.

OBSERVATION.

Hence we may observe, every saint of God, in a common calamity, is to think that God aimed at his punishment, and intended his reformation in particular. "The hand of the Lord" was gone out also against Orpah and Ruth, in taking away their husbands; yet Naomi appropriateth the stroke to herself,—"is gone out against me."

How contrary is this to the practice of the world! Men in a public and a general affliction, each shifteth it off from themselves; and no one man will be brought to confess that his sins are punished or his amendment intended in particular, if the scourge be universal. As the Philistines (1 Sam. v.) posted the ark of God from Ashdod to Ekron, from one place to another, and none would receive it; so, in a common calamity, none will acknowledge that he himself is especially inter-

ested in it, but plead, " What is that to us ?   Let
others look unto it."   " O," saith the people,
" God hath justly sent this plague for the corruption of the magistrates."   " It is justly inflicted,"
saith the magistrate, " for the disobedience of the
people."   " Herein," saith the poor man, " God
hath met with the oppression and extortion of the
rich."   " Herein," saith the rich man, " God hath
paid home the muttering and the repining of the
poor."   " Now," saith the prodigal, " God punisheth the covetousness of old men."   " Now,"
saith the old man, " He scourgeth the prodigality
of such as be young."   Far otherwise Naomi,
who, though the arrows of God did glance and
rebound, to the wounding of Orpah and Ruth, yet
she thought she herself was the mark at whom
God did level His shafts : " The hand of the Lord
is gone out against me."

VERSE 14.

*And Orpah kissed her mother-in-law ; but Ruth
clave unto her.*

These words contain two general parts.

First. A blazing meteor falling down out of
the air : " And Orpah," &c.

Secondly. A fixed star fairly shining in the
heaven : " But Ruth," &c.

And Orpah kissed her mother.

Is this she which even now was so promising in her words, and so passionate in her weeping? See how soon a forward professor may turn to a fearful apostate. Though she standeth or falleth to her own Master, yet, as the Psalmist saith, "I am horribly afraid for those that forsake Thy law," so have we just cause to suspect the fearful final estate of Orpah.

Kissed her mother.

That is, gave her this last salutation of her departure. Here we see, that those who want grace and true sanctity may notwithstanding have manners and good civility. Now, had Orpah changed the corporal kiss she gave to her mother, into a spiritual kiss to her Saviour,— "Kiss the Son, lest He be angry," (Psalm ii. 12,) —her case had been as happy as now it may seem to be hopeless. But, leaving her, we come to ourselves, and gather this doctrine.

DOCTRINE.

Those who at the first were forward in religion, may afterward altogether fall away. (1 Tim. i. 20; Heb. vi. 4; Matth. xiii. 20.) It may therefore serve to abate the proud carriage of such, who, as if it were not enough to be sure, will also be presumptuous of their salvation, and thereby take leave and liberty to themselves to live more licentiously.

But as once one of the children of the prophets cried out to Elisha, "O man of God, there is death in the pot;" so may the weak Christian complain against this doctrine: "O, it is a deadly and dangerous one, containing much matter of despair, too bitter for the palate of a poor Christian to taste, or his stomach to digest. It quencheth all the sparks of my comfort, and hacketh asunder all the sinews of my hope. I fear lest, Orpah-like, I also should fall away. What shall I do, that I may be saved?"

ANSWER.

Let not the "smoking flax" be dismayed, which in time may be a blazing flame; nor the "bruised reed" be discouraged, which may prove a brazen pillar in the temple of God. That therefore thou mayest finally persevere, observe these four rules.

RULE I.

First: Utterly renounce all sufficiency in thyself. Who but a madman will now-a-days warrant the paper shields of his own strength, that knows that Adam's complete armour of original integrity was shot through in Paradise?

RULE II.

Secondly: Place all thy confidence on the undeserved mercy of God. Perseverance cometh neither from the east, nor from the west, nor as yet from the south; but God suffereth one to fall, and holdeth up another. The temple of Solomon had two pillars; one called *Jachin,* sounding in Hebrew, "The Lord will stablish;" the other, *Boaz,* signified, "In Him is strength." So every Christian ("the temple of the Holy Ghost") is principally holden up by these two pillars,—God's power, and will, to support him. Wherefore in every distress let us cry out to God, as the disciples did to our Saviour in the midst of a tempest, "Help, Master, or else we perish."

RULE III.

Thirdly: Use all those means which God hath chalked out for the increase of grace in thee; as prayer, meditation, reverent receiving the sacraments, accompanying with God's children, reading, hearing the word, &c.

RULE IV.

Fourthly: Always preserve in thyself an awful fear, lest thou shouldst fall away from God.

Fear to fall, and Assurance to stand, are two sisters; and though Cain said he was not his "brother's keeper," sure I am that this Fear doth watch and guard her sister Assurance. *Tantus est gradus certitudinis, quantus sollicitudinis:* they that have much of this fear, have much certainty; they that have little, little certainty; they that have none, have none at all. It is said in building, that those chimneys which shake most, and give way to the wind, will stand the longest: the moral in divinity is true: those Christians that shiver for fear by sins to fall away, may be observed most courageous to persist in piety.

COMFORT.

To those that diligently practise these rules, I will add this comfort: Encourage thyself, that God will keep thee from apostasy unto the end, because already hitherto He hath preserved thee. For God's former favours are pawns and pledges of His future love.   David's killing of a lion and a bear were the earnests of his victory over Goliath.   Thus St. Paul reasoneth, 2 Cor. i. 10 : "Who delivered us from so great a death, and doth deliver : in whom we trust that He will yet deliver us."   When Rachel bare her first son, (Gen. xxx.,) she called him Joseph, and said, "The Lord shall add to me another son."   So, when God hath already blessed us and supported us for the time past, let us say with Rachel, "' Joseph,—the Lord will add:' He will not stay, or stint, or stop here; but as He hath kept me from my mother's womb, and ever since I was born, so I trust He will not forsake me when I am aged, and full of grey hairs."

But, to return to her which returned again to Moab. We read in 2 Sam. xx. that the people which passed by the corpse of murdered Amasa, being moved with such a hideous and uncouth spectacle, they " stood still: " but when we read this Book of Ruth, and come to Orpah's apostasy, there let us a while pause and demur, to read in her fall a lecture of our own infirmity. For if we stand, it is not because we have more might in ourselves, but because God hath more mercy on us. Let us therefore " work out our salvation with fear and trembling: " ever trembling, lest we should be cast to hell; ever triumphing, that we shall come to heaven: ever fearful, lest we should fall; ever certain, that we shall stand: ever careful, lest we should be damned; ever cheerful, that we shall be saved. Concerning Ruth's perseverance we intend to treat hereafter.

VERSE 15.

*And Naomi said, Behold, thy sister-in-law is gone
   back unto her people, and unto her gods: return
   thou after thy sister-in-law.*

In these words Naomi seeks to persuade Ruth
to return; alleging the example of Orpah, who,
she saith, was " gone back to her people, and to
her gods."

OBSERVATION.

Where, first, we find that all the heathen, and
the Moabites amongst the rest, did not acknowledge one true God, but were the worshippers of
many gods; for they made every attribute of God
to be a distinct deity. Thus, instead of that attribute, the wisdom of God, they feigned Apollo
the god of wisdom; instead of the power of God,
they made Mars the god of power; instead of
that admirable beauty of God, they had Venus
the goddess of beauty. But no one attribute was
so much abused as God's providence: for the
heathen supposing that the whole world, and all
the creatures therein, was too great a diocese to be
daily visited by one and the same Deity, they
therefore assigned sundry gods to several creatures. Thus God's providence in ruling the
raging of the seas was counted Neptune; in

stilling the roaring winds, Æolus; in commanding the powers of hell, Pluto: yea, sheep had their Pan, and gardens their Pomona; the heathens then being as fruitful in feigning of gods, as the Papists since in making of saints.

DOCTRINE.

Now, because Naomi used the example of Orpah as a motive to work upon Ruth to return, we gather from thence, examples of others set before our eyes are very potent and prevalent arguments to make us follow and imitate them: whether they be good examples,—so the forwardness of the Corinthians to relieve the Jews provoked many,—or whether they be bad,—so the dissembling of Peter at Antioch drew Barnabas and others into the same fault. But those examples, of all others, are most forcible with us, which are set by such who are near to us by kindred, or gracious with us in friendship, or great over us in power.

USE I.

Let men in eminent places, as magistrates, ministers, fathers, masters, and the like, (seeing that others love to dance after their pipe, to sing after their tune, to tread after their track,) endeavour to propound themselves patterns of pity and religion to those that be under them.

USE II.

When we see any good example propounded unto us, let us strive with all possible speed to imitate it. What a deal of stir is there in the world for civil precedency and priority! Every one desires to march in the forefront, and thinks it a shame to come lagging in the rearward. O that there were such a holy ambition and heavenly emulation in our hearts, that, as Peter and John ran a race, which should come first to the grave of our Saviour, so men would contend, who should first attain to true mortification! And when we see a good example set before us, let us imitate it, though it be in one who in outward respects is far our inferior. Shall not the master be ashamed to see that his man, whose place on earth is to come behind him, in piety towards heaven goes before him? Shall not the husband blush to see his wife, which is the weaker vessel in nature, to be the stronger vessel in grace? Shall not the elder brother dye his cheeks with the colour of virtue, to see his younger brother, who was last born, first re-born by faith and the Holy Ghost? Yet let him not therefore envy his brother, as Cain did Abel; let him not be angry with his brother, because he is better than himself; but let him be angry with himself, because he is worse than his brother; let him turn all his

malice into imitation, all his fretting at him into
following of him. Say unto him, as Gehazi did of
Naaman, "As the Lord liveth, I will run after
him:" and though thou canst not over-run him,
nor as yet over-take him, yet give not over to run
with him; follow him, though not as Asahel did
Abner, hard at the heels; yet as Peter did our
Saviour, "afar off;" that, though the more
slowly, yet as surely thou mayest come to heaven;
and though thou wert short of him whilst he
lived, in the race, yet thou shalt be even with him
when thou art dead, at the mark.

USE III.

When any bad example is presented unto us,
let us decline and detest it, though the men be
never so many, or so dear unto us. Imitate
Micaiah, (1 Kings xxii.,) to whom when the messengers sent to fetch him said, " Behold now, the
words of the prophets declare good to the king
with one mouth: let thy word therefore, I pray
thee, be like to one of them; " Micaiah answered,
" As the Lord liveth, whatsoever the Lord saith
unto me, that will I speak." If they be never so
dear unto us, we must not follow their bad practice. So must the son please him that begat him,
that he do not displease Him that created him : so
must the wife follow him that married her, that she
doth not offend Him that made her. Wherefore,

as Samson, though bound with new cords, snapped them asunder as tow when it feeleth the fire ; so, rather than we should be led by the lewd examples of those which be near and dear unto us, let us break in pieces all ties, engagements, relations whatsoever.

QUESTION.

Yea, but one may say, " What if I find in the Scripture an action recorded, whose doer is known to have been a godly and gracious man ? may I not, without any further doubt or scruple, follow the same ? "

ANSWER.

For the better satisfying hereof, I will rank the actions of godly men, registered in the Scriptures, into nine several ranks, and will show how far forth we may safely proceed in the imitation of them.

1. We find some actions set down which are extraordinary, the doers whereof had peculiar strength and dispensation from God to do them. Thus Samson slew himself and the Philistines in the temple of Dagon; Elias caused fire to descend on the two captains and their fifties ; Elisha cursed the children of Bethel. Now these are recorded rather for our instruction than imitation : for when the " sons of thunder " would have been the sons of lightning, and have had

fire from heaven to burn the Samaritans, which refused to receive our Saviour, after the example of Elias, Christ checked their ill-tempered zeal, and told them, " You know not what spirit you are of."

2. Some examples are set down which are founded in the ceremonial law; as, the eating of the paschal lamb; the circumcising of their children the eighth day. Now the date of these did expire at the death of Christ : the substance being come, the shadows are fled; and therefore they may in no wise still be observed.

3. Such examples as are founded in the judicial law, which was only calculated for the elevation of the Jewish commonwealth; as, to put men to death for adultery. Now these examples tie us no farther to imitate them, than they agree with the moral law, or with those statutes by which every particular country is governed.

4. Some there be founded in no law at all, but only in an ancient custom by God tolerated and connived at; as, polygamy in the patriarchs, divorces in the Jews upon every slight occasion. From these also we must in these days abstain, as which were never liked or allowed by God, though permitted in some persons and ages, for some special reasons.

5. Doubtful examples ; which may so be termed, because it is difficult to decide whether the actors

of them therein did offend or no ; so that, should a jury of learned writers be empanneled to pass their verdict upon them, they would be puzzled whether to condemn or acquit them, and at length be forced to find it an *Ignoramus ;* as, whether David did well to dissemble himself frantic, thereby to escape the cruelty of Achish, king of Gath. Now our most advised way herein is altogether to abstain from the imitation of them, because there is a deal of difficulty and danger, and our judgments may easily be deceived.

6. Mixed examples; which contain in them a double action, the one good, the other bad, both so closely couched together that it is a very hard thing to sever them. Thus, in the unjust steward, there was his wisdom to provide for himself, and his wickedness to purloin from his master : the first God did commend, we may imitate ; the latter He could not but loathe, we may not but shun. In the Israelitish midwives, Exod. i., there was *fides mentis, et fallacia mentientis,* " the faith of their " love, " and the falseness of their lying : " the first God rewarded, and we may follow ; the latter He could not but dislike, and we must detest. Behold, here is wisdom, and let the man that hath understanding discreetly divide betwixt the dross and the gold, the chaff and the wheat, in these mixed examples; that so he may practise the one, eschew and avoid the other.

7. Those which be absolutely bad, that no charitable comment can be fastened upon them; as, the drunkenness of Noah, the incest of Lot, the lying of Abraham, the swearing of Joseph, the adultery of David, the denial of Peter. Now God forbid we should imitate these: far be it from us, with king Ahaz, to take a pattern from the idolatrous altar of Damascus. The Holy Spirit hath not set these sins down with an intent they should be followed; but first to show the frailty of His dearest saints, when He leaves them to themselves; as also to comfort us when we fall into grievous sins, when we see that as heinous offences of God's servants stand upon the record in the Scripture.

8. Actions which are only good as they are qualified with such a circumstance, as David's eating of the show-bread, provided for the priests, in a case of absolute necessity. These we may follow; but then we must have a special eye and care that the same qualifying circumstance be in us; for otherwise the deed will be impious and damnable.

9. Examples absolutely good; as, the faithfulness of Abraham, the peaceableness of Isaac, the painfulness of Jacob, the chastity of Joseph, the patience of Moses, the valour of Joshua, the sincerity of David. These it is lawful and laudable with our best endeavours to imitate. Follow not the adultery of David, but follow the chastity of

Joseph; follow not the dissembling of Peter, but follow the sincerity of Nathanael; follow not the testiness of Jonah, but follow the meekness [of] Moses; follow not the apostasy of Orpah, but follow the perseverance of Ruth, which comes in the next text to be treated of.

VERSES 16, 17.

And Ruth answered, Entreat me not to leave thee,
nor to depart from thee ; for whither thou goest,
I will go ; and where thou dwellest, I will dwell :
thy people shall be my people, and thy God my
God :
Where thou diest, will I die, and there will I be
buried : the Lord do so to me, and more also, if
aught but death part thee and me.

Here we have the resolution of Ruth portrayed in lively colours : so that if we consider her sex,— a woman ; her nation,—a Moabite ; one may boldly pronounce of her what our Saviour did of the centurion, "Verily I say unto you, I have not found so great faith, no, not in Israel."

Entreat me not to leave thee.

Some read it, " Be not thou against me," as it is in the margin of the new translation. Where we see, that those are to be accounted our adversaries, and against us, who dissuade us from our voyage to Canaan, from going to God's true religion. They may be our fathers, they cannot be our friends. Though they promise us all outward profits and pleasures, yet in very deed they are not with us, but against us, and so must be accounted of.

Where thou lodgest, I will lodge.

A good companion, saith the Latin proverb, is *pro viatico*,*—I may add also, *pro diversorio*.† Ruth, so be it she may enjoy Naomi's gracious company, will be content with any lodging, though happily it may be no better than Jacob had. (Gen. xxviii.) And yet we see how some have been discouraged even from the company of our Saviour, for fear of hard lodging. Witness the scribe, to whom when our Saviour said, " The foxes have their holes, and the fowls of the air have nests, but the Son of Man hath not where to lay His head; " this cold comfort presently quenched his forward zeal, and he never appeared afterward ; whereas he ought to have said to our Saviour, as Ruth to Naomi, " Where Thou lodgest, will I lodge."

Thy people shall be my people.

Haman, being offended with Mordecai, as if it

---

* [Serves "instead of baggage, provender, and all the necessaries of travelling."—ED.]

† [" Instead of an inn or lodging."—ED.]

had been but lean and weak revenge to spit his
spite upon one person, hated all the Jews for
Mordecai's sake. The mad bear, stung with one
bee, would needs throw down the whole hive.
But clean contrary, Naomi had so graciously demeaned herself that Ruth for her sake is fallen in
love with all the Jews. Farewell, Melchom;
farewell, Chemosh; farewell, Moab! Welcome,
Israel; welcome, Canaan; welcome, Bethlehem!
All of a sudden she will turn convert, she will
turn proselyte.

OBSERVATION.

The godly carriage of one particular person
may beget a love of that country and people whereof he is, even in a stranger and foreigner. Do we
then desire to gain credit to our country, praise to
our people, honour to our nation, repute to our
religion? Let us deport and behave ourselves
graciously, if we live amongst strangers. On the
other side, the base and debauched manners of
some one man are able to make his country stink
in the nostrils of those foreigners amongst whom
he lives. *Ex uno discite omnes :* in one faithless
Sinon one may read the treachery of all the
Grecians.

Thy God shall be my God.

Jehoshaphat, when he joined with Ahab, (1

Kings xxii.,) said unto him, " My people is as thy people, and my horses are as thy horses; " that is, he would comply with him in a politic league : but Ruth goes further, to an unity in religion, " Thy God shall be my God." Yea, but one may say, " How came Ruth to know who was the God of Naomi ? " I answer, As God said of Abraham, " I know that Abraham will instruct his children ; " so may one confidently say of Naomi,—I know that Naomi had catechized and instructed her daughter-in-law, and often taught her that the God of the Israelites was the only true God, who made heaven and earth, and that all others were but idols, the works of men's hands. Yet, as the Samaritans believed our Saviour first upon the relation of the woman that came from the well, but afterwards said unto her, " Now we believe, not because of thy saying : for we have heard Him ourselves, and know that this is indeed the Christ, the Saviour of the world ; " (John iv. 42 ;) so happily Ruth was induced first to the liking of the God of Israel upon the credit of Naomi's words ; but afterwards her love of Him proceeded from a more certain ground, the motions of God's Holy Spirit in her heart.

Where thou diest, will I die.

Here Ruth supposeth two things. First, that she and her mother-in-law should both die : " It is appointed for all once to die." Secondly, that Naomi, as the eldest, should die first; for, according to the ordinary custom of nature, it is most probable and likely that those that are most stricken in years should first depart this life. Yet I know not whether the rule or the exceptions be more general; and therefore let both young and old prepare for death: the first may die soon, but the second cannot live long.

And there will I be buried.

Where she supposeth two things more. First, that those that survived her would do her the favour to bury her; which is a common courtesy, not to be denied to any. It was an epitaph written upon the grave of a beggar,—

*Nudus eram vivus; mortuus, ecce, tegor.**

Secondly, she supposeth that they would bury her, according to her instructions, near to her mother Naomi.

OBSERVATION.

As it is good to enjoy the company of the godly while they are living, so it is not amiss, if it will stand with conveniency, to be buried with them

---

* [" Naked on the earth I hover'd:
Now, stone dead, behold, I 'm cover'd."—Ed.]

after death. The old prophet's bones escaped a
burning by being buried with the other prophets;
and the man who was tumbled into the grave of
Elisha was revived by the virtue of his bones.
And we read in the " Acts and Monuments," that
the body of Peter Martyr's wife was buried in a
dunghill; but afterward, being taken up in the
reign of Queen Elizabeth, it was honourably
buried in Oxford, in the grave of one Frideswick,
a Popish she-saint; to this end, that if Popery—
which God forbid!—should overspread our kingdom again, and if the Papists should go about to
untomb Peter Martyr's wife's bones, they should
be puzzled to distinguish betwixt this woman's
body and the relics of their saint. So, good it is
sometimes to be buried with those whom some
do account pious, though perchance in very deed
they be not so.

The Lord do so to me, and more also.

To ascertain Naomi of the seriousness of her
intentions herein, Ruth backs what formerly she
had said with an oath, lined with an execration.

OBSERVATION.

Whence we may gather, it is lawful for us to
swear upon a just cause: but then these three
rules must be warily observed.

First: That we know that the thing whereto

we swear be true, if the oath be assertory; and if it be promissory, that we be sure that it is in our intent, and in our power, God blessing us, to perform that which we promise.

Secondly : That the occasion whereupon we use it be of moment and consequence, not trifling and trivial.

Thirdly : That we swear by God alone, and not by any creature. Swear then neither by the heaven, nor by the earth, nor by Jerusalem, nor by the temple, nor by the gold of the temple, nor by the altar, nor by the sacrifice on the altar, but by God alone : for He only is able to reward thee, if that thou affirmest be true; He only is able to punish thee, if that thou avouchest be false. Yet this doth no ways favour the practice of many now-a-days, who make oaths their language. Our Saviour said to the Jews, " Many good works have I showed you from the Father : for which of them go you about to stone Me ? " So may the Lord say to many riotous gallants now-a-days, " Many good deeds have I done to thee: I created thee of nothing; I sent My Son to die for thee; by My providence I continually protect and preserve thee: for which of these deeds dost thou go about by oaths to blaspheme Me ? "

Now whereas Ruth doth not say, " God damn me," " God confound me," " I would I might never stir; " but shrouds the execration under general terms, " God do so to me, and more also ; " we learn, it is not good to particularize in any kind of punishment when we swear, but only to express the curse in general terms, leaving it to the discretion of God Almighty, to choose that arrow out of His quiver which He shall think most fit to shoot at us.

If aught but death.

See here the large extent of a saint's love; it lasts till death : and no wonder ; for it is not founded upon honour, beauty, or wealth, or any other sinister respect in the party beloved; which is subject to age or mutability, but only on the grace and piety in him ; which foundation because it always lasteth, that love which is built upon it is also perpetual.

Part thee and me.

Death is that which parteth one friend from another. Then the dear father must part with his dutiful child ; then the dutiful child must forgo his dear father : then the kind husband must leave his constant wife ; then the constant wife must lose her kind husband : then the careful master must be sundered from his industrious servant ; then the industrious servant must be severed from his careful master. Yet this may be some comfort to those whose friends death hath taken away, that as our Saviour said to the disciples, " Yet a little while, and you shall not see Me ; and yet a little while, and you shall see Me again : " so yet a little while, and we shall not see our friends ; and yet a little while, and we shall see them again in the kingdom of heaven ; for, *non mittuntur, sed præmittuntur,*—we do not forgo them, but they go before us.

To conclude : we see many women so strangely disguised with fantastic fashions, as if they desired to verify the nickname of the philosopher, and to prove themselves in very deed to be very monsters. Yea, many of them so affect man-like clothes and shorn hair, it is hard to discover the sex of a woman through the attire of a man. But we see in my text worthy Ruth taking upon her, not the clothes, but the courage ; not the hair, but the heart ; not the attire, but the resolution of a man, yea, and more than of a man. Witness her worthy speech, " Entreat me not to depart," &c.

VERSE 18.

And when she saw that she was steadfastly minded
to go with her, she left off speaking unto her.

Orpah and Ruth may be compared to two strong forts ; Naomi, to one that besieged them ; who

made three sore assaults upon them :—the first, in
the eighth verse; which assault both of them
resisted with equal constancy :—the second, in the
eleventh verse; to which Orpah basely yieldeth,
and accepteth terms of composition :—the last, in
the fifteenth verse; which Ruth most valiantly
defeated, and stood upon terms of defiance to the
mention of any return.   Now as soldiers, when
they have long besieged a city with the loss of
time, money, and men, being hopeless to take it,
they even sound a retreat, and retire home,
without accomplishing their desire; so Naomi,
perceiving that all her arguments which she used
to conquer Ruth, like water in the smith's forge
cast on coals, did more intend * the heat of her
constancy, gives over in my text : " And when
she saw," &c.

Which words do probably persuade what formerly we affirmed, namely, that Naomi dissuaded
her daughter, only to search and sound her sincerity, not with any true desire she should go back
to Moab.   For even as it is plain that the replier
in his disputation aimeth not at the suppressing,
but at the advancing, of a truth, who surceaseth
and cavils no longer, when he sees the neck of his
argument broken with a sufficient answer; so it
appeareth that Naomi, what she had said formerly,

* [" Intensify."—Ed.]

spake it only to try her daughter ; because, having now had sufficient experience of her constancy, she so willingly desisted. God wrestled with Jocob, with a desire to be conquered ; so Naomi no doubt opposed Ruth, hoping and wishing that she herself might be foiled.

And when she saw that she was steadfastly minded.

The Hebrew reads it, " that she strengthened herself; " that being their phrase to express an oath.

OBSERVATION.

Where we observe, oaths taken upon just occasion are excellent ties and bands to strengthen men in the performance of those things to which they swear. The greater pity it is, then, that a thing in itself so sovereign should be so daily and dangerously abused. Witness Herod, who by reason of a rash oath cast himself into a worse prison than that wherein he had put the Baptist, making that which, being well used, might have confirmed in piety, to be a means to enforce him to murder.

USE.

Let this teach us, when we find ourselves to lag and falter in Christianity, to call to mind that solemn vow, promise, and profession, which our godfathers in our name made for us at our baptism,—to " forsake the devil and all his works, the vain pomps and vanities of this wicked world ; and to fight valiantly under Christ's standard." Let us remember from whence we are fallen, and do our first work. We need not make a new vow, but only renew the old ; and so settle and establish ourselves in the practice of piety, as Ruth in my text by an oath strengthened herself.

She left off speaking unto her.

She saw she had now enough expressed and declared her integrity, and therefore she would not put her to the trouble of any farther trial.

OBSERVATION.

Hence the doctrine is this : After proof and trial made of their fidelity, we are to trust our brethren, without any farther suspicion. Not to try before we trust, is want of wisdom ; not to trust after we have tried, is want of charity. The goldsmith must purify the dross and ore from the gold ; but he must be wary lest he makes waste of good metal, if over-curious in too often refining. We may search and sound the sincerity of our brethren ; but, after good experience made of their uprightness, we must take heed lest by continual sifting and proving them we offend a weak Christian. Christ tried the woman of Syrophœnicia first with silence, then with two sharp answers; at last, finding her to be sound, He dismissed her with granting her request, and commending of her faith. When He had said to Peter the third time, "Lovest thou Me?" He rested satisfied with Peter's answer, and troubled him with no more questions.

USE.

It may confute the jealous and suspicious minds of such who still think that their brethren are rotten at the heart, hypocritical, dissemblers, though they have made never so manifest proof of their uprightness. Thomas would not take his Master's resurrection on the credit of his fellow apostles' relation : his faith would not follow, except his own sense was the usher to lead it the way. So these men are altogether incredulous and very infidels in the point of their brethren's sincerity, though it be never so surely warranted unto them on the words of those whom they ought to believe. Hence oftentimes it comes to pass, that they scandalize and offend many weak Christians, whose graces are true, though weak; faith unfeigned, though feeble. Yea, it maketh weak saints to be jealous of themselves, to see others so jealous of them. But we must be

wonderful careful how we give offence to any of
God's "little ones." When Esau (Gen. xxxiii.
13) would have persuaded Jacob to drive on
faster, Jacob excused himself, saying, that the
children were "tender," and the ewes big with
young; and if they should be overdriven one day,
they would die. Thus, if any would persuade us
to sift and winnow, and try the integrity of our
brethren, after long experience of them, we may
answer, This is dangerous to be done, because
"smoking flax" and "bruised reeds," tender profes-
sors, may utterly be discouraged and disheartened
by our restless pressing and disquieting of them.
Wherefore Naomi, having now seen the reality of
Ruth's resolutions, left off from any further mo-
lesting of her.

VERSES 19, 20, 21, 22.

*So they went both until they came to Bethlehem.
And when they came to Bethlehem, all the city
was moved at them, and they said, Is not this
Naomi?*

*And she said, Call me not Naomi, but call me Marah:
for the Lord hath dealt bitterly with me.*

*I went out full, and the Lord hath caused me to re-
turn empty: why call you me Naomi, sithence**

* ["Since," or "seeing."—ED.]

the Lord hath testified against me, and the Almighty hath afflicted me?

So Naomi returned, and Ruth the Moabitess, her daughter-in-law, with her, when she came out of the country of Moab: and they came to Bethlehem in the beginning of barley harvest.

The Holy Spirit mentioneth not what discourse they exchanged by the way; yet no doubt they were neither silent, nor busied in unprofitable talk.

And all the city was moved, &c.

See here, Naomi was formerly a woman of good quality and fashion, of good rank and repute: otherwise her return in poverty had not been so generally taken notice of. Shrubs may be grubbed to the ground, and none miss them; but every one marks the felling of a cedar. Grovelling cottages may be evened to the earth, and none observe them; but every traveller takes notice of the fall of a steeple. Let this comfort those to whom God hath given small possessions. Should He visit them with poverty, and take from them that little they have, yet their grief and shame would be the less: they should not have so many fingers pointed at them, so many eyes staring on them, so many words spoken of them; they might lurk in obscurity: it must be a Naomi, a person of eminency and estate, whose poverty must move a whole city.

And they said, Is not this Naomi?

Remarkable it is, that so many people should jump in the same expression; but as Abraham laughed, and Sarah laughed,—both used the same outward gesture, yet arising from different causes; his laughter from joy, hers from distrust, —so all these people might meet in the same form of words, yet far dissent in their minds wherewith they spake them. Some might speak out of admiration: "Strange! wonderful! is this she who once was so wealthy? How quickly is a river of riches drained dry! She that formerly was so fair, now one can scarce read the ruins of beauty in her face. 'Is not this Naomi?'" Some out of exprobration: "See, see, this is she that could not be content to tarry at home to take part of the famine with the rest of her fellows, but needs with her husband and sons must be gadding to Moab. See what good she hath got by removing: by changing her country, she hath changed her condition. 'Is not this Naomi?'" Some might speak it out of commiseration: "Alas, alas! is not this that gracious woman, that godly saint, which formerly by her charity relieved many in distress? How soon is a full clod turned into parched earth! one that supplied others, into one that needeth to be supplied by others!　' Is not this Naomi?' "

*And she said, Call me not Naomi, but call me
Marah.*

Naomi signifieth "Beautiful;" *Marah*, "Bitter:" (Exod. xv. 23:) where we see, that the godly in poverty are unwilling to have names and titles disagreeing and disproportioned to their present estates; which may confute the folly of many, which, being in distress, and living little better than upon the alms of others, will still stand upon their points, bear themselves bravely on their birth, not lose an inch of their place, not abate an ace of their gentry.　Far otherwise was Naomi affected: being poor, she would not be over-named or title-heavy: "Call me not Naomi, but call me Marah."

OBSERVATION.

Here also we may see, that it was a custom of great antiquity in the world, that men and women should have several names whereby they were called; and that for these three reasons.

1. That they might be differenced and distinguished from others.

2. That they might be stirred up to verify the meanings and significations of their names.

Wherefore let every Obadiah strive to be "a servant of God," each Nathanael to be " a gift of God," Onesimus to be "profitable," every Roger "quiet and peaceable," Robert "famous for counsel," and William "a help and defence" to many: not like Absalom, who was not a "father of peace," as his name doth import, but a son of sedition; and Diotrephes, not "nursed by God," as his name sounds, but puffed up by the devil, as it is 3 John 9.

3. That they might be incited to imitate the virtues of those worthy persons who formerly have been bearers and owners of their names. Let all Abrahams be faithful, Isaacs quiet, Jacobs painful, Josephs chaste; every Lewis pious, Edward confessor of the true faith, William conqueror over his own corruptions. Let them also carefully avoid those sins for which the bearers of the names stand branded to posterity. Let every Jonah beware of frowardness, Thomas of distrustfulness, Martha of worldliness, Mary of wantonness. If there be two of our names, one exceedingly good, the other notoriously evil, let us decline the vices of the one, and practise the virtues of the other. Let every Judas not follow Judas Iscariot, who betrayed our Saviour, but Judas the brother of James, the writer of the General Epistle:—each Demetrius not follow him in the Acts who made silver

shrines for Diana, but Demetrius, 3 John 12, who had a " good report of all men : "—every Ignatius not imitate Ignatius Loyola the lame father of blind obedience, but Ignatius the worthy martyr in the primitive church. And if it should chance, through the indiscretion of parents and god-fathers, that a bad name should be imposed on any, O let not " folly" be " with " them, because Nabal is their name; but in such a case let them strive to falsify, disprove, and confute their names. Otherwise, if they be good, they must answer them.

In the days of Queen Elizabeth, there was a royal ship called " The Revenge," which, having maintained a long fight against a fleet of Spa-niards, (wherein eight hundred great shot were dis-charged against her,) was at last fain to yield : but no sooner were her men gone out of her, and two hundred fresh Spaniards come into her, but she suddenly sunk them and herself; and so "The Revenge" was revenged. Shall lifeless pieces of wood answer the names which men impose upon them, and shall not reasonable souls do the same ? But, of all names, I pray God that never just occasion be given that we be christened " Icha-bod," but that the glory may remain in our Israel so long as the faithful Witness endur h in heaven. And so much of those words, " Call me not Naomi, but," &c.

For the Lord hath dealt bitterly with me.

Afflictions relish sour and bitter even to the palates of the best saints.

Now bitter things are observed in physic to have a double operation : first, to strengthen and corroborate the liver; and secondly, to cleanse and wipe away choler, which cloggeth the stomach. Both these effects afflictions by their bitterness produce: they strengthen the inward vitals of a Christian, his faith and patience; and cleanse God's saints from those superfluous excrements which the surfeit of prosperity hath caused in them. It may therefore serve to comfort such as groan under God's afflicting hand. (Hebrews xii. 11.) The book which St. John ate, (Rev. x. 10,) was "sweet" in his mouth, but "bitter" in his belly: clean contrary, afflictions are bitter in the mouth, but sweet in the belly; God, by sanctifying them, extracting honey out of gall, and sugar out of wormwood. And let it teach us also not to wonder if the children of God winch [wince], and shrug, and make sour faces, when afflicted. Wonder not at David, if he crieth out in the anguish of his heart; at Job, if he complaineth in the bitterness of his soul; at Jeremiah, if he lamenteth in the extremity of his grief: for even then they are swallowing of a potion which is bitter unto flesh and blood.

I went out full, and the Lord hath caused me to return empty.

Here may we see the uncertainty of all outward wealth.

OBSERVATION.

How quickly may a Crassus, or Crœsus, be turned into a Codrus; the richest, into the poorest of men! Whom the sun-rising seeth in wealth, him the sun-setting may see in want. Set not up then your horns so high, neither speak presumptuous words, ye wealthy men; for God, if it pleaseth Him, can in a moment dispossess you of all your riches. And let us all " not lay up treasures here on earth, where rust and moths do corrupt, and thieves break through and steal: but lay up your treasure in heaven, where rust and moth do not corrupt, and thieves do not break through and steal."

Why call you me Naomi, sithence the Lord, &c.

The mention of their former wealth is grievous to the godly, when they are in present poverty.

OBSERVATION.

When the children of Israel are captives in

Babylon, it cuts them to the heart to be twitted with the songs of Sion. And it may teach this point of wisdom to such as repair to give comfort to men in affliction, not to mention that tedious and ingrateful subject, what happiness that party formerly enjoyed. Sum not up to Job in distress the number of his camels; tell not his sheep, reckon not his oxen; read not unto him an inventory of those goods whereof he before was possessed: for this will but add to his vexation. Rather descend to apply solid and substantial comfort unto him.

Sithence [Seeing] the Lord hath testified against me, and the Almighty hath afflicted me?

Every affliction is a witness that God is angry with us for our sins.

OBSERVATION.

Who then is able to hold out suit with God in the court of heaven? For God Himself is both Judge and Witness, and also the executor and inflicter of punishment. It is therefore impossible for sinful man to plead with Him; and it is our most advised course, as soon as may be, to come to terms of composition with Him, and to make means unto Him through the mediation of our

Saviour.   Now, that all afflictions are immediately
inflicted by God, we have showed formerly.

*And they came to Bethlehem in the beginning of
barley harvest.*

The Jews had two distinct harvests, of wheat
and barley ; and barley was the first. (2 Sam. xxi.
9.)   So here we see the providence of God, in ordering and disposing the journey of Naomi, to end
it in the most convenient time.   Had she come
before harvest, she would have been straitened for
means to maintain herself ; if after harvest, Ruth
had lost all those occasions which paved the way
to her future advancement.   God therefore, who
ordered her going, concludes her journey in the
beginning of harvest.

And thus have we gone over this chapter.   Now,
as Samuel, in the First Book, chap. vii., verse 12,
erected an altar, and called it Eben-ezer ; for, said
he, " Hitherto the Lord hath helped us : " so here
may I raise an altar of gratitude unto God, with
the same inscription : " Eben-ezer : Hitherto the
Lord of His goodness hath assisted us."

CHAPTER II.

And Naomi had a kinsman of her husband's, a mighty man of wealth, of the family of Elimelech; and his name was Boaz.

And Ruth the Moabitess said unto Naomi, I pray thee, let me go into the field, and gather ears of corn after him in whose sight I find favour. And she said unto her, Go, my daughter.

This first verse presents us with two remarkable things.

1. Poor Naomi was allied to powerful Boaz.

2. Boaz was both a powerful man, and a godly man.

Of the first. Poor people may be allied and of great kindred to those that are wealthy; and those that be wealthy, to such as are poor. Joseph, though governor of Egypt, had poor Jacob to his father, and plain shepherds to his brethren. Esther, though queen to Ahasuerus, hath poor Mordecai for her uncle.

USE I.

Let this confute such as having gotten a little

more thick clay than the rest of their family, the getting of new wealth and honour makes them to lose their old eyes, so that they cannot see and discern their poor kindred afterwards. When Joseph was governor of Egypt, it is said that he knew his brethren, but his brethren knew not him; but now-a-days it happeneth clean contrary. If one of a family be advanced to great honour, it is likely that his kindred will know him, but he oftentimes comes to forget them. Few there be of the noble nature of the Lord Cromwell, who, sitting at dinner with the lords of the council, and chancing to see a poor man afar off which used to sweep the cells and the cloisters, called for the man, and told the lords, " This man's father hath given me many a good meal; and he shall not lack so long as I live." *

USE II.

Let it teach those who are the top of their kindred, the best of their house, to be thankful to God's gracious goodness, who hath raised them to such a height. He hath not dealt thus with every one, neither are all of their kindred so well provided for outward maintenance. And also let them learn to be bountiful and beneficial to their kindred in distress. Mordecai said to Esther, (Esth. iv. 14,) " Who knoweth whether thou art

* Foxe, page 1188.

come to the kingdom for such a time?" namely, to deliver her countrymen the Jews from that imminent danger.

So, who knoweth whether God hath raised thee up, who art the best of thy kindred, to this very intent, that thou mightest be the treasure and the storehouse to supply the want of others which are allied unto thee? But if one should chance to be of so wealthy a stock as that none of his alliance stood in need of his charity, let such a one cast his eye upon such as are of kindred unto him by his second birth, and so he shall find enough widows, orphans, and poor Christians, to receive his liberality.

Notwithstanding, let poor people be wary and discreet, that through their idleness they be not a burden to wealthy men of their alliance. When a husbandman claimed kindred in Grosted,* bishop of Lincoln, and would fain on the instant turn a gentleman, and to this end requested his lordship to bestow an office upon him; the bishop told him, that if his plough were broken, he would mend it; if he wanted a plough, he would make him a new one; telling him withal, that he should by no means leave that calling and vocation wherein God had set him. So ought all poor people in-

* [Spelt variously by old writers, according as they inclined to an English or French form of the name,—Grosthead, Grouthead, Grotehead, and Grosseteste.—Ed]

dustriously to take pains for themselves, and not
to give themselves over to ease, relying and de-
pending for their maintenance on their reference
and relation to a rich kinsman.

Come we now to the second observation,—that
the same man may be godly, and also mighty in
wealth, like Boaz. Behold your calling: "not many
wise," yet some wise, as Solomon, and Sergius
deputy of Cyprus; "not many rich," yet some
rich, as Abraham, Job; "not many noble," yet
some noble, as Theophilus. For it is not the
having of wealth, but the having confidence in
wealth; not the possessing it, but the relying on
it, which makes rich men incapable of the kingdom of heaven : otherwise wealth well used is a
great blessing, enabling the owner to do God
more glory, the church and commonwealth more
good.

USE.

Let all wealthy men strive to add inward grace
unto their outward greatness. O 'tis excellent
when Joash and Jehoiada meet together; when
prince and priest, power and piety, are united in
the same person; that so greatness may be seasoned and sanctified by grace, and grace credited
and countenanced by greatness; that so kings
may be nursing-fathers, and queens nursing-
mothers, to God's church. Contrary to which,

how many be there, that think themselves privileged from being good, because they are great !
Confining Piety to hospitals, for their own parts
they disdain so base a companion.　Hence, as
hills, the higher, the barrener ; so men commonly,
the wealthier, the worse ; the more honour, the
less holiness.　And as rivers, when content with
a small channel, run sweet and clear ; when
swelling to a navigable channel, by the conflu-
ence of several tributary rivulets, gather mud and
mire, and grow salt and brackish, and violently
bear down all before them : so many men, who in
mean estates have been pious and religious, being
advanced in honour, and enlarged in wealth, have
grown both impious and profane towards God,
cruel and tyrannical over their brethren.

*And Ruth the Moabitess said unto Naomi, I pray
thee, let me go into the field, and gather ears of
corn, &c.*

Herein two excellent graces appear in Ruth.
First, obedience : she would not go to glean,
without the leave of her mother-in-law.　Verily,
I say unto you, I have not found so much duty,
no, not in natural daughters to their own mothers.
How many of them now-a-days, in matters of
more moment, will betroth and contract themselves, not only without the knowledge and con-

sent, but even against the express commands, of
their parents !

Secondly, see her industry, that she would con-
descend to glean. Though I think not, with the
Jewish Rabbins, that Ruth was the daughter to
Eglon, king of Moab; yet no doubt she was descended of good parentage, and now, see, fain to
glean. Whence we may gather, that those that
formerly have had good birth and breeding, may
afterward be forced to make hard shifts to maintain themselves. Musculus was forced to work
with a weaver, and afterwards was fain to delve
in the ditch about the city of Strasburg; as
Pantaleon in his Life. Let this teach even those
whose veins are washed with generous blood, and
arteries quickened with noble spirits, in their
prosperity to furnish, qualify, and accommodate
themselves with such gentile [gentle] arts and
liberal mysteries as will be neither blemish nor
burthen to their birth; that so, if hereafter God
shall cast them into poverty, these arts may
stand them in some stead towards their maintenance and relief.

And Naomi said, Go, my daughter.

See here how meekly and mildly she answers
her. The discourse of God's children, in their
ordinary talk, ought to be kind and courteous:

so betwixt Abraham and Isaac, Gen. xxii. 7 ;
betwixt Elkanah and Hannah, 1 Sam. i. 23.   Indeed, it is lawful and necessary for Jacob to chide
Rachel speaking unadvisedly ; (Gen. xxx. 2 ;) for
Job to say to his wife, " Thou speakest like a foolish wife."   But otherwise, when no just occasion
of anger is given, their words ought to be meek
and kind, like Naomi's, " Go, my daughter."

VERSES 3, 4.

*And she went, and came, and gleaned in the field
after the reapers : and it happened that she met
with the portion of the field of Boaz, who was
of the family of Elimelech.*

*And, behold, Boaz came from Bethlehem, and said
unto the reapers, The Lord be with you ; and
they answered him, The Lord bless thee.*

Formerly we have seen the dutifulness of Ruth,
which would not leave her mother until she had
leave from her mother.   Proceed we now to her
industry, and God's providence over her.   As the
star (Matt. ii.) guided the wise men to Judea, to
Bethlehem, to the inn, to the stable, to the manger ;
so the rays and beams of God's providence con-
ducted Ruth, that, of all grounds within the compass and confines, within the bounds and borders
of Bethlehem, she lighted on the field of Boaz.

And it happened.

OBJECTION.

How comes the Holy Spirit to use this word; a profane term, which deserves to be banished out of the mouths of all Christians? Are not all things ordered by God's immediate providence, without which "a sparrow lighteth not on the ground?" Is not that sentence most true?— " God stretcheth from end to end strongly, and disposeth all things sweetly. Strongly, Lord, for Thee; sweetly, Lord, for me." So St. Bernard. Or was the providence of God solely confined to His people of Israel, that so Ruth, being a stranger of Moab, must be left to the adventure of hazard? How comes the Holy Spirit to use this word, "hap?"

ANSWER.

Things are said to " happen," not in respect of God, but in respect of us ; because oftentimes they come to pass, not only without our purpose and forecast, but even against our intentions and determinations. It is lawful therefore in a sober sense to use these expressions, " It chanced," or, " It fortuned." (Luke x. 31.) Nor can any just exception be taken against those words in the Collect, " Through all changes and chances of this mortal life : " provided always that in our forms of speech we dream not of any heathen chance. It is observed, that τυχή is not used in all the works of Homer : but sure St. Austin, in the first of his " Retractations," complaineth, that he had too often used the word *fortuna ;* and therefore, in the pagans' sense thereof, we ought to abstain from it.

OBSERVATION.

Now whereas Ruth by chance lighteth on Boaz his field, we may observe, Admirable is the providence of God, in the ordering of contingent events to His glory and His children's good. The Scripture swarmeth with precedents in this behalf, which at this time I surcease to recite, and conclude with the Psalmist : " O Lord, how wonderful are Thy works ! In wisdom hast Thou made them all. The earth is full of Thy riches." To which I may add : " O that men would therefore praise the name of the Lord, and show forth the wonderful works that He doth for the children of men ! "

And, behold, Boaz came unto his reapers.

He had a man over them, yet himself came to oversee them.

OBSERVATION.

Where note, it is the part of a thriving husband, not to trust the care of his affairs to his servants, but to oversee them himself. "The master's eye maketh a fat horse:" and one asking, what was the best compost to manure land, it was answered, "The dust of the master's feet;" meaning, his presence to behold his own business. Hushai would not counsel Absalom to let Ahithophel go with his army, but advised him, "Thou shalt go to battle in thine own person." However he herein had a secret intent, yet thus far the proportion holds: things thrive best, not when they are committed to surrogates, deputies, delegates, and substitutes; but when men themselves oversee them. Let masters therefore of families carefully attend on their own business; and let the daughters of Sarah, whom the meekness of their sex hath privileged from following without-doors affairs, imitate the wise woman, Proverbs xxxi. 15, 27 : "She rises whiles as yet it is night, and giveth her meat to her household, and their portions to her maids. She looks well to all the ways of her household, and eateth not the bread of idleness." And such servants which have careless masters, let them look better to their masters' estate, than their masters do to their own: let them be neither idle nor unfaithful in their place, knowing that though their earthly master be negligent to eye them, yet they have a Master in heaven who both beholds and will punish or reward them according to their deserts. And as for the sons of the prophets, let them feed tho flock over which they are placed, and not think to shuffle and shift off their care to their curates and readers in their own unnecessary absence. And yet how many are there, that preach as seldom as Apollo laughs,—once in the year! Indeed, Elijah fasted forty days and forty nights in the strength of one meal; but surely these think that their people can hold out fasting a twelvemonth. Well, let them practise Boaz' example: as they have curates, so had he one to care for his affairs; and yet, behold, in person he comes forth unto his reapers.

And said unto them, The Lord be with you.

Observe, courteous and loving salutations beseem Christians. Indeed, our Saviour (Matt. x.) forbade His disciples to salute any in the way: but His meaning was, that they should not lag or delay, whereby to be hindered from the service wherein they were employed. And St. John, in his Second Epistle, saith, that to some we must not say, " God speed," lest we be made " partakers of their evil deeds: " but that is meant of

2

notorious sinners, which have discovered their impious intents. It is commonly said, that the small-pox is not infectious until it be broken out, so that before the time one may safely converse, eat, drink, lie with them; but after the pox is broken out, it is very dangerous: so we may safely salute and exchange discourse with the most wicked sinners, whiles yet they smother and conceal their bad designs; but when once they declare and express them, then it is dangerous to have any further familiarity with them; for such Marcions "the first-born of the devil," and "the eldest son of Satan," are salutations good enough.

USE.

Those are justly to be reproved, which lately have changed all hearty expressions of love into verbal compliments; which etymology is not to be deduced *à completione mentis,* but *à completè mentiri.* And yet I cannot say, that these men lie in their throat; for I persuade myself, their words never came so near their heart, but merely they lie in their mouths, where all their promises—

" Both birth and burial in a breath they have;
  That mouth which is their womb, it is their
    grave."

Yea, those words which St. Paul to the Corinthians thought to be the most affectionate expression of love, is now made the word of course, commonly bandied betwixt superficial friends at the first encounter,—" YOUR SERVANT." Worse than these are the ambitious saluters, like Absalom, (2 Sam. xv. 4,) who at the same time, by taking his father's subjects by their hands, stole away their hearts ; and the lower his body did couch, the higher his mind did aspire.   Worst of all is the treacherous salutation of Judas and Joab, who at one instant pretend lip love, and intend heart hatred ; who both kiss and kill,— embrace another with their hands, and imbrue their hands in his blood whom they embrace.

And they answered him, The Lord bless thee.

When one offers us a courtesy, especially being our superior, it is fitting we should requite him. It is a noble conquest for to be overcome with wrongs; but it is a sign of a degenerous nature to be outvied with courtesies ; and therefore, if one begin a kindness to us, let us (if it lie in our power) pledge him in the same nature.

VERSES 5, 6, 7.

And Boaz said unto the servant which was appointed over the reapers, Whose is this maid ?

And the servant which was appointed over the
reapers answered and said, This is the Moab-
itish maid which came with Naomi from the
country of Moab ;
Which came and said, Let me gather, I pray, among
the sheaves after the reapers : and so she came,
and stayed here from morning until now ; only
she tarried a little in the house.

And Boaz said unto the servant which was appointed
over the reapers.

Here we learn, that it is a part of good husbandry in a numerous family, to have one servant
as steward, to oversee the rest. Thus Abraham
had his Eliezer of Damascus ; Potiphar, his
Joseph ; Joseph, his man which put the cup into
Benjamin's sack ; Ahab, his Obadiah ; Hezekiah,
his Eliakim, the son of Hilkiah.

OBSERVATION.

Let masters therefore, in choosing these
stewards to be set above the rest, take such as
are qualified like Jethro's description of inferior
judges, (Exod. xviii. 21,) "men of courage, fearing God, dealing truly, hating covetousness."
And however they privilege them to be above the
rest of their servants, yet let them make them to
know their duty and their distance to their

masters, lest that come to pass which Solomon foretelleth, Prov. xxix. 21 : "He that bringeth up his servant delicately in his youth, will make him like his son at the last." Let stewards not be like that unjust one in the Gospel, who made his master's debtors write down fifty measures of wheat, and fourscore measures of oil, when both severally should have been a hundred; but let them carefully discharge their conscience in that office wherein they are placed : whilst inferior servants, that are under their command, must neither grieve nor grudge to obey them, nor envy at their honour. But let this comfort those underlings, that if they be wronged by these stewards, their appeal lies open from them to their master, who, if good, will no doubt redress their grievances.

Now if stewards be necessary in ordering of families, surely men in authority are more necessary in governing the church, and managing the commonwealth. If a little cock-boat cannot be brought up a tributary rivulet without one to guide it, how shall a caravan,* a galleon, or argosy, sailing in the vast ocean, be brought into a harbour without a pilot to conduct it ? Let us therefore with all willingness and humility submit ourselves to our superiors, that so under them we

---

* [Sometimes used to denote a *naval* expedition.—ED.]

"may live a peaceable life, in all godliness and honesty."

Whose is this maid?

Boaz would know what those persons were that gleaned upon his land; and good reason: for we ought not to prostitute our liberality to all, though unknown; but first we must examine who, and whence, they be; otherwise, that which is given to worthless persons, is not given, but thrown away. I speak not this to blunt the charity of any who have often bestowed their benevolence upon beggars unknown and unseen before; but if easily and with conveniency (as Boaz could) they may attain to know the qualities and conditions of such persons, before they dispose their liberality unto them.

And the servant which was appointed.

He herein performed the part of a careful servant; namely, fully to inform his master. Servants ought so to instruct themselves as thereby to be able to give an account to their lords, when they shall be called thereunto, and give them plenary satisfaction and contentment in any thing belonging to their office, wherein they shall be questioned. Now, whereas he doth not derogate or detract from Ruth, though a stranger, but sets her forth with her due commendation; we gather, servants, when asked, ought to give the pure character of poor people to their masters, and no way to wrong or traduce them.

Which came and said, Let me gather, I pray.

See here Ruth's honesty; she would not presume to glean before she had leave. Clean contrary is the practice of poor people now-a-days, which oft-times take away things not only without the knowledge, but even against the will, of the owners. The boy of the priest, (1 Sam. ii. 13–16,) when the sacrifice was in offering, used to come with a flesh-hook of three teeth, and used to cast it into the fat of the sacrifice, making that his fee, which so he fetched out. If any gainsaid him, he answered, " Thou shalt give it me now; or if thou wilt not, I will take it by force." Thus poor people now-a-days, they cast their hook, their violent hands, (gleaning the lean will not content them,) into the fat, the best and principal of rich men's estates; and breaking all laws of God and the king, they by main force draw it unto themselves. Not so Ruth; she would not glean without leave.

And stayed here from morning until now.

See here her constancy in industry. Many are very diligent at the first setting forth, for a fit and a gird, for a snatch and away : but nothingviolent is long permanent; they are soon tired, quickly weary, and then turn from labour to laziness. But Ruth continued in her labour "from the morning till now;" till night, till the end of the harvest. O that we would imitate the constancy of Ruth, in the "working out of our salvation with fear and trembling!"—not only to be industrious in the morning, when we first enter into Christianity, but to hold out and to persevere even to the end of our lives.

Only she tarried a little in the house.

No doubt some indispensable business detained her there; and probable it is that a principal one was, to say her matins, to do her devotions, commend herself with fervent prayer unto the Lord, to bless her and her endeavours the day following. "A whet is no let," saith the proverb: mowers lose not any time which they spend in whetting or grinding of their scythes. Our prayer to God in the morning, before we enter on any business, doth not hinder us in our day's work, but rather whets it, sharpens it, sets an edge on our dull souls, and makes our minds to undertake our labours with the greater alacrity.

And here may I take just occasion to speak concerning gleaning. Consider, First, the antiquity therefore, as being commanded by God, Levit. xix. 9, and xxiii. 22. Secondly, consider the equity thereof: it doth the rich no whit of harm; it doth the poor a great deal of good. One may say of it, as Lot of Zoar, "Is it not a little one, and my soul shall live?" Is it not a petty, a small, exile * courtesy, and the hearts of poor people shall be comforted thereby? *Reliquiæ Danaûm atque immitis Achillis*,†—the remnant which hath escaped the edge of the scythes, and avoided the hands of the reapers. Had our reapers the eyes of eagles, and the claws of harpies, they could not see and snatch each scattered ear, which may well be allowed for the relief of the poor. When our Saviour said to the woman of Syrophœnicia, "It is not good to take the children's bread, and cast it to the dogs;" she answered, "Yea, Lord, but the dogs eat of the children's crumbs that fall from their table." So, if any misers mutter, "It is not meet that my bread should be cast unto poor people, to glean corn upon my lands;" yea, but let them know that poor people (which are no "dogs," but, setting a little thick clay aside, as good as themselves) may eat the falling "crumbs," the scattered ears, which they gather on the ground.

USE.

It may confute the covetousness of many, which

---

* ["Slender," "trifling;" from the Latin *exilis*.—ED.]

† [VIRGILII *Æneid*. i., 30; iii., 87.—ED.]

repine that the poor should have any benefit by them; and are so far from suffering the poor to glean, that even they themselves glean from the poor, and speak much like to churlish Nabal: (1 Sam. xxv. 11:) "Shall I take my wheat, my rye, and my barley, which I have prepared for my family, and give it to the poor, which I know not whence they be?" Yea, some have so hard hearts that they would leave their grain to be destroyed by beasts and vermin, rather than that the poor should receive any benefit thereby. Cruel people, which prefer their hogs before Christ's sheep, mice before men, crows before Christians!

But withal, poor people must learn this lesson, to know the meaning of these two pronouns, "mine" and "thine;" what belongs to their rich masters, and what pertains to themselves. The sheep which had little spots, those were Jacob's fee; so the little spots, the loose, straggling, and scattered ears, those are the poor's: but as for the great ones, the handfuls, the armfuls, the sheaves, the shocks, the cocks, these are none of theirs, but the rich owner's; and therefore let the poor take heed how they put forth their hands to their neighbours' goods.

MOTIVE.

One forcible motive to persuade the rich to

suffer the poor to glean, may be this : Even the greatest, in respect of God, is but a gleaner. God, He is the Master of the harvest; all gifts and graces, they are His, in an infinite measure; and every godly man, more or less, gleans from Him. Abraham gleaned a great glean of faith; Moses, of meekness; Joshua, of valour; Samson, of strength; Solomon, of wealth and wisdom; St. Paul, of knowledge, and the like. Now, if we would be glad at our hearts that the Lord would give us free leave and liberty for to glean graces out of His harvest, let us not grudge and repine that poor people glean a little gain from our plenty. To conclude : when God hath multiplied our " five loaves," that is, when of our little seed He hath given us a great deal of increase, let poor people, like Ruth in the text, be the " twelve baskets " which may take up the fragments of gleanings which are left.

VERSES 8, 9, 10.

Then said Boaz unto Ruth, Hearest thou, my daugh-
ter ?   Go to no other field to gather, neither go
from hence, but abide here by my maidens :
Let thy eyes be on the field which they do reap, and
go after the maidens.   Have I not charged the
servants that they touch thee not ?   Moreover,

when thou art thirsty, go unto the vessels, and
drink of that which the servants have drawn.
Then she fell on her face, and bowed herself to the
ground, and said unto him, Why have I found
favour in thy eyes, that thou shouldest know me,
since I am a stranger?

Mothers and nurses are very careful tenderly to handle infants when they are but newly born. So Ruth: Christ was newly formed in her, a young convert, a fresh proselyte; and therefore Boaz useth her with all kindness, both in works and words: "Hearest thou, my daughter?"

OBSERVATION.

Aged persons may term younger people their sons and daughters. (1 Sam. iii. 6.) And if they were persons in authority, though they were well-nigh equal in age, they used the same expression. Thus Joseph to his brother Benjamin, Gen. xliii. 29: "God be merciful to thee, my son." Let young people therefore reverently observe their duty and distance to their seniors in age, and superiors in authority. Yet, I am afraid, men keep not the method of Jacob's children, the eldest sitting down according to his age, and the youngest according to his youth; but fulfil the complaint of the prophet, "The young presume against the aged, and the base against the honourable." Let aged persons strive to deserve their respect, by demeaning themselves gravely, and striving to add gracious hearts to grey hairs : otherwise, if they discover any lightness, looseness, wantonness in their carriage, young men will hereupon take occasion, not only to slight and neglect, but also to contemn and despise their paternal distance and father-like authority. Now, as for young ministers, they have not this advantage, to speak unto young people in the phrase of Boaz, " Hearest thou, my daughter? " but must practise St. Paul's precept, 1 Tim. v. 1 : " Rebuke not an elder, but exhort him as a father; and the younger men as brethren ; the elder women as mothers ; the younger as sisters, in all pureness."

But abide here by my maidens.

OBSERVATION.

Hence we gather, 't is most decent for women to associate and accompany themselves with those of their own sex. Miriam, (Exod. xv. 20,) with a feminine choir, " with timbrels and dances," answered the men; and the disciples wondered (John iv. 27) that Christ talked with a woman ; showing hereby that it was not His ordinary course to converse alone with one of another sex : for herein the apostle's precept deserves to take place, namely, to " avoid from all appearance of evil."

Have I not commanded the servants that they should not touch thee ?

Boaz had just cause to fear lest some of his servants might wrong her : to prevent which, he gave them strict charge to the contrary.

OBSERVATION.

Here we see, that servile natures are most prone and proclive to wrong poor strangers. Indeed, generous spirits disdain to make those the subjects of their cruelty, which rather should be the objects of their pity : but it complies with a servile disposition to tyrannize and domineer over such poor people as cannot resist them. Like petty brooks pent within a narrow channel, on every dash of rain they are ready to overflow, and wax angry at the apprehension of the smallest distaste. The locusts, Rev. ix. 10, had " tails like scorpions, and stings in their tails ; " which by some is expounded, that of those people which are meant by the scorpions, the poorest were the proudest ; the meanest, the most mischievous ; the basest, the bloodiest. And surely he that readeth the story of our English martyrs shall find, that one Alexander, a jailor, and one drunken Warwick, an executioner, were most basely and barbarously cruel to God's poor saints.

Secondly, from these words observe, that it is the part of a good master not only to do no harm himself, but also to take order that his servants do none. (Gen. xii. 20; and xxvi. 11.) When Elisha would take nothing of Naaman, (2 Kings v. 20,) Gehazi said, "As the Lord liveth, I will run after him, and take something of him." Thus may base servants (if not prevented with a command to the contrary) wrong their most right and upright masters, by taking gifts and bribes privately. The water (though it ariseth out of a most pure fountain) which runneth through minerals of lead, copper, brimstone, or the like, hath with it a strange taste and relish in the mouth. So justice, which should run down like a stream, though it ariseth out of a pure fountain, out of the breast of a sincere and incorrupted judge; yet, if formerly it hath passed through the mines of gold and silver, I mean, through bad servants, who have taken bribes to prepossess the judge their master with the prejudice of false informations, justice hereby may be strangely perverted and corrupted. Many masters themselves have been honest and upright, yet much wrong hath been done under them by their wicked servants. It is said of Queen Mary, that, for her own part, *she* did not so much as bark; but she had them under her which did more than bite; such were Gardiner, Bonner, Story, Woodroffe, Tyrrell. Now she should have tied up these ban-dogs, and chained and fettered up these bloodhounds from doing any mischief. Camden, in his *Elizabetha*, in the year 1595, writeth thus of the then Lord Chancellor of England: *Ob sordes et corruptelas famulorum in beneficiis ecclesiasticis nundinandis, ipse vir integer ab ecclesiasticis haud bene audivit.* He ought to have imitated the example of Boaz, not only to have done no harm himself, but also to have enjoined the same to his servants: "Have I not commanded my servants that they should not touch thee?"

Thirdly, in these words Boaz doth intimate, that if he gave a charge to the contrary, none of his servants durst presume once to molest her.

OBSERVATION.

Where we see, masters' commands ought to sound [as] laws in the ears of their servants, if they be lawful. Indeed, if Absalom (2 Sam. xiii. 28) saith to his servants, "Kill Amnon, fear not; for have I not commanded you?" this command did not oblige, because the thing enjoined was altogether ungodly. Otherwise, men must imitate the obedience of the centurion's servants; who said to the one, "Go," and he goeth; and to another, "Come," and he cometh; and to his servant, "Do this," and he doth it.

COROLLARY.

Now, if we ought to be thus dutiful to our earthly masters, surely, if the Lord of Heaven enjoineth us any thing, we ought to do it without any doubt or delay. Were there no hell to punish, no heaven to reward, no promises pronounced to the godly, no threatenings denounced to the wicked; yet this is a sufficient reason to make us do a thing,—because God hath enjoined it; this a convincing argument to make us refrain from it, —because He hath forbidden it.

Then she fell on her face, and bowed.

QUESTION.

Was not this too much honour to give to any mortal creature? And doth it not come within the compass of the breach of the second commandment, "Thou shalt not bow down and worship them?" Especially seeing godly Mordecai refused to bend his knee to Haman.

ANSWER.

Civil honour may and must be given to all in authority, according to the usual gestures of the country. Now such bowing was the custom of the Eastern people. (Gen. xxxiii. 3.) As for Mordecai's instance, it makes not against this; he being therein either immediately warranted by

God; or else he refused to bow to Haman as being an Amalekite, betwixt which cursed brood and the Israelites the Lord commanded an eternal enmity.

COROLLARY.

Now, if Ruth demeaned herself with such reverent gesture to Boaz, how reverent ought our gesture to be, when we approach into the presence of God! Indeed, " God is a Spirit," and He will be worshipped " in spirit and truth;" yet so that He will have the outward decent posture of the body to accompany the inward sincerity of the soul.

And said, Why have I found favour ?

As if she had said, " When I reflect my eyes upon myself, I cannot read in myself the smallest worth, to deserve so great a favour from thy hands; and therefore I must acknowledge myself exceedingly beholden to you. But principally I lift up my eyes to the providence of the Lord of Heaven: men's hearts are in His hand as 'the rivers of water;' He 'turneth them whither He pleaseth.' He it is that hath mollified thy heart, to show this undeserved kindness unto me." Here we see Ruth's humility. Many now-a-days would have made a contrary construction of Boaz his charity, and reasoned thus : " Surely he seeth in me some extraordinary worth, whereof as yet I have not taken notice in myself; and therefore hereafter I will maintain a better opinion of my own deserts." But Ruth confesseth her own unworthiness : and from her example let us learn to be humbly and heartily thankful to those which bestow any courtesy or kindness upon us.

Since I am a stranger.

She amplifies his favour, from the indignity of her own person, being a stranger.

COROLLARY.

O, then, if Ruth interpreted it such a kindness that Boaz took notice of her, being a stranger; how great is the love of God to us, who loved us in Christ when we were " strangers, and aliens from the commonwealth of Israel ! " As the never-failing foundation of the earth is firmly fastened for ever fleeting, yet settled on no other substance than its own ballasted weight; so God's love was founded on neither cause nor condition in the creature, but issued only out of His own free favour. So that in this respect we may all say unto God what Ruth doth unto Boaz in the text, " Why have we found favour in Thine eyes, that Thou shouldest take knowledge of us, seeing we were but strangers ? "

And Boaz answered and said unto her, It hath fully been showed me, all that thou hast done unto thy mother-in-law since the death of thine husband; and how thou hast left thy father and thy mother, and the land of thy nativity, and art come unto a people which thou knewest not heretofore.

The Lord recompense thy work, and a full reward be given thee of the Lord God of Israel, under whose wings thou art come to trust.

It hath been fully showed me, all.

More than probable it is, that Boaz had received his intelligence immediately from Naomi.

OBSERVATION.

However, here we may see, the virtues of worthy persons will never want trumpets to sound them to the world. The Jews were the centurion's trumpet to our Saviour; (Luke vii. 5;) and the widows, Dorcas her trumpet to St. Peter. (Acts ix. 39.) Let this encourage men in their virtuous proceedings, knowing that their worthy deeds shall not be buried in obscurity, but shall find tongues in their lively colours to express them. Absalom, having no children, and desirous to perpetuate his name, erected " a pillar in the king's dale ; " and the same " is called Absalom's pillar unto this day." But the most compendious way for men to consecrate their memories to eternity, is to erect a pillar of virtuous deeds ; which shall ever remain, even when the most lasting monuments in the world shall be consumed, as not able to satisfy the boulimee * of all-consuming Time. And to put the worst, grant the envious men with a cloud of calumnies should eclipse the beams of virtuous memories from shining in the world, yet this may be their comfort, that God, that " sees in secret," will " reward them openly." Moreover, it is the duty of such who have received courtesies from others, to profess and express the same as occasion shall serve ; that so their benefactors may publicly receive their deserved commendation. Thus surely Naomi had done by Ruth ; from whose mouth, no doubt, though not immediately, her virtues were sounded in the ears of Boaz : " It hath been fully showed me, all."

Here now followeth a summary, reckoning up of the worthy deeds of Ruth ; which, because they have been fully discoursed of in the former chapter, it would be needless again to insist upon them. Proceed we therefore to Boaz his prayer.

* [*Boulimy,* or *bulimy,* "ravenous appetite."—ED.]

The Lord recompense thee.

As if he had said: "Indeed, Ruth, that courtesy which I afforded thee, to glean upon my land without any disturbance, comes far short both of thy deserts and my desires. All that I wish is this, that what I am unable to requite, the Lord Himself would 'recompense.' May He give thee 'a full reward' of graces internal, external, eternal; here, hereafter; on earth, in heaven; while thou livest, when thou diest; in grace, in glory, 'a full reward.'"

Where first we may learn, that when we are unable to requite people's deserts of ourselves, we must make up our want of works with good wishes to God for them. Indeed, we must not do like those in the second of St. James, verse 16, who only said to the poor, "Depart in peace; warm yourselves, and fill your bellies," and yet bestowed nothing upon them. We must not both begin and conclude with good wishes, and do nothing else; but we must observe Boaz his method: first, to begin to do good to those that, being virtuous, are in distress; and then, where we fall short in requiting them, to make the rest up with hearty wishes to God for them.

OBSERVATION.

But the main observation is this: There is a

recompence of a full reward upon the good works of His servants. (Gen. xv. 1.) "Moreover by them is Thy servant taught; and in keeping them there is great reward." (Psalm xix. 11.) Verily, there is a reward for the righteous; doubtless, there is a God that judgeth the earth. Godliness hath the promises of this life, and of the life to come.

USE I.

It may serve to confute such false spies as raise wrong reports of the land of Canaan,—of the Christian profession; saying with the wicked, Mal. iii. 14, "It is in vain to serve God: and what profit is it that we have kept His commandments, and that we have walked mournfully before the Lord of Hosts?" Slanderous tongues! which one day shall be justly fined in the Star-Chamber of Heaven, *ob scandala magnatum*, for slandering of God's noble servants, and their profession. For, indeed, the Christian life is most comfortable: for we may both take a liberal portion, and have a sanctified use of God's creatures: besides, within we have peace of conscience, and joy in the Holy Ghost, in some measure; one dram whereof is able to sugar the most wormwood affliction.

USE II.

When we begin to feel ourselves to lag in Christianity, let us spur on our affections with the

meditation of that " full reward " which we shall
in due time receive; with our Saviour, let us
" look to the joys which are set before " us ; and,
with Moses, let us have " an eye to the recompence of reward; " yet so that, though we look
at this reward, yet also we must look through it
and beyond it. This meditation of the reward is
a good place for our souls to bait at, but a bad
place for our souls to lodge in. We must mount
our minds higher, namely, to aim at the glory of
God; at which all our actions must be directed,
though there were no reward propounded unto
them. Yet, since it is God's goodness to propound unto us a reward, over and besides His
own glory, this ought so much the more to incite
us to diligence in our Christian calling. For, if
Othniel (Judges i.) behaved himself so valiantly
against the enemies of Israel, in hope to obtain
Achsah, Caleb's daughter, to wife; how valiantly
ought we to demean ourselves against our spiritual enemies, knowing that we shall one day be
married unto our Saviour in eternal happiness !
And this is " a full reward."

OBJECTION.

But some may say, " These terms of ' recompence ' and ' reward ' may seem to favour the
Popish tenet, that our good works merit at God's
hand."

Reward and recompence unto our good works are not due unto us for any worth of our own, but merely from God's free favour and gracious promise. For, to make a thing truly meritorious of a reward, it is required, First, that the thing meriting be our own, and not another's. Now our best works are none of ours, but God's Spirit in us. Secondly, it is requisite that we be not bound of duty to do it. Now we are bound to do all the good deeds which we do, and still remain but "unprofitable servants." Thirdly, there must be a proportion between the thing meriting, and the reward merited. Now there is no proportion between our stained and imperfect works, (for such are our best,) and that infinite weight of glory wherewith God will reward us. It remains, therefore, that no reward is given us for our own inherent worth, but merely for God's free favour, who crowns His own works in us.

Under whose wings thou art come to trust.

A metaphor: it is borrowed from a hen, which with her clocking summons together her straggling chickens, and then outstretcheth the fan of her wings to cover them. Familiarly it is used in Scripture; and amongst other places, by our Saviour, Matth. xxiii. 37: " How oft would I have gathered thee together, as a hen gathereth her chickens under her wings, and ye would not!" And just it was with God,—because the foolish chickens of the Jews would not come to Christ, the hen, calling them,—to suffer them to be devoured by the eagle, the imperial army of the Romans.

OBSERVATION.

God's love and care over His children is as great as a hen's over her chickens. Now the hen's wings do the chickens a double good.

First. They keep them from the kite. So God's providence protecteth His servants from that kite, the devil. For as the kite useth to fetch many circuits and circles, and long hovers and flutters round about, and at length, spying her advantage, pops down on the poor chicken for a prey; so the devil, who, as it is Job i. 7, "compasseth the earth to and fro, and walketh through it," and at length, spying an opportunity, pitcheth and settleth himself upon some poor soul, to devour it, if the wings of God's providence (as the city of refuge) do not rescue him from his clutches.

Secondly. The hen with her chickens broods her chickens, and makes them thereby to thrive and grow. In summer her wings are a canopy, to keep her chickens from the heat of the scorching sun; and in winter they are a mantle, to defend them from the injury of the pinching cold. So God's providence and protection makes His children to sprout, thrive, and prosper under it. In prosperity God's providence keepeth them from the heat of pride: in adversity, it preserveth them from being benumbed with frozen despair.

Let us all then strive to run to hide ourselves under the wings of the God of heaven. Hark how the hen clocks in the Psalms: "Call upon Me in the time of trouble, and I will hear thee, and thou shalt praise Me." How she clocks in the Canticles: "Return, O Shulamite; return, return, that we may behold thee." How she clocketh, Matth. vii. 7: "Ask, and ye shall have; seek, and ye shall find; knock, and it shall be opened unto you." How she clocks, Matth. xi. 28: "Come unto Me, all ye that are weary and heavy laden, and I will ease you." Let not us now be like sullen chickens, which sit moping under a rotten hedge, or proating under an old wood-pile, when the hen calleth them. Let not us trust to the broken wall of our own strength, or think to lurk under the tottering hedge of our own wealth, or wind-shaken reeds of our unconstant friends; but fly to God, that He may stretch His wings over us, as the cherubim did over the mercy-seat. And as always in day-time, so especially at night, when we go to bed, (for chickens, when going to roost, always run to the hen,) let us commend ourselves with prayer to His providence, that He would be pleased to preserve us from the dangers of the night ensuing; "trusting," with Ruth in the text, "under the wings of the Lord God of Israel.

VERSES 13, 14.

Then she said, Let me find favour in the sight of my lord; for thou hast comforted me, and spoken comfortably unto thy maid, though I be not like to one of thy maids.

And Boaz said unto her, At the meal-time come thou hither, and eat of the bread, and dip thy morsel in the vinegar. And she sate beside the reapers: and he reached her parched corn; and she did eat, and was sufficed, and left thereof.

Boaz had formerly called Ruth "daughter;" now Ruth styleth him "lord." When great ones carry themselves familiarly to meaner persons, meaner persons must demean themselves respectively [respectfully] to great ones. Indeed, with base and sordid natures familiarity breeds contempt; but ingenuous natures will more awfully observe their distance towards their superiors, of whom they are most courteously entreated. And if great personages should cast up their accounts, they should find themselves, not losers, but gainers of honour, by their kind usage of their inferiors. Those stars seem to us the greatest, and shine the brightest, which are set the lowest.   Great men, which sometimes stoop, and stoop low, in their humble carriage to others, commonly get the greatest lustre of credit and esteem in the hearts of those that be virtuous.

And spoken comfortably unto thy maid.

In Hebrew, " hast spoken unto the heart." A comfortable speech is a word spoken to the heart.

MEDITATION.

O that ministers had this faculty of Boaz his speech! not to tickle the ears, teach the heads, or please the brains of the people, but that their sermons might soak and sink to the root of their hearts.   But though this may be endeavoured by them, it cannot be performed of them without God's special assistance.   We may leave our words at the outward porch of men's ears; but His Spirit must conduct and lodge them in the closet of their hearts.

Though I be not like to one of thy maids.

Meaning, because she was a Moabitess, a stranger and alien, they natives of the commonwealth of Israel.   In this respect she was far their inferior.

OBSERVATION.

The godly ever conceive very humbly and meanly of themselves: Moses, Exod. iv. 10; Gideon, Judg. vi. 15; Abigail, 1 Sam. xxv. 41; Isaiah, vi. 5; Jeremiah, i. 6; John Baptist, Matth. iii. 11; [Paul], 1 Tim. i. 15. And the reason hereof is, because they are most privy to and sensible of their own infirmities; their corruptions, which cleave unto them, are ever before their eyes. These black feet abate their thoughts, when puffed up with pride for their painted train of other graces. On the other side, the wicked set ever the greatest price on their own worth: they behold their own supposed virtues through magnifying glasses, and think with Haman, that none deserves better to be honoured by the king but themselves.

USE.

Let us endeavour to obtain humility with Ruth; a virtue of most worth, and yet which costeth least to keep. Yet notwithstanding, it is both lawful and needful for us to know our own worth, and to take an exact survey of those graces which God hath bestowed upon us. First, that we may know thereby the better to proportion our thanks to God. Secondly, that we may know how much good the church and commonwealth expecteth to be performed by us. And lastly, that if any should basely insult and domineer over us, we may in humility stand upon the lawful justification of ourselves, and our own sufficiency, as St. Paul did against the false apostles at Corinth ; always provided that we give God the glory, and profess ourselves to be but " unprofitable servants."

And Boaz said unto her, At the meal time come thou hither, and eat of the bread.

Two things herein are commendable in Boaz, and to be imitated by masters of families.

First : That he had provided wholesome and competent food for his own servants. So ought all householders to do. And herein let them propound God for their president [precedent] ; for He maintaineth the greatest family ; all creatures are His servants, and " He giveth them meat in due season ; He openeth His hand, and filleth with His blessing every living thing."

Secondly : As Boaz provided meat for his servants, so he allowed them certain set convenient times wherein they might quietly eat their meat. But as the people of the Jews pressed so fast upon our Saviour (Mark iii. 20) that He had not so much leisure as to " eat bread," and take necessary sustenance ; so, such is the gripple * nature of many covetous masters, that they will

* [" Griping," " grasping," " stingy."—Ed.]

so task and tie their servants to their work, as not to afford them seasonable respite to feed themselves.

And dip thy morsel in the vinegar.

OBSERVATION.

The fare of God's servants in ancient time, though wholesome, was very homely. Here they had only bread and vinegar, and parched corn. For a thousand five hundred and sixty years the world fed upon herbs; and the Scripture maketh mention since of mean and sparing fare of many godly men. It may therefore confute the gluttony and epicurism of our age, consisting both in the superfluous number of dishes, and in the unlawful nature of them. We rifle the air for dainty fowl; we ransack the sea for delicious fish; we rob the earth for delicate flesh, to suspend the doubtful appetite betwixt variety of dainties. As for the nature of them, many are mere needless whetstones of hunger, which, instead of satisfying, do increase it. And as in the Spanish Inquisition such is their exquisite cruelty, that, having brought one to the door of death by their tortures, they then revive him by cordials; and then again, re-killing him with their torments, fetch him again with comfortable things; thus often re-iterating their cruelty: so men, having killed their appetite with good cheer, seek with dishes made for the nonce to enliven it again, to the superfluous wasting of God's good creatures, and much endamaging the health of their own bodies. But, leaving them, let us be content with that competent food which God hath allotted us, knowing that "better is a dinner of herbs with peace, than a stalled ox with strife;" and God, if it pleaseth Him, can so bless Daniel's pulse unto us, that by mean fare we shall be made more strong and healthful than those who surfeit on excess of dainties.

And she did eat, and was sufficed.

It is a great blessing of God, when He gives such strength and virtue to His creatures as to satisfy our hunger; and the contrary is a great punishment: for as, (1 Kings i. 1,) when they heaped abundance of clothes on aged King David, yet his decayed body felt no warmth at all; so God so curseth the meat to some, that though they cram down never so much into their bellies, yet still their hunger increaseth with their meat, and they find that nature is not truly contented and satisfied therewith.

And left thereof.

Hence we learn, the overplus which remaineth

after we have fed ourselves, must neither be
scornfully cast away, nor carelessly left alone, but
it must be thriftily kept; imitating herein the
example of our Saviour; who, though He could
make five loaves swell to sufficient food for five
thousand men, yet gave He command, that "the
fragments" should be carefully basketed up.

VERSES 15, 16, 17.

*And when she arose to glean, Boaz commanded his
servants, saying, Let her gather among the
sheaves, and do not rebuke her:*

*Also let fall some of the sheaves for her, and let it
lie, that she may gather it up, and rebuke her
not.*

*So she gleaned in the field until evening, and she
threshed that she had gathered: and it was
about an ephah of barley.*

Before I enter into these words, behold, an
objection stands at the door of them, which must
first be removed.

OBJECTION.

One may say to Ruth, as our Saviour to the
young man in the Gospel, "One thing is wanting." Here is no mention of any grace she said
to God either before or after meat.

ANSWER.

Charity will not suffer me to condemn Ruth of forgetfulness herein. She who formerly had been so thankful to Boaz, the conduit pipe, how can she be thought to be ungrateful to God, the Fountain of all favours? Rather I think it is omitted of the Holy Spirit to be written down; who, had He registered each particular action of God's saints, (as it is John xxi. 25,) "the world would not have been able to contain the books which should be written."

Let none therefore take occasion to omit this duty, because here not specified; rather let them be exhorted to perform it, because in other places it is both commanded by precept, and commended by practice. (Deut. viii. 10; 1 Cor. x. 31.) Yea, in the twenty-seventh of the Acts, the mariners and soldiers, (people ordinarily not very religious,) though they had fasted fourteen days together, yet none of them were so unmannerly, or rather so profane, as to snatch any meat, before St. Paul had given "thanks." Let us not, therefore, be like Esau, who, instead of giving a blessing to God for his pottage, sold his blessing to his brother for his pottage; but, though our haste or hunger be never so great, let us dispense with so much time as therein to crave a blessing from God, wherein His creatures are sanctified; as no doubt Ruth did, though not recorded.

And when she arose to glean.

The end of feeding is to fall to our calling.
Let us not, therefore, with Israel, sit down to eat
and to drink, and so rise up again to play; but
let us eat to live, not live to eat. 'T is not matter,
we need not make the clay cottage of our body
much larger than it is by immoderate feasting:
it is enough if we maintain it so with competent
food, that God, our Landlord, may not have just
cause to sue us for want of reparations.

Boaz commanded his servants, saying, Let her gather
among the sheaves, and do not rebuke her.

OBSERVATION.

It is lawful for us, according to our pleasure, to
extend our favours more to one than to another.
Ruth alone, not all the gleaners, was privileged to
gather among the sheaves uncontrolled.   Give
leave to Jacob to bequeath a double portion to
Joseph, his best beloved son; for Joseph to make
the mess of Benjamin five times greater than any
other of his brethren; for Elkanah to leave a
worthier portion to Hannah than to Peninnah.
The reason is, because there can be no wrong
done in those things which are free favours. I
am not less just to him, to whom I give less; but
I am more merciful to him, to whom I give more.
Yet, in the dealing and distributing of liberality,

let those of the family of faith be especially respected; and of these, those chiefly which, as the
apostle saith, are worthy of a "double honour."

COROLLARY.

Shall it not therefore be lawful for the Lord of
Heaven to bestow wealth, honour, wisdom,
effectual grace, blessings outward and inward, on
one, and deny them to another? You, therefore,
whom God hath suffered to glean among the
sheaves, and hath scattered whole handfuls for
you to gather; you that abound and flow with
His favours, be heartily thankful unto Him. He
hath not dealt so with every one, neither have all
such a large measure of His blessings. And ye
common gleaners, who are fain to follow far after,
and glad to take up the scattered ears, who have
a smaller proportion of His favour, be neither
angry with God, nor grieved at yourselves, nor
envious at your brethren; but be content with
your condition. It is the Lord, and let Him do
what is good in His eyes. Shall not He have
absolute power to do with His own what He
thinketh good, when Boaz can command that
Ruth, and no other, may glean among the sheaves
without "rebuke?"

Had the servants of Boaz, without express warrant and command from their master, scattered
handfuls for her to glean, their action had not

been charity, but flat theft and robbery; for they were to improve their master's goods to his greatest profit. On the other side, it had been a great fault to withhold and withdraw anything from her, which their master commanded them to give. Yet, as the unjust steward in Luke made his master's debts to be less than they were, so many servants now-a-days make their master's gifts to be less than they are, giving less than he hath granted, and disposing less than he hath directed. Men commonly pay toll for passing through great gates, or over common bridges: so, when the liberality of masters goeth through the gate of their servants' hands, and bridges of their fingers, it is constrained to pay tribute and custom to their servants, before it cometh to those poor to whom it was intended. Thus many men make the augmentation of their own estates from the diminution of their master's bounty.

QUESTION.

But some may say, " Why did not Boaz bestow a quantity of corn upon Ruth, and so send her home unto her mother ? "

ANSWER.

He might have done so, but he chose rather to keep her still a working. Where we learn, that is the best charity which so relieves people's wants as that they are still continued in their calling. For, as he who teacheth one to swim, though happily [haply] he will take him by the chin, yet he expecteth that the learner shall nimbly ply the oars of his hands and feet, and strive and struggle with all his strength to keep himself above water : so those who are beneficial to poor people, may justly require of them that they use both their hands to work and feet to go in their calling, and themselves take all due labour, that they may not sink in the gulf of penury. Relieve a husbandman, yet so as that he may still continue in his husbandry ; a tradesman, yet so as he may still go on in his trade; a poor scholar, yet so as he may still proceed in his studies. Hereby the commonwealth shall be a gainer. Drones bring no honey to the hive ; but the painful hand of each private man contributes some profit to the public good. Hereby the able poor, the more diligent they be, the more bountiful men will be to them; while their bodies are freed from many diseases, their souls from many sins, whereof idleness is the mother. Laziness makes a breach in our soul, where the devil doth assault us with greatest advantage ; and when we are most idle in our vocations, then he is most busy in his temptations. A reverend minister was wont to say, that the devil never tempted him more than on Mondays, when (because his former week's task was newly done, and that for the week to come six days distant) he took most liberty to refresh himself.

Since, therefore, so much good cometh from industry, I could wish there were a public vineyard, into which all they should be sent, who stand lazing in the market place till the eleventh hour of the day. Would all poor and impotent were well placed in a hospital; all poor and able well disposed in a workhouse; and the common stocks of towns so laid out as they thereby might be employed!

So she gleaned in the field until evening.

The night is only that which must end our labours: only the evening must beg us a play, to depart out of the school of our vocation, with promise next morning to return again: "Man goeth out to his labour until evening." Let such then be blamed, who in their working make their night to come before the noon, each day of their labour being shorter than that of St. Lucy [Luke]; and after a spurt in their calling for some few hours, they relapse again to laziness.

And she threshed what she had gathered.

The materials of the temple were so hewed and carved, both stone and wood, before that they were brought unto Jerusalem, that there was not

so much as the noise of a hammer heard in the
temple. So Ruth fits all things in a readiness,
before she goes home : what formerly she gleaned,
now she threshed; that so no noise might be
made at home, to disturb her aged mother. Here
we see God's servants, though well descended,
disdain not any homely, if honest, work for their
own living. Sarah kneaded cakes; Rebekah
drew water; Rachel fed sheep, Tamar baked
cakes. Suetonius reporteth of Augustus Cæsar,
that he made his daughters to learn to spin; and
Pantaleon relates the same of Charles the Great.
Yet now-a-days (such is the pride of the world)
people of far meaner quality scorn so base
employments.

And it was about an ephah of barley.

An " ephah " contained ten " omers." (Exod.
xvi. 36.) An " omer " of manna was the proportion allowed for a man's one day meat. Thus
Ruth had gleaned upon the quantity of a bushel :
such was her industry, in diligent bestirring herself; Boaz his bounty, in scattering for her to
gather; and, above all, God His blessing, who
gave so good success unto her. Ruth, having
now done gleaning, did not stay behind in the
field, as many now-a-days begin their work when
others end ; if that may be termed work, to filch
and steal; as if the dark night would be a veil to

cover their deeds of darkness : but home she hasteneth to her mother, as followeth.

VERSES 18, 19.

And she took it up, and went into the city : and her
mother-in-law saw what she had gathered : also
she took forth, and gave to her that which she
had reserved when she was sufficed.

Then her mother-in-law said unto her, Where hast
thou gleaned to-day? and where wroughtest
thou? Blessed be he that knew thee. And she
showed her mother-in-law with whom she had
wrought, and said, The man's name with whom
I wrought to-day is Boaz.

And she took it up.

See here, the shoulders of God's saints are wonted to the bearing of burthens. Little Isaac carried the faggot wherewith himself was to be sacrificed; our Saviour, His own cross, till His faintness craved Simon of Cyrene to be His successor. Yet, let not God's saints be disheartened : if their Father hath a " bottle," wherein He puts the tears which they spend, sure He hath a balance, wherein He weighs the burthens which they bear; He keeps a note, to what weight their burthens amount, and, no doubt, will accordingly comfort them.

Those are to be confuted who, with the scribes, (Matt. xxiii. 4,) " bind heavy burthens and grievous to be borne, and lay them on the backs of others; but for their own part they will not so much as touch them with one of their fingers." Yea, some are so proud that they will not carry their own provender, things for their own sustenance. Had they been under Ruth's ephah of barley, with David in Saul's armour, they could not have gone under the weight of it, because never used unto it.

And her mother-in-law saw what she had gathered.

Namely, Ruth showed it unto her, and then Naomi saw it. Children are to present to their parents' view all which they get by their own labour. Otherwise do many children now-a-days. As Ananias and Sapphira brought "part of the money, and deposed it at the apostles' feet," but reserved the rest for themselves; so they can be be content to show to their parents some parcel of their gains, whilst they keep the remnant secretly to themselves.

Also she took forth, and gave to her.

Learn we from hence, children, if able, are to cherish and feed their parents, if poor and aged. Have our parents performed the parts of pelicans

to us? let us do the duty of storks to them.
Would all children would pay as well for the
party-coloured coats which their parents do give
them, as Joseph did for his, who maintained his
father and his brethren in the famine in Egypt!
Think on thy mother's sickness, when thou wast
conceived; sorrow, when thou wast born;
trouble, when thou wast nursed. She was cold,
whilst thou wast warm; went, whilst thou layest
still; waked, whilst thou sleptest; fasted, whilst
thou feddest. These are easier to be conceived
than expressed, easier deserved than requited.
Say not, therefore, to thy father according to
the doctrine of the Pharisees, *Corban*, "It is a
gift, if thou profitest by me;" but confess that
it is a true debt, and thy bounden duty, if thou
beest able, to relieve them. So did Ruth to
Naomi, who was but her mother-in-law.

Which she had reserved when she was sufficed.

OBSERVATION.

We must not spend all at once, but providently
reserve some for afterwards: we must not speak
all at once, without Jesuitical reservation of some
things still in our hearts; not spend all at once,
without thrifty reservation of something still in
our hands. Indeed, our Saviour saith, "Care
not for to-morrow; for to-morrow shall care for

itself:" but that is not meant of the care of providence, which is lawful and necessary; but of the care of diffidence, which is wicked and ungodly. Those are to be blamed which, as Abishai said to David concerning Saul, "I will strike him but once, and I will strike him no more;" so many men, with one act of prodigality, give the bane and mortal wound to their estates; with one excessive feast, one costly suit of clothes, one wasteful night of gaming, they smite their estates under the fifth rib, which always is mortal in Scripture, so that it never reviveth again. But let us spare where we may, that so we may spend where we should: in the seven years of plenty let us provide for the seven years of famine; and to make good construction of our estates, let us as well observe the future as the present tense.

Then her mother-in-law said unto her, Where hast thou gleaned to-day?

These words were not uttered out of jealousy, as if Naomi suspected that Ruth had dishonestly come by her corn; (for charity is not suspicious, but ever fastens the most favourable comments upon the actions of those whom it affects;) but she did it out of a desire to know who had been so bountiful unto her. Yet hence may we learn, that parents, after the example of Naomi, may

and ought to examine their children, how and
where they spend their time: for hereby they
shall prevent a deal of mischief, whilst their
children shall be more watchful what company
they keep, as expecting with fear at night to be
examined. Neither can such fathers be excused,
who never say to their children, as David to
Adonijah, "Why doest thou so?" but suffer
them to rove and range at their own pleasure.
"Am I," say they, "my son's keeper? He is old
enough, let him look after himself."

Now, as for those Joashes, whose Jehoiadas are
dead,—those young men whose friends and fathers
are deceased,—who now must have reason for
their ruler, or rather grace for their guide and
governor; let such know, that indeed they have
none to ask them, as the angel did Hagar,
"Whence comest thou, and whither goest thou?"
—none to examine them, as Eliab did David,
"Wherefore art thou come down hither?"—none
to question them, as Naomi did Ruth, "Where
wroughtest thou to-day?" But now, as St. Paul
said of the Gentiles, that, "having no law," they
were "a law unto themselves;" so must such
young persons endeavour that, having no examiners, they may be examiners to themselves,
and at night, accordingly as they have spent their
time, either to condemn or acquit their own
actions.

Blessed be he that knew thee.

1 Kings xxii., the man shot an arrow at unawares, yet God directed it to the chink of the armour of guilty Ahab. But Naomi doth here dart and ejaculate out a prayer, and that at rovers, aiming at one particular mark : " Blessed be he that knew thee : " yet, no doubt, was it not in vain ; but God made it light on the head of bountiful Boaz, who deserved it.

Learn we from hence, upon the sight of a good deed, to bless the doer thereof, though by name unknown unto us. And let us take heed that we do not recant and recall our prayers, after that we come to the knowledge of his name ; as some do, who, when they see a laudable work, willingly commend the doer of it; but after they come to know the author's name, (especially if they be prepossessed with a private spleen against him,) they fall then to derogate and detract from the action, quarrelling with it as done out of ostentation, or some other sinister end.

And she showed her mother-in-law with whom she had wrought.

Children, when demanded, are truly to tell their parents where they have been. Rather let them hazard the wrath of their earthly father by tell-

ing the truth, than adventure the displeasure of
their heavenly Father by feigning a lie. Yet, as
David, when Achish asked him where he had been,
(1 Sam. xxvii. 10,) told him that he had been
"against the south of Judah, and against the
south of the Jerahmeelites, and against the
south of the Kenites;" when indeed he had been
the clean contrary way, "invading the Geshurites,
and Gezrites, and the Amalekites:" so many children flap their parents in the mouth with a lie, that
they have been in their study, in their calling, in
good company, or in lawful recreations; when the
truth is, they have been in some drinking school,
tavern, or alehouse, misspending of their precious
time. And many serve their masters as Gehazi
did the prophet; who, being demanded, answered,
"Thy servant went no whither," when he had
been taking a bribe of Naaman.

The man's name with whom I wrought to-day is Boaz.

We ought to know the names of such who are
our benefactors. Those are counted to be but
basely born, who cannot tell the names of their
parents; and surely those are but of a base nature,
who do not know the names of their patrons and
benefactors. To blame therefore was that lame
man cured by our Saviour, (John v. 13,) of whom
it is said, "And he that was healed knew not the

name of Him that said unto him, Take up thy bed, and walk." Yet let not this discourage the charity of any benefactors, because those that receive their courtesies oftentimes do not remember their names. Let this comfort them,—though they are forgotten by the living, they are remembered in the Book of Life. The Athenians out of superstition erected an altar with this inscription, " Unto the unknown God : " but we out of true devotion must erect an altar of gratitude to the memory, not of our once unknown, but now forgotten benefactors, whose names we have not been so careful to preserve as Ruth was the name of Boaz : " And the man's name was Boaz."

VERSE 20.

And Naomi said unto her daughter-in-law, Blessed be he of the Lord; for he ceaseth not to do good to the living and to the dead. Again Naomi said unto her, The man is near unto us, and of our affinity.

These words consist of three parts. 1. Naomi's praying for Boaz. 2. Her praising of Boaz. 3. Her reference and relation unto Boaz. Of the first :—

2

Blessed be he of the Lord.

The Lord is the Fountain from whom all blessedness flows.   Indeed, Jacob blessed his sons;
Moses, the twelve tribes; the priests, in the law,
the people: but these were but the instruments,
God the Principal; these the pipe, God the Fountain; these the ministers to pronounce it, God the
Author who bestowed it.

For he ceaseth not.

OBSERVATION.

Naomi never before made any mention of Boaz,
nor of his good deeds; but now, being informed
of his bounty to Ruth, it puts her in mind of his
former courtesies.   Learn from hence, new favours
cause a fresh remembrance of former courtesies.
Wherefore, if men begin to be forgetful of those
favours which formerly we have bestowed upon
them, let us flourish and varnish over our old
courtesies with fresh colours of new kindnesses;
so shall we recall our past favours to their memories.

USE.

When we call to mind God's staying of His killing angel, *anno* 1625,* let that mercy make us to

* [This "killing angel" was the plague, which in London swept off
35,417 persons in the summer of 1625.—ED.]

be mindful of a former,—His safe bringing back of our (then prince, now) king from Spain ; * when the pledge of our ensuing happiness was pawned in a foreign country. Let this blessing put us in mind of a former,—the peaceable coming in of our gracious sovereign, of happy memory,† when the bounds of two kingdoms were made the middle of a monarchy. Stay not here, let thy thankfulness travel further. Call to mind the miraculous providence of God in defending this land from invasion in '88. On still : be thankful for God's goodness in bringing Queen Elizabeth to the crown, when our kingdom was like the woman in the Gospel, " troubled with an issue of blood," (which glorious martyrs shed,) but stanched at her arriving at the sceptre. We might be infinite in prosecution of this point : let present favours of God renew the memories of old ones, as the present bounty of Boaz to Ruth made Naomi remember his former courtesies : " For he ceaseth not to do good to the living and the dead."

He ceaseth not.

Our deeds of piety ought to be continued with-

---

* [Charles I. is the king here alluded to ; our author retaining the language of his Lectures, delivered at Cambridge in 1630–1, although Charles had long been dead when the Lectures were printed and published as a " Comment."—ED.]

† [James I. of England and VI. of Scotland.—ED.]

out interruption or ceasing. Some men there be, whose charitable deeds are as rare as an eclipse or a blazing star. These men deserve to be pardoned for their pious deeds, they are so seldom guilty of them. With Nabal, they prove themselves by excessive prodigality at one feast: but he deserves the commendation of a good housekeeper, who keeps a constant table, who, with Boaz, " ceaseth not to do good."

To the dead.

The meaning is, to those who now are dead, but once were living; or to their friends and kindred. Whence we learn, mercy done to the kindred of the dead is done to the dead themselves. Art thou, then, a widower, who desirest to do mercy to thy dead wife; or a widow, to thy dead husband; or a child, to thy deceased parent? I will tell thee how thou mayest express thyself courteous. Hath thy wife, thy husband, or thy parent, any brother, or kinsman, or friends surviving? be courteous to them; and, in so doing, thy favours shall redound to the dead. Though old Barzillai be uncapable of thy favours, let young Chimham taste of thy kindness. Though the dead cannot, need not have thy mercy, yet may they receive thy kindness by a proxy,—by their friends that still are living.

Mercy, then, to the dead makes nothing for the

Popish purgatory; and yet no wonder if the Papists fight for it. 'T is said of Sicily and Egypt, that they were anciently the barns and granaries of the city of Rome : but now-a-days purgatory is the barn of the Romish court, yea, the kitchen, hall, parlour, larder, cellar, chamber, every room of Rome. David said, (2 Sam. i. 24,) " Ye daughters of Israel, weep for Saul, which clothed you in scarlet with pleasure, and hanged ornaments of gold upon your apparel : " but should purgatory once be removed, weep, pope, cardinals, abbots, bishops, friars ; for that is gone which maintained your excessive pride. When Adonijah sued for Abishag the Shunammite, Solomon said to his mother, " Ask for him the kingdom also." But if once the Protestants could wring from the Papists their purgatory, nay, then would they say, " Ask the triple crown, cross keys, St. Angelo, Peter's Patrimony, and all." In a word, were purgatory taken away, the pope himself would be in purgatory, as not knowing which way to maintain his expensiveness.

The man is near unto us, and of our affinity.

Naomi never before made any mention of Boaz. Some, had they had so rich a kinsman, all their discourse should have been a survey and inventory of their kinsman's goods ; they would have made an occasion at every turn to be talking of them.

Well, though Naomi did not commonly brag of her kinsman, yet, when occasion is offered, she is bold to challenge her interest in him.

OBSERVATION.

Poor folks may with modesty claim their indred in their rich alliance.   Let not therefore great personages scorn and contemn their poor kindred.   Camden reports of the citizens of Cork, that all of them in some degrees are of kindred one to the other : but I think that all wealthy men will hook in the cousin, and draw in some alliance one to other.   But as they will challenge kindred where there is none, in rich folks ; so they will deny kindred where it is, in poor.   Yet is there no just reason they should do so.   All mankind knit together in the same father in the creation, and at the deluge ; I know not who lay higher in Adam's loins, or who took the wall in Eve's belly.   I speak not this to pave the way to an Anabaptistical parity, but only to humble and abate the conceits of proud men, who look so scornful and contemptuous over their poor kindred.

USE.

Let such as are allied to rich kindred be heartily thankful to God for them ; yet so as they under God depend principally on their own labour, and not on their reference to their friends.   And let them not too earnestly expect help from their kindred, for fear they miscarry. A scholar being maintained in the university by his uncle, who gave a basilisk for his arms, and expecting that he should make him his heir, wrote these verses over his chimney :—

Falleris aspectu basiliscum occidere, Plini ;
Nam vitæ nostræ spem basiliscus alit.

Soon after it happened that his uncle died, and gave him nothing at all; whereupon the scholar wrote these verses under the former :—

Certè aluit, sed spe vanâ ; spes vana venenum ;
Ignoscas, Plini, verus es historicus.

So soon may men's expectations be frustrated, who depend on rich kindred. Yea, I have seen the twine-thread of a cordial friend hold, when the cable-rope of a rich kinsman hath broken.

Let those therefore be thankful to God, to whom God hath given means to be maintained of themselves, without dependance on their kindred. Better it is to be the weakest of substances, to subsist of themselves, than to be the bravest accidents, to be maintained by another.

VERSE 21.

And Ruth the Moabitess said, He said unto me also, Thou shalt keep fast by my young men, until they have ended all my harvest.

He said unto me also.

Ruth, perceiving that Naomi kindly resented Boaz his favour, and that the discourse of his kindness was acceptable unto her, proceeds in her relation.

DOCTRINE.

People love to enlarge such discourses which they see to be welcome to their audience.

What maketh talebearers so many, and their tales so long, but that such persons are sensible that others are pleasingly affected with their talk? Otherwise, "a frowning look" (Prov. xxv. 23) will soon put such to silence. When Herod saw (Acts xii. 3) that the killing of James "pleased the Jews, he proceeded farther, to take Peter also." Detractors, perceiving that killing of their neighbours' credits is acceptable to others, are encouraged thereby to imbrue their tongues in the murdering of more reputations.

Secondly. Whereas Ruth candidly confesseth what favour she found from Boaz, we learn, we ought not sullenly to conceal the bounty of our benefactors, but express it to their honour, as occasion is offered. The *giver* of alms may not, but the *receiver* of them may, "blow a trumpet."

This confuteth the ingratitude of many in our age; clamorous to beg, but tongue-tied to confess what is bestowed upon them. What the "sin against the Holy Ghost" is in divinity, that ingrati-tude is in morality,—an offence unpardonable. Pity it is but that moon should ever be in an eclipse, that will not confess the beams thereof to be borrowed from the sun. He that hath a hand to take, and no tongue to thank, deserves neither hand nor tongue, but to be lame and dumb here-after.

Observe by the way, that Ruth expresseth what tends to the praise of Boaz, but conceals what Boaz said in the praise of herself. He had com-mended her (verse 11) for a dutiful daughter-in-law, and for leaving an idolatrous land. But Ruth is so far from commending herself in a direct line, that she will not do it by reflection, and at the second hand, by reporting the commendations which others gave her.

DOCTRINE.

"Let another praise thee, and not thine own mouth."

How *large* are the penmen of the Scripture, in relating their own faults! How *concise* (if at all) in penning their own praises!

It is generally conceived that the Gospel of St. Mark was indited by the apostle Peter; and that from his mouth it was written by the hand of John Mark, whose name now it beareth. If so, then we may observe, that Peter's *denying of his Master,* with all the circumstances thereof, his cursing and swearing, is more largely related in the Gospel of St. Mark than in any other: but as for his *repentance,* it is set down more shortly there than in other Gospels.

Matthew xxvi. 75: "And he went out, and wept bitterly."

Luke xxii. 62: "And Peter went out, and wept bitterly."

But Mark xiv. 72, it is only said, "When he thought thereon, he wept."

So short are God's servants in giving an account of their own commendations, which they leave to be related by the mouths of others.

Thou shalt keep fast by my young men.

OBJECTION.

"Here either Ruth's memory failed her, or else she wilfully committed a foul mistake. For Boaz never bad her to 'keep fast by his young men,' but, (verse 8,) 'Abide here fast by my maidens.' It seems she had a better mind to male company, who had altered the gender in the relating of his words."

ANSWER.

Condemn not the "generation of the righteous," especially on doubtful evidence. Boaz gave a command (verse 15) to his young men to permit her to glean: she mentioneth them therefore in whom the authority did reside, who had a commission from their master to countenance and encourage her in her extraordinary gleaning, which privilege his maidens could not bestow upon her.

VERSE 22.

And Naomi said unto Ruth her daughter-in-law, It is good, my daughter, that thou go out with his maidens, that they meet thee not in any other field.

And Naomi said unto Ruth her daughter-in-law.

DOCTRINE.

It is the bounden duty of parents to give the best counsel they can to their children; as Naomi here prescribes wholesome advice unto her daughter-in-law.

It is good.

That is, it is better. It is usual, both in the Old and New Testament, to put the positive for the comparative in this kind. Luke x. 42: "Mary hath chosen that good part," that is, the better part. "It is profitable for thee that one of thy members perish, and not thy whole body;" (Matt. v. 29;) "profitable," that is, more profitable; and, as it is expounded, Matt. xviii. 8, "better." "It is good for a man not to touch a woman;" (1 Cor. vii. 1;) that is, it is better; it is more convenient, and freer from trouble, in time of persecution. "It is good for thee that thou go out with his maidens;" that is, it is better.

DOCTRINE.

Maids are the fittest company for maids; amongst whom a chaste widow, such as Ruth was, may well be recounted. Modesty is the life-guard of chastity.

That they meet thee not in any other field.

Here she rendereth a reason of her counsel, because Ruth thereby should escape suspicion, or appearance of evil.

OBJECTION.

"What hurt or harm had it been, if they had met her in another field? She might have been met there, and yet have departed thence as pure and spotless as she came thither."

ANSWER.

It is granted. Yet, being a single woman, slanderous tongues and credulous ears meeting together had some colour to raise an ill report on her reputation. Besides, being a Moabite, she ought to be more cautious of her credit; lest, as she was a stranger, she might be taken for a " strange woman," in Solomon's sense. And therefore *nimia cautela non nocet.* In some ears it is not enough to be honest, but also to have *testes honestalis;* many a credit having suffered, not for want of clearness, but clearing of itself, surprised on such disadvantages.

VERSE 23.

So she kept fast by the maidens of Boaz to glean unto the end of barley harvest and of wheat harvest; and dwelt with her mother-in-law.

So she kept fast by the maidens of Boaz.

Here was good counsel well given, because thankfully accepted and carefully practised.

DOCTRINE.

It is the duty of children to follow the advice of their parents.

We meet with two examples in wicked persons, which in this respect may condemn many unduti- ful children of our days. The one, Ishmael; who, though he be charactered to be "a wild man," (Gen. xvi. 12,) "his hand against every man, and every man's hand against him;" yet it seems his hand was never against his mother Hagar, whom he obeyed in matters of most moment;—in his marriage, Gen. xxi. 21: "His mother took him a wife out of the land of Egypt."

The second is Herodias; of whom no good at all is recorded, save this alone, that she would not beg a boon of her father Herod, until first she went in to her mother Herodias, to know what she should ask. How many now-a-days make deeds of gift of themselves, without the knowledge and consent of their parents!

Unto the end of barley harvest.

Commendable is the constancy and the continu- ance of Ruth in labour. Many there are who at the first have a ravenous appetite to work, but quickly they surfeit thereof. Ruth gleans one day so as she may glean another. It is the constant pace that goeth farthest, and freest from being tired. Matt. xxiv. 13: "But he that shall endure unto the end, the same shall be saved."

And dwelt with her mother-in-law.

It was Christ's counsel unto His disciples, (Matt. x. 11,) to "abide" in the place wherein they did enter, and not to go from house to house. Such the settledness of Ruth,—where she first fastened, there she fixed: she "dwelt with her mother." Naomi affords Ruth house-room, Ruth gains Naomi food; Naomi provides a mansion, Ruth purveys for meat; and so [they] mutually serve to supply the wants of each other.

If envy, and covetousness, and idleness were not the hinderances, how might one Christian reciprocally be a help unto another! All have something, none have all things; yet all might have all things in a comfortable and competent proportion, if seriously suiting themselves as Ruth and Naomi did, that what is defective in one might be supplied in the other.

FINIS.

[Here ends this beautiful Comment, to the regret of all its readers. Why Fuller did not proceed to draw quaint lessons of wisdom and piety from each line of the last two chapters of Ruth, we are not informed. It may be that his course of Lectures was broken off by fresh preferment in the Church, with a corresponding increase of duties. That he was not deterred by any difficulties in the third chapter, is obvious from the skill with which he handled the previous two; not forcing the meaning, as was the wont of many of his contemporaries, but with ready ease pressing choice wine from the ripe fruit of each phrase of the text.

While perusing this Comment, some readers will be reminded, as we have been, of the lines written on "RUTH" by a man of kindred genius, who, cast in a more mirth-loving age than Fuller's, fed the public with lighter food than he did, but whose powers were really as great in serious as in comic prose and verse.—ED.

> " She stood breast high among the corn,
> Clasp'd by the golden light of morn;
> Like the sweetheart of the sun,
> Who many a glowing kiss had won.
>
>   *   *   *   *
>
> Thus she stood among the stooks,
> Praising God with sweetest looks.
> ' Sure,' I said, ' Heaven did not mean
> Where I reap thou shouldst but glean :
> Lay thy sheaf adown and come,
> Share my harvest and my home.' "

Works of THOMAS HOOD, 1862, vol. i., p. 336.]

NOTES UPON JONAH.

BY

THOMAS FULLER.

NOTES UPON JONAH.

CHAPTER I. VERSE 1.

*The word of the Lord came also unto Jonah.the son
of Amittai, saying.*

SOMETHING must be premised of the name,
parentage, time, and place of this prophet.

His name: JONAH, signifying a "dove" in
Hebrew: but he answered his name rather in
flying so fast away, than in want of gall, wherewith he abounded.

Parentage: "son of Amittai." Men are differenced in the Bible, 1. By their fathers : as " Benaiah son of Jehoiada." 2. Mothers : as "Joab
son of Zeruiah." 3. Husbands : as "Mary the
wife of Cleophas." 4. Brothers : as "Judas the
brother of James." 5. Sons : as "Simon of
Cyrene, the father of Alexander and Rufus."
But that this prophet was son to the widow
of Sarepta, I believe no more than that Dinah,
Jacob's daughter, was wife to Job ; or that Ruth

was daughter to Eglon king of Moab: both which are as fondly fabled by the Jews as justly rejected by Christians.

As for the time and place of this prophet, when and where he lived, though here omitted, is supplied, 2 Kings xiv. 25. He was of Gath-hepher, a city of the tribe of Zebulon, and lived in the time of Joash king of Israel.

The word of the Lord came.

All prophets and preachers ought to have their patent and commission from God. "How can they preach, except they be sent?" (Rom. x. 15.) That is, How can they preach lawfully and profitably? though *de facto* they preach, to their own great harm and others' little good. But as long as there is current coin, there will be counterfeit: Jeroboam's priests under the Law, and Sheva's sons in the Gospel, and at this day some who leap from the loom to the pulpit. I must confess, an ass's head was good food in a famine; coarse meat is dainty when no other can be had. But now (thanks be to God) great is the company of preachers, able and learned; and, for aught I see, the universities afford more vine-dressers than the country can yield them vineyards. No necessity, therefore, that such blind guides should be admitted.

VERSE 2.

Arise, and go to Nineveh, that great city, and cry against it ; for their wickedness is come up before Me.

The words contain Jonah's commission ;—the place whither he was sent ;—what he should do there.

The commission : " Arise." As if He had said, " Thou hast long preached in Israel to little purpose : great the pains, small the profit, of thy ministry. I will therefore transplant thy preaching, to see if it will bring more fruit in another soil." It is a sign of a ruin of a church, when their pastors are called from their flocks to go to foreigners : as Jonah, who was here made non-resident against his will. When the eye-strings are broken, the heart-strings hold out not long after. The prophets are called " seers : " their departure presageth that their parishes soon after will die and decay. For sure the children of Israel prospered not long after that Jonah, a star of the first bigness, was fallen from that firmament, to arise into the horizon of Nineveh.

Go to Nineveh, that great city.

It is more than probable that this city, being

the metropolis of Assyria, was not a little proud
of the greatness of it, as able thereby to outface
the judgments of God, and to blunt the edge of
His revenging sword with the populousness of her
nhabitants, before it could cut clean through them.
But let no city, though never so great, thus presume upon her multitudes.   The greater, the
fairer mark she is for the arrows of God's judgments ; (though indeed nothing seems great in
His eyes, save that man that seems little in his
own ;) and God can quickly subtract in a day, by
sword, plague, and famine, what health, peace,
and plenty hath multiplied in seven years. This
island, since the ends of two kingdoms were made
the middle of cne monarchy, hath got the addition
of " Great Britain ; " yet, if compared to the continent, we may say of it, as Lot of Zoar, " Is it
not a little one ? " Isaiah xl. 15 : " Behold, the
nations are as the drop of a bucket, and are
counted as the small dust in the balance : He
taketh up the isles as a very little thing." Let
us, the inhabitants thereof, not be proud of the
greatness of it, which probably puffed up Nineveh,
the " great city."

And cry against it.

Ministers must not mutter, but publicly and
strongly cry, against sinners.   First, because

sinners are *afar off.* Isaiah lix. 2 : "But your iniquities have separated betwixt you and your God." Matt. xv. 8 : "Their heart is far from Me." Ephes. ii. 13 : "You who sometimes were afar off." Secondly, because they are *deaf.* Thirdly, *asleep.* Fourthly, *dead.* If any object, "Why, then, it is lost labour to cry against sinners : preaching to the dead is as unprofitable as praying for them ; " I answer, Not so. For it is said, John v. 25, " The hour is coming, and now is, when the dead shall hear the voice of the Son of God : and they that hear shall live." To blame, then, are those that are cruelly kind unto their people in sewing pillows under their elbows. Honey-dews, though they be sweet in taste, do blast and black the corn : and smoothing of people in their sins, though pleasant to the palate of flesh, damneth and destroyeth the soul. And yet this command to " cry " no whit favours their practice, who change the strength of matter into stentoriousness of voice. Such pieces make a great report with powder, but are charged with no shot, and are useless to the beating down of sin. And it may be said of their "crying," that they do but whisper whilst they holloa.

For their wickedness is come up before Me.

What the particular sin of Nineveh was, is not

expressed. Some think, had that city been arraigned for the sins of Sodom, it would have been found guilty. And no doubt sorcery, the sin of the East, was no stranger in her own country; and therefore the Ninevites thereto much addicted. But that *oppression* was certainly their predominant sin, may be gathered out of the third of Nahum, verse 1: "O bloody city! it is full of lies and robbery; the prey departeth not." Not content to be a queen of those countries she had subdued, she was a tyrant. So then we see, all sins, but oppression especially, though naturally they tend downwards to their centre, and with their weight press sinners to hell, yet they do mount upwards by their cry and clamour. (Gen. iv. 10; and xviii. 20.) It were then an advised way for us to make some counter-sounds to drown the noise of our sins, that God may not hear them. First, by sending up sighs from a penitent heart. Secondly, prayers and alms. Acts x. 31: "Cornelius, thy prayer is heard, and thine alms are had in remembrance in the sight of God." Thirdly, by pleading Christ His merits; that the loud language of His blood may out-noise and silence the cry of our sins. (Heb. xii. 24.) Yet let oppressors take notice, that theirs being the sin of Nineveh, as it is of a higher nature, so is it of a higher cry than other sins. And let the remorseless extortioner take this into his consideration:—

hand-mills, though they grind not so much, yet they grind as much to powder as either wind-mills or water-mills, which are far greater :— though these oppressors do not mischief to so many as Nineveh did, yet to so many as come within their clutches they show as merciless cruelty ; and this is a sin [which] will come up before God.

VERSE 3.

But Jonah rose up to flee into Tarshish from the presence of the Lord, and went down to Japho [Joppa]; for he found a ship going to Tarshish ; so he paid the fare thereof, and went down into it, that he might go with them into Tarshish from the presence of the Lord.

But Jonah rose up.

Whose superscription doth this book bear? Jonah's. Why did he not, like Alexander, when he was painted, lay his finger on his wart ? Why did he not conceal in silence his own faults and infirmities? Why did he paint his own deformity with his own pencil? Because the penmen of the Holy Word are unpartial relators of their own faults, and [those] of them who are dearest and nearest unto them. Who speaks more against David than David? " So ignorant was I and foolish, even as a beast before Thee."

Who accuseth St. Paul more than St. Paul?
1 Tim. i. 13: "I was a blasphemer, and a perse-
cutor, and an oppressor." We learn from St.
Stephen, (Acts vii. 22,) that Moses " was learned
in all the wisdom of the Egyptians; " but in
Moses, in his own writings, we find no mention or
commendation of this his learning. He spared
not himself in registering his passion in smit-
ing of the rock ; neither spared he to record the
cruelty of Levi his grandfather, the shrewishness
of Zipporah his wife, the idolatry-promoting of
Aaron his brother, the murmuring of Miriam his
sister, the profaneness of Nadab and Abihu his
nephews. This, amongst other reasons, may be
one to prove, that no " Scripture is of private interpretation ; but that holy men of God wrote it, as
as they were inspired by God's Holy Spirit."
Whereas the books of heathen writers are
nothing else but the inventories of their own
virtues. What are Cæsar's Commentaries, but
commentaries on the text of his own valour ?
But, for a man thus far to be unmanned as to
banish self-love from himself, and, with Jonah, to
put his own flight and fault into the calendar of
eternity ;—who sees not the finger of God in
Jonah's hand writing this prophecy ?

Sundry carnal reasons may be alleged for
Jonah's flight. First, fear of extreme and cruel
usage from the wicked Ninevites. Secondly,

despair that his preaching, barren in Israel, should be fruitful in Asshur. Thirdly, the strangeness of the message; distasteful to a Jewish palate, to be sent to the Gentiles. Fourthly, a zeal to his country: he might perceive that the conversion of the Gentiles would be the eversion of the Jews; and therefore he was loth to be accessory to the destruction of his own nation. Fifthly, the reason alleged by himself in the fourth chapter and verse 2: he feared to be disproved, because God was so merciful. But let his reasons, though never so many and weighty, be put into one scale, and God's absolute command weighed against them in the other, TEKEL; They are "weighed in the balance, and found too light." Prosper: *Obedientia non discutit Dei mandata, sed facit.* The Popish tenet of blind obedience is true doctrine in this case: what God commands let us put in speedy execution, without denying, or delaying, or disputing the difficulties that attend it.

To flee.

God bids Jonah go, and he flies; he supererogates, but in a wrong work. In him the proverb finds truth, "The more haste, the worse speed." We see, then, those that want legs to go in goodness, can find wings to fly in wickedness. The elders of the Jews, (probably aged grandsires,)

how late were they up that night our Saviour was
betrayed! How early did they rise that morning
He was condemned! How duly did they attend
the whole day He was crucified!—who otherwise,
no doubt, would have been in their beds as drowsy
as dormice. It is not therefore the greatness of
the strides, nor the swiftness of the pace, but the
rightness of the way, which maketh our going
pleasing unto God. 1 Cor. ix. 24: "So run, that
ye may obtain." And if, with David, we cannot
run the way of God's commandments, let us go
them; if not go, let us creep. And this may comfort us, that though we go not so swift in our
calling as we could desire, yet we go in our calling: our pace, though not fast, is firm; and still
by degrees we draw nearer and nearer to that
Nineveh to which God hath sent us.

To Tarshish.

What and where this Tarshish was, authors only
agree in disagreeing. Let this suffice: be this
Tarshish in Asia, be it in Africa; be it city, be it
country; be it sea, be it continent; this sure I am,
it was not that Nineveh to which Jonah was sent.

From the presence of the Lord.

It were great ignorance in us to charge Jonah

with such ignorance, as if he thought it absolutely possible to fly from God's presence. And if he had been so erroneous, he made the most unadvised choice,—to fly to the sea, where there appears the most evident demonstration of God's powerful presence. Psalm cvii. 23 : "They that go down to the sea in ships," &c. The sight of the sea might have been a remembrancer to an atheist, and put him in mind of a God. Esau went to kill his brother Jacob; but when he met him, his mind was altered, he fell a kissing him, and so departed. Thus the waves of the sea march against the shore, as if they would eat it up : but when they have kissed the utmost brink of the sand, they melt themselves away to nothing. And this spectacle must needs make a man acknowledge a Deity. So, then, these words, "to fly away from the presence of the Lord," are not simply to be understood ; there being no flying from God but thus :—from God, an angry Judge for our sins ; to God, a merciful Father in our Saviour. By this phrase, then, is meant, he deserted the office of a prophet ; he forsook and relinquished the ministerial function, whereabout God had employed him. Thus to be *in God's presence* is used in Holy Writ : Deut. x. 8 : "The Lord separated the tribe of Levi to stand before the Lord." 1 Kings xvii. 1 : "As the Lord liveth," saith Elias [Elijah], "before whom I stand." What kind of men, then, ought

we ministers to be ?   How decently ought we to
demean and behave ourselves, who are chaplains
in ordinary to the King of Heaven !   Every month
is our waiting month : we are bound to constant
and continual attendance.   It was the title of the
angel Gabriel, (Luke i. 19,) " I am Gabriel that
stands in the presence of God," *i. e.*, ever ready to
be sent of Him in any employment.   Now, as
angels are God's ministers in heaven, so ministers
are God's angels on earth, and stand in His presence, from which Jonah did fly.

*And he went down to Japho ; for he found a ship
going to Tarshish.*

Japho was the port of Jerusalem, distant from
thence some thirty miles, in the tribe of Dan ;
afterwards called Joppa.   Here Jonah finds a ship
for his purpose.   How all things seem to favour
and flatter his flight !   He lights on a ship, the
ship sets sail, and at the first the tide serves, the
wind seconds them.   Let us suspect ourselves, and
search our actions, whether they be not wrong,
when we run without rub, and sail without *re-
mora :* * for the first entrance into sin is easy and
pleasant ; whereas in good actions, when we begin
them, it is a thousand to one but that the devil or
our corruptions start some enemies or obstacles to
hinder us.

* [" Hindrance," " obstacle," " delay."   A Latin word of frequent
occurrence in the writings of Fuller and his contemporaries.—ED.]

So he paid the fare thereof.

Jonah herein seems to be a man of a good conscience. Hearken, ye detainers of the wages of the hirelings: know that Oppression, the master whom you serve, will deal otherwise with you than you deal with your servants: for " the wages of sin is death," and that shall duly be paid you. And you servants who have received your hire aforehand, deal not worse with your masters for dealing the better with you, but conscionably do your work, that the outlandish proverb may not be verified in you, " He that pays his servant's wages aforehand, cuts off his right arm; " that is, occasions him to be lazy and slothful.

That he might go with them to Tarshish from the presence of the Lord.

Pharaoh's dreams were doubled, because it was a thing determined by God. (Gen. xli. 32.) So these words were doubled in the text, to show that it was no sudden motion or project whereon Jonah stumbled unawares, but it was a purpose consulted, concluded, debated, determined. He would, *that* he would, fly from the presence of the Lord. Now, it is the opinion of some, that Jonah altered his calling, and turned merchant; but this is more

than can be proved out of the words.   Traffic in
itself is lawful, making those wooden bridges
over the sea, which join the islands to the continent; adopting those commodities to countries,
whereof they are barren themselves by nature. But
it is not fitting that the tribe of Levi should change
lots with the tribe of Asshur; or that those who
have *curam animarum,* should take upon them
curam animalium ; apply themselves to husbandry,
grazing, or any mechanical trade.

VERSE 4.

But the Lord sent out a great wind into the sea, and
*   there was a mighty tempest in the sea, so that the*
*   ship was like to be broken.*

But the Lord.

Though the man did thus leave his Master, yet
the Master will not leave His man; but sends a
pursuivant after him.   Learn from hence, God is
careful for His servants, though they be careless
for themselves. (Gen. xix. 16.) Thus also was God
merciful to Thomas, (who, for his temper, may be
called the Jonah of the apostles,) making a new
apparition for the confirming of his faith. (John
xx. 26.)   Let us pray to God, that He would love
us to the end ; that, though we forsake Him, He
would not forsake us; that, though we forget the

duty of children to Him, He would be pleased to remember the love of a Father to us. And here we may admire God's goodness to take such pains about the recalling of a froward sinner. Lord! what was Jonah, that Thou shouldst regard him? or the son of Amittai, that Thou shouldst visit him?

Sent out a great wind into the sea.

God is the Commander of the winds, and hath them at His beck, as the centurion had his servants. He saith to the east wind, "Go;" and he goeth; (Exod. x. 13;) and the west wind, "Come;" and he cometh; (Exod. x. 19;) and to the south wind, "Do this;" and he doth it. (Psal. lxxviii. 26.) If it be objected, that the devil is styled, (Ephes. ii. 2,) "the prince of the power of the air;" and therefore, (to give the devil his due,) sithence [since] wind is nothing else but air moved by vapours, it may seem to be a subject of the devil's dominions: I answer, The devil is no absolute prince of the air, no monarch, but only he hath a deputed command therein under the God of Heaven. And Satan dares not, for the fear of a *præmunire*, exceed his commission, and endeavour anything in the air, without God's express command or permission. Much less can witches and conjurers (lieutenants under the devil) per-

2

form anything therein. And as for the heathen's fancy, which make Æolus god of the wind, it is lighter than the wind itself.

So that the ship was like to be broken.

Here a difficult objection may be started. "How could it stand with God's justice to put so many innocent mariners in hazard and jeopardy of their lives for the sin of Jonah alone? 'But these sheep, what have they done?' 'Will God destroy the righteous with the wicked?' 'Shall not the Judge of all the earth do righteously?'" I answer, first, at large: In God's proceedings what we cannot conceive to be good, we must not condemn to be bad; but suspect ourselves, suspend our censures, admire His works, which are never against right, though often above reason. To come nearer: God need not pick a quarrel with man; He hath just matter enough at any time to have a controversy with him, and to commence actions against him. These mariners, though not guilty with Jonah in this particular act, yet had deserved this punishment of God for their manifold transgressions, from which no man is free.

Yet God hastened this punishment upon them for Jonah's presence with them. Wash not in the same bath with Cerinthus; decline the society of notorious sinners. (Rev. xviii. 4.) Gold, though the noblest metal, loseth of his lustre by being continually worn in the same purse with silver: and the best men, by associating themselves with the wicked, are often corrupted with their sins, yea, and partake of their plagues. Yet when men are implunged in misery through the faults of others, and suffer for company for the sins of others, (as men in suretiship, undone by the prodigality of their friends for whom they were bound,) let them reflect their eyes on their own faults, and know that, though they be innocent in this particular, yet they have deserved this punishment of God for some other sin; and God may justly take advantage at His own pleasure to inflict the punishment. However, let *them* know themselves for sinners in a high degree, who involve others within the very latitude of their own punishments; as drunken husbands, who by their prodigality drowned their whole family in a sea of want, making their wives, children, servants, cattle, pinch and pine through their riot and excess. For our parts, let us labour to attain to true piety; that so we may rather be a Joseph, whose goodness may make a whole family to prosper; rather one of those ten righteous, for whose righteousness a whole Sodom might be saved; than an Achan, for whose sins an army may be routed; or a Jonah, for whose fault a whole ship full of men was like to be broken.

Then the mariners were afraid, and cried every man
unto his god, and cast the wares that were in
the ship into the sea, to lighten it of them. But
Jonah was gone down into the sides of the ship ;
and he lay down, and was fast asleep.

Then the mariners were afraid.

These words afford a harder than Samson's
riddle. Out of the bold came fear; out of the
profane, piety; out of the covetous came casting
away of goods. Mariners, they are the hardiest
of all people, so always in danger that they are
never in danger, as if their hearts were made of
those rocks amongst which they use to sail.
Yet see, they feared. They are accounted a profane kind of people, a-kin'd unto the unjust
judge. (Luke xviii. 2.) They are esteemed the
Nazareth of the world, out of which cometh no
good. Yet see, they pray. They are generally
covetous, venturing their lives for lucre. Yet see,
they cast away their goods. Whence we may
learn, that afflictions are able to affright most
profane men into piety : whether really inflicted,
as unto Pharaoh; or certainly denounced, as
unto Ahab. Wherefore, let us labour that we be
as good when afflictions are removed, as when

they are inflicted; as pious in wealth as in want; as well affected in health as in sickness; that in prosperity we prove not apostates from those pious resolutions which we made in adversity. When David had appointed Solomon king, (1 Kings i. 36,) "Benaiah the son of Jehoiada answered, AMEN. And the Lord God of my lord the king say, AMEN." So, when in afflictions we have made any vows of future piety, if we have deliverance, let us pray to God to ratify and confirm our resolutions, and to give us strength to fulfil and perform them; lest otherwise we take but a lease of piety, during the term that the tempest doth last, and relapse to our former wickedness when the calm begins.

And cried every man unto his god.

General punishments must have general prayer and humiliation; otherwise the plaster will be too narrow for the sore.

To his god.

The ship was fraught with a miscellany of all nations: it was a Babel, and contained a confusion of as many religions as that of languages: none were at a loss for a deity to pray to. (So an unnatural sin was atheism.) Yet woful then was the estate of the world, when one could not

see GOD for gods. But let us now be thankful,
that as the true serpent of Moses ate up and
devoured the seeming serpents which Jannes and
Jambres, the Egyptian enchanters, did make; so
now in the civilized world the knowledge of the
true God hath devoured and done away all fancies
and fables of feigned gods. Nevertheless, as the
heathens in this ship, so every Christian may still
pray to his proper GOD. "My Lord and my
God," saith Thomas. "I thank my God." (1
Cor. i. 4.) The same is God to all in general,
and to each in particular.

And cast the wares that were in the ship into the sea.

"Skin for skin, and all that a man hath will he
give for his life."* (Acts xxvii.) Now, if life be so
dear, how dear is the life of our life, the eternal
happiness of our souls! "What shall a man
gain, if," &c.? Therefore, when it cometh in
competition whether we shall lose our souls or
our goods, let us drown our outward pelf, lest it
drown us; let us cast it away, lest we be cast
away by it. "Woe be to him that loadeth himself of thick clay!" (Hab. ii. 6.) Rather, as
Joseph saved himself from his mistress, though

* [Job ii. 4. Fuller gives the reference, "Acts xxvii.," simply to
draw the reader's attention to the illustration of this *dictum* afforded
by the account of St. Paul's shipwreck, when "they lightened the ship,
and cast the wheat into the sea," &c.—ED.]

he left his garment behind him ; so it matters
not though we lose (the clothes of our souls) our
earthly possessions, so be it our souls themselves
still remain safe and entire. And if in such a
case we must forgo our goods, much more must
we forsake our sins, which are good for nothing,
but to sink us down to destruction. (Heb. xii. 1.)
" Let us lay aside every weight, and the sin that
doth so easily beset us ; " and not only pray to
God to assist us, but, with the mariners in the
text, back and second our prayers by using all
lawful means for our own safety.

*But Jonah was gone down into the sides of the
ship.*

I here read a contradiction in Jonah's actions.
He went " down into the sides of the ship : " this
savours of flight and of fear. And there he
" slept : " this, of confidence and security. Yet
wonder I not that I cannot make sense of Jonah's
actions, who surely at this time could scarce
make sense of his own. Sin distracts men, and
makes them at the same time embrace contra-
dicting purposes; so that their resolutions fight
as the twins in Rebekah's womb, and are as contrary to themselves as to God's laws. See, Jonah
at one instant *formidat et audet.*

And lay down, and was fast asleep.

An emperor, hearing of the death of one of his subjects, who was deeply indebted, sent to buy his bed, supposing there was some opium or soporiferous virtue therein, that he could sleep so soundly thereon and be so much engaged. Surely this emperor would have proved a frank chapman to have purchased Jonah's ship; who, notwithstanding he had so many things within, without, about, above, beneath, to disturb him, yet, as if the tossing of the waves had been the rocking of this cradle, and the roaring of the winds lullabies in his ear, " was fast asleep."

Learn, First : It is a great sin, with Jonah, to be drowsy, when the rest are at their devotion; and yet many such separatists and non-conformists we have, who by their sluggishness divide themselves from the whole congregation. Indeed, Eutychus had some plea for his sleeping, because St. Paul's sermon was continued until midnight. But we may say to our people, as our Saviour to His disciples, " What! can ye not watch with me one hour ? "

Secondly : It is a great sin with us (with Jonah) to be secure, whilst we, with others, are in a common danger and calamity. Consider the present estate of the Christian church. Is it not tossed with the tempest of war, as bad as Jonah's ship? It lost an anchor, when the Palatinate was lost. It sprung a leak, when Rochelle was taken. One of the main-masts thereof was split, when the king of Sweden was killed.* Though we in this island be safe in the sides of the ship, yet let us not be sleepy as Jonah; but with our prayers commend to God the distresses of our beyond-sea brethren; and thank God that we, like Gideon's fleece, are dry, when the ground round about is wet with weeping, steeped in tears, bedewed with mourning.

Thirdly: Persevering in sin besots men, and makes them insensible of the greatest dangers. It makes men like Nabal; their "heart dies within" them, and they "become like a stone;" so frozen in their sins that no fear of hell fire can thaw them. Thus David, when he killed Uriah, seemed to kill his own conscience. How was he bereft of sense of sin and punishment for nine months together! Yea, the time of Bathsheba's deliverance was come, but the time of David's repentance was not come. Who ever saw the sun so long in an eclipse? Let us, therefore, stop sin in the beginning: for profaneness, as well as piety, is advanced by degrees, and in the progress thereof hath certain stages before it comes to the

* [Gustavus Adolphus, at the battle of Lutzen, November 6th, 1632.—Ed.]

journey's end. Crush it, therefore, in the first motion, before it comes to be a settled thought; in the thought, before it break forth into action; in the action, ere it become a disposition; in the disposition, ere it be a habit; in the infant habit, before it become inveterate and another nature.

And here also we may see how desperate security in wicked men hath by usurpation entituled itself to be true valour. Men count wicked men full of fortitude, which run on God's drawn sword without any fear; when, alas! it is nothing but a sottish security, arising from a seared conscience. Will any say, that it is true valour in a Bedlam that he feels no pain, whose limbs are benumbed and past sense?

VERSE 6.

So the shipmaster came to him, and said unto him, What meanest thou, O sleeper? Arise, call upon thy God, if so be that God will think upon us, that we perish not.

So the shipmaster.

The shipmaster that was,—but now no master of it, the tyranny of the tempest commanding both it and him,—begins to bestir him. Great men must not think to be privileged from danger by the eminency of their place. Mordecai to

Esther : "Think not thou shalt escape in the king's house, more than all the Jews." Yea, sometimes great men are in the greatest dangers ; they are most aimed at. " Fight neither against small nor against great, save only against the king of Israel." (1 Kings xxii. 31.) Now sithence [seeing] there was a governor in a ship, it teacheth us that no company can long subsist without order and superiority one above another. From the courtiers to the prisoners, (Gen. xxxix. 22,) Joseph had all the prisoners in the prison committed to his hand. Ten is but a small number, yet Moses made governors over ten. (Exod. xviii. 21.) Yea, as there is Michael the archangel in heaven, so is there Beelzebub the prince of devils in hell : so much order there is in the very place of confusion. Away then with the Anabaptist, who would set all men at odds by making all men even ! For a commonwealth to want [a] chief, it is the chief of all wants ; every man will do what he list, few what they should. Too much liberty would make men slaves to their own self-will. Let us therefore be " subject to the higher powers," knowing that " there are no powers but of God."

Came unto him, and said.

Every one in authority ought to look unto those which are under their command : otherwise they shall answer to God for such faults as those

commit which are under their charge, through
their oversight and neglect.   Christ is said to
have baptized, John iii. 22; and yet it is said,
John iv. 2, that He "Himself baptized not, but
His disciples."   We see that the deed of the servants, being done by the countenance and command of the Master, is attributed 'and ascribed to
the Master as His own proper work.   If the
master hears of his servant's drunkenness, and
punisheth it not, it is the master's drunkenness.
If the master hears of his servant's profaneness,
and reproves him not for it, it is his profaneness.
Blameworthy, then, are those magistrates who
would have the profit, not the pain; the credit,
not the care, of their place and charge: so that
they deal with those that are under them as
David did with Adonijah; they will not so much
as trouble themselves to say to offenders, "Why
doest thou so?"

What meanest thou, O sleeper?

See here, the Gentile teacheth the Jew, the
Pagan preacheth to the Prophet, and he is content to hear him.   How faulty is their pride, who
count it an imbasing of their knowledge to listen
to the advice of others who in any respect are
their inferiors!   (John   ix.   34.)   Yet David
hearkened to the advice of Abigail; Abraham, to
the counsel of Sarah; Apollos, to the instruction

of Aquila and Priscilla ; yea, Solomon, the wisest of earthly kings, had a council of aged men which stood before him. Neither need any man think much to learn of the meanest of men, who may be taught by pismires and lilies. Yet, when inferiors on just occasion adventure to counsel those that are above them, that their counsel may better relish, let it be seasoned with these three ingredients. First : secrecy. This alone was good in Peter's reproving of our Saviour, (Matt. xvi. 22,) προσλαβόμενος, he " took him aside." Secondly : seasonableness. Abigail (1 Sam. xxv. 36) told drunken Nabal neither more nor less, till the next morning : she thought her physic would work the better, if she gave it him fasting. Thirdly : humility. Naaman's servants : " Father, if the prophet had bid thee some great thing, wouldst not thou have done it? " (2 Kings v. 13.) They brought not only good logic, reasoning from the greater to the less; but also good ethics, " Father." These cautions observed, meaner persons, by God's assistance, with hope of success may take upon them to advise their betters.

Arise, and call upon thy God.

He doth not only reprove him for what he hath done amiss, but also directeth him in what he should do well. They are miserable guides, that tell the wandering traveller that he hath lost the way, but tell him not how to find it.

Arise.

Men must put away all laziness, when they prepare themselves to prayer. Indeed, when in sickness we are God's prisoners, then we can only rouse up our souls, and not arise in our bodies. Then, with Hezekiah, we may lie on our bed and pray, pleading to God, as Mephibosheth to David, that His "servant is lame." But otherwise, "Cursed is he that doth the work of the Lord negligently." The first fruits of the ass was not to be dedicated to God in the Levitical law, but the neck thereof was to be broken. Let us break the ass's neck; let us banish all sloth and laziness, when we go about to perform any service of God.

Call upon thy God.

Because perchance the shipmaster had a great opinion of the sufficiency of Jonah's God; or because he might have a conceit that Jonah's prayers might be more prevalent than his own. Æschinus said unto his uncle Micio, in the comedy :—

Tu potius deos comprecare ; nam tibi eos certò scio,
Quo vir melior es, quàm ego sum, obtemperaturos
*magis.**

* [Terentii *Adelphi*, iv., v., 70, 71.—Ed.]

Or else he only aimed at a general collection of prayers, hoping that that cable-rope would be strongest that was twisted of most several cords.

If so be that God will think upon us, that we perish not.

It is worth our search to know when these words, " If so be God will," are to be inserted into our prayers, and when they must be omitted. When we pray for pardon of our sins, then we must omit them : for God hath said, " At what time," &c., " I will put all his wickedness out of My remembrance." Now let us not dispute of what is determined, suspect what is sure. God saith, He will : let us not say, " If so be God will." If our repentance be unfeigned, our pardon may be undoubted. In such a case, let us come to the throne of grace with boldness in the assurance of faith, with reasoning, trust perfectly in grace. But when we pray for the removal of punishment, then these words are no parenthesis, but an essential part of our prayers. Then we must submit ourselves : not our wills, but " Thy will be done." Then, with children, we must not cry to carve our own meat, but eat that which God our Father cuts for us : though it be untoothsome for our palates to taste, it is never unwholesome for our stomachs to digest.

VERSE 7.

And they said every one to his fellow, Come, and let
us cast lots, that we [may] know for whose
cause this evil is upon us. So they cast lots,
and the lot fell upon Jonah.

And they said every one to his fellow.

The apprehension of the present danger was
the cement that did glue and unite their different
judgments and affections to resolve on that which
they conceived was for their general good. It is
likely that the beasts in the ark, when they were
in a common danger of drowning, did agree
together, and for that time dispense with their
mutual antipathies. Grant, then, that we have
several tempers, humours, opinions; yet the apprehension that we have one grand unpartial
enemy, the devil, who like a roaring lion seeks to
devour us,—this should make us centre our votes
in such resolutions which are behoof-ful for all
our goods.

Come, let us cast lots.

The use of lots was very ancient amongst both
Jews and Gentiles. They were of three natures.
First, the lot divinatory, used by Haman.
(Esther iii. 7.) And as for this kind of lot, it
is utterly unlawful: " We have no such custom,
nor yet the churches of God."   Secondly,

divisory. (Obad. 11; Matt. xxvii. 35.) Thirdly, consultory. (Lev. xvi. 21; Josh. vii. 18; 1 Sam. xiv. 42.) These are lawful, if used lawfully, with these cautions:—First: in matters of difficulty; as quicksilver in the *iliaca passio*, when nothing else can untwine the guts; in perplexed and intricate causes. Secondly: in matters of consequence: otherwise there may [be] *difficiles nugæ*, riddles not worth the reading; hard shells without a kernel, not worth the cracking; difficulties which deserve not the resolving. Thirdly: they are to be ushered with prayer, as in the choice of Matthias. (Acts i.) Fourthly: that nothing therein be attributed to chance. Prov. xvi. 33: " The lot is cast into the lap; but the whole disposition thereof is from the Lord; "—" whole." Fortune, that god of man's making, is a mere idol of Dagon, and falls down at the approach of the ark of God's providence; losing both head and hands, power both to plot and perform. It is not Fortune, blind through ignorance, that cannot see; but Divine Justice, blind through impartiality, that will not see, which ordereth the matter. Lastly: no cozenage or deceit is to be used in them. Lots are God's scales, wherein He weigheth matters of seeming equality, and shows which preponderates: they therefore that falsify this balance of the sanctuary must needs be abomination in the sight of God.

Now, because lots may say to cards what Naomi said to [of] Boaz, " They are near unto us, and of our affinity," something also of the use of them. It were no great harm if there were no other cards used than those of clothiers about wool, and of mariners in the ship. But as for cards to play with, let us not wholly condemn them, lest, lacing our consciences too strait, we make them to grow awry on the wrong side.

Such recreations are lawful, if we use them as Jonathan tasted the honey : putting forth the end of his rod, he touched a little of it, and his eyes were cleared. But let us take heed of a surfeit, into which those do fall who either play out of covetousness, or for more than their estates can bear, or constantly and continually. All their meat is sauce ; all the days in their almanack play-days, though few holy-days. The creation lasted but a week, but these men's recreations all the days of their lives. Such using of lawful exercises is altogether unlawful.

That we may know for whose cause this evil is
upon us.

The best man in the ship carried sin enough about him to drown himself, ship, and passengers. But this milk we suck from the breasts of our mother Eve, to shift and post off the fault from ourselves, how guilty soever we are. 1 Sam. xv.

9 : "But *Saul* and the people spared Agag, and the best sheep." Now, verse 15, it is said, "They have brought them from the Amalekites: for the people spared the best of the sheep." He that was the greatest in the sin, would not be at all in the shame. Should God scourge this land with famine, or any other general punishment, the courtiers would impute the cause thereof to the covetousness of the citizens; the citizens to the prodigality of the courtiers : the rich to the un- thankfulness, discontented murmuring of the poor; the poor to the hard-heartedness of the rich: the laity to the clergy's want of preaching; the clergy to the laity's want of practising. Every one would post the fault from himself, and be inquisitive, with these mariners, "for whose fault this evil was upon" them.

FINIS.

1982-83 TITLES

Code	Author	Title	Price
0203	Dolman, Dirk H.	The Tabernacle	19.75
0603	Lang, John M.	Studies in the Book of Judges	17.75
0701	Cox, S. & Fuller, T.	The Book of Ruth	14.75
0902	Deane, W. J. & Kirk, T.	Studies in the First Book of Samuel	19.00
1301	Kirk, T. & Rawlinson, G.	Studies in the Books of Kings	20.75
2102	Wardlaw, Ralph	Exposition of Ecclesiastes	16.25
4603	Jones, John Daniel	Exposition of First Corinthians 13	9.50
4902	Pattison, R. & Moule, H.	Exposition of Ephesians: Lessons in Grace and Godliness	14.75
5104	Daille, Jean	Exposition of Colossians	24.95
5803	Edwards, Thomas C.	The Epistle to the Hebrews	13.00
5903	Stier, Rudolf E.	Commentary on the Epistle of James	10.25
6202	Morgan, J. & Cox, S.	The Epistles of John	22.95
7000	Tatford, Frederick Albert	The Minor Prophets(3 vol.)	44.95
7107	Cox, S. & Drysdale, A. H.	The Epistle to Philemon	9.25
8403	Jones, John Daniel	The Apostles of Christ	10.00
8404	Krummacher, Frederick W.	David, King of Israel	20.50
8405	MacDuff, John Ross	Elijah, the Prophet of Fire	13.75
8406	MacDuff, John Ross	The Footsteps of St. Peter	24.25
8801	Lidgett, John Scott	The Biblical Doctrine of the Atonement	19.50
8802	Laidlaw, John	The Biblical Doctrine of Man	14.00
9513	Innes, A. T. & Powell, F. J.	The Trial of Christ	10.75
9514	Gloag, P. J. & Delitzsch, F.	The Messiahship of Christ	23.50
9515	Blaikie, W. G. & Law, R.	The Inner Life of Christ	17.25
9806	Ironside, H. A. & Ottman, F.	Studies in Biblical Eschatology	16.00

TITLES CURRENTLY AVAILABLE

Code	Author	Title	Price
0101	Delitzsch, Franz	A New Commentary on Genesis (2 vol.)	30.50
0102	Blaikie, W. G.	Heroes of Israel	19.50
0103	Bush, George	Genesis (2 vol.)	29.95
0201	Murphy, James G.	Commentary on the Book of Exodus	12.75
0202	Bush, George	Exodus	22.50
0301	Kellogg, Samuel H.	The Book of Leviticus	21.00
0302	Bush, George	Leviticus	10.50
0401	Bush, George	Numbers	17.75
0501	Cumming, John	The Book of Deuteronomy	16.00
0602	Bush, George	Joshua & Judges (2 vol. in 1)	17.95
1101	Farrar, F. W.	The First Book of Kings	19.00
1201	Farrar, F. W.	The Second Book of Kings	19.00
1701	Raleigh, Alexander	The Book of Esther	9.75
1802	Green, William H.	The Argument of the Book of Job Unfolded	13.50
1901	Dickson, David	A Commentary on the Psalms (2 vol.)	32.50
1902	MacLaren, Alexander	The Psalms (3 vol.)	45.00
2001	Wardlaw, Ralph	Book of Proverbs (3 vol.)	45.00
2101	MacDonald, James M.	The Book of Ecclesiastes	15.50
2201	Durham, James	An Exposition on the Song of Solomon	17.25
2301	Kelly, William	An Exposition of the Book of Isaiah	15.25
2302	Alexander, Joseph	Isaiah (2 vol.)	29.95
2401	Orelli, Hans C. von	The Prophecies of Jeremiah	15.25
2601	Fairbairn, Patrick	An Exposition of Ezekiel	18.50
2701	Pusey, Edward B.	Daniel the Prophet	19.50
2702	Tatford, Frederick Albert	Daniel and His Prophecy	9.25
3001	Cripps, Richard S.	A Commentary on the Book of Amos	13.50
3201	Burn, Samuel C.	The Prophet Jonah	11.25
3801	Wright, Charles H. H.	Zechariah and His Prophecies	24.95
4001	Morison, James	The Gospel According to Matthew	24.95
4101	Alexander, Joseph	Commentary on the Gospel of Mark	16.75

TITLES CURRENTLY AVAILABLE

4102	Morison, James	The Gospel According to Mark	21.00
4201	Kelly, William	The Gospel of Luke	18.50
4301	Brown, John	The Intercessory Prayer of Our Lord Jesus Christ	11.50
4302	Hengstenberg, E. W.	Commentary on the Gospel of John (2 vol.)	34.95
4401	Alexander, Joseph	Commentary on the Acts of the Apostles (2 vol. in 1)	27.50
4402	Gloag, Paton J.	A Critical and Exegetical Commentary on Acts (2 vol.)	29.95
4403	Stier, Rudolf E.	Words of the Apostles	18.75
4501	Shedd, W. G. T.	Critical and Doctrinal Commentary on Romans	17.00
4502	Moule, H. C. G.	The Epistle to the Romans	16.25
4601	Brown, John	The Resurrection of Life	15.50
4602	Edwards, Thomas C.	A Commentary on the First Epistle to the Corinthians	18.00
4801	Ramsay, William	Historical Commentary on the Epistle to the Galatians	17.75
4802	Brown, John	An Exposition of the Epistle of Paul to the Galatians	16.00
5001	Johnstone, Robert	Lectures on the Book of Philippians	18.25
5102	Westcott, F. B.	The Epistle to the Colossians	7.50
5103	Eadie, John	Colossians	10.50
5401	Liddon, H. P.	The First Epistle to Timothy	6.00
5601	Taylor, Thomas	An Exposition of Titus	20.75
5801	Delitzsch, Franz	Commentary on the Epistle to the Hebrews (2 vol.)	31.50
5802	Bruce, A. B.	The Epistle to the Hebrews	17.25
5901	Johnstone, Robert	Lectures on the Epistle of James	16.50
5902	Mayor, Joseph B.	The Epistle of St. James	20.25
6201	Lias, John J.	The First Epistle of John	15.75
6601	Trench, Richard C.	Commentary on the Epistles to the Seven Churches	8.50
7001	Orelli, Hans C. von	The Twelve Minor Prophets	15.50
7002	Alford, Dean Henry	The Book of Genesis and Part of the Book of Exodus	12.50
7003	Marbvry, Edward	Obadiah and Habakkuk	23.95
7004	Adeney, Walter	The Books of Ezra and Nehemiah	13.00
7101	Mayor, Joseph B.	The Epistle of St. Jude and The Second Epistle of Peter	16.50
7102	Lillie, John	Lectures on the First and Second Epistles of Peter	19.75
7103	Hort, F. J. A. & Hort, A. F.	Expository and Exegetical Studies	29.50
7104	Milligan, George	St. Paul's Epistles to the Thessalonians	12.00
7105	Stanley, Arthur P.	Epistles of Paul to the Corinthians	20.95
7106	Moule, H. C. G.	Colossia. and Philemon Studies	12.00
7107	Fairbairn, Patrick	The Pastoral Epistles	17.25
8001	Fairweather, William	Background of the Gospels	17.00
8002	Fairweather, William	Background of the Epistles	16.50
8003	Zahn, Theodor	Introduction to the New Testament (3 vol.)	48.00
8004	Bernard, Thomas	The Progress of Doctrine in the New Testament	9.00
8401	Blaikie, William G.	David, King of Israel	17.50
8402	Farrar, F. W.	The Life and Work of St. Paul (2 vol.)	43.95
8601	Shedd, W. G. T.	Dogmatic Theology (4 vol.)	52.50
8602	Shedd, W. G. T.	Theological Essays (2 vol. in 1)	26.00
8603	McIntosh, Hugh	Is Christ Infallible and the Bible True?	27.00
8701	Shedd, W. G. T.	History of Christian Doctrine (2 vol.)	31.50
8703	Kurtz, John Henry	Sacrificial Worship of the Old Testament	16.50
8901	Fawcett, John	Christ Precious to those that Believe	10.00
9401	Neal, Daniel	History of the Puritans (3 vol.)	54.95
9402	Warns, Johannes	Baptism	13.25
9501	Schilder, Klass	The Trilogy (3 vol.)	48.00
9502	Liddon, H. P. & Orr, J.	The Birth of Christ	15.25
9503	Bruce, A. B.	The Parables of Christ	15.50
9504	Bruce, A. B.	The Miracles of Christ	20.00
9505	Milligan, William	The Ascension of Christ	15.00
9506	Moule, H. C. & Orr, J.	The Resurrection of Christ	20.00
9507	Denney, James	The Death of Christ	12.50
9508	Farrar, F. W.	The Life of Christ	24.95
9509	Dalman, Gustaf H.	The Words of Christ	13.50
9510	Andrews, S. & Gifford, E. H.	Man and the Incarnation & The Incarnation (2 vol. in 1)	15.00
9511	Baron, David	Types, Psalms and Prophecies	14.00
9512	Stier, Rudolf E.	Words of the Risen Christ	8.25
9801	Liddon, H. P.	The Divinity of Our Lord	20.50
9802	Pink, Arthur W.	The Antichrist	12.00
9803	Shedd, W. G. T.	The Doctrine of Endless Punishment	8.25
9804	Andrews, S. J.	Christianity and Anti-Christianity in Their Final Conflict	15.00
9805	Gilpin, Richard	Biblical Demonology: A Treatise on Satan's Temptations	20.00